Anthropometry, Body Composition and Resting Energy Expenditure in Human

Anthropometry, Body Composition and Resting Energy Expenditure in Human

Special Issue Editors

Josep A. Tur
Maria del Mar Bibiloni

MDPI • Basel • Beijing • Wuhan • Barcelona • Belgrade

Special Issue Editors

Josep A. Tur
University of the Balearic Islands &
CIBEROBN, IdISBa, Campus UIB,
Guillem Colom Bldg
Spain

Maria del Mar Bibiloni
University of the Balearic Islands &
CIBEROBN, Guillem Colom Bldg
Spain

Editorial Office
MDPI
St. Alban-Anlage 66
4052 Basel, Switzerland

This is a reprint of articles from the Special Issue published online in the open access journal *Nutrients* (ISSN 2072-6643) from 2018 to 2019 (available at: https://www.mdpi.com/journal/nutrients/special_issues/Anthropometry_Body_Energy_Human)

For citation purposes, cite each article independently as indicated on the article page online and as indicated below:

LastName, A.A.; LastName, B.B.; LastName, C.C. Article Title. *Journal Name* **Year**, *Article Number*, Page Range.

ISBN 978-3-03921-461-7 (Pbk)
ISBN 978-3-03921-462-4 (PDF)

© 2019 by the authors. Articles in this book are Open Access and distributed under the Creative Commons Attribution (CC BY) license, which allows users to download, copy and build upon published articles, as long as the author and publisher are properly credited, which ensures maximum dissemination and a wider impact of our publications.

The book as a whole is distributed by MDPI under the terms and conditions of the Creative Commons license CC BY-NC-ND.

Contents

About the Special Issue Editors vii

Josep A. Tur and Maria del Mar Bibiloni
Anthropometry, Body Composition and Resting Energy Expenditure in Human
Reprinted from: *nutrients* **2019**, *11*, 1891, doi:10.3390/educsci11081891 1

Enrique Albert Pérez, Victoria Mateu Olivares, Rosa María Martínez-Espinosa, Mariola D Molina Vila and Manuel Reig García-Galbis
New Insights about How to Make an Intervention in Children and Adolescents with Metabolic Syndrome: Diet, Exercise vs. Changes in Body Composition. A Systematic Review of RCT
Reprinted from: *nutrients* **2018**, *10*, 878, doi:10.3390/educsci10070878 4

Edward Bitok, Sujatha Rajaram, Karen Jaceldo-Siegl, Keiji Oda, Aleix Sala-Vila, Mercè Serra-Mir, Emilio Ros and Joan Sabaté
Effects of Long-Term Walnut Supplementation on Body Weight in Free-Living Elderly: Results of a Randomized Controlled Trial
Reprinted from: *nutrients* **2018**, *10*, 1317, doi:10.3390/educsci10091317 28

Yoshinori Ozeki, Takayuki Masaki, Yuichi Yoshida, Mitsuhiro Okamoto, Manabu Anai, Koro Gotoh, Yuichi Endo, Masayuki Ohta, Masafumi Inomata and Hirotaka Shibata
Bioelectrical Impedance Analysis Results for Estimating Body Composition Are Associated with Glucose Metabolism Following Laparoscopic Sleeve Gastrectomy in Obese Japanese Patients
Reprinted from: *nutrients* **2018**, *10*, 1456, doi:10.3390/educsci10101456 39

Kaitlin Day, Alastair Kwok, Alison Evans, Fernanda Mata, Antonio Verdejo-Garcia, Kathryn Hart, Leigh C. Ward and Helen Truby
Comparison of a Bioelectrical Impedance Device against the Reference Method Dual Energy X-Ray Absorptiometry and Anthropometry for the Evaluation of Body Composition in Adults
Reprinted from: *nutrients* **2018**, *10*, 1469, doi:10.3390/educsci10101469 49

Aimee L. Dordevic, Maxine Bonham, Ali Ghasem-Zadeh, Alison Evans, Elizabeth Barber, Kaitlin Day, Alastair Kwok and Helen Truby
Reliability of Compartmental Body Composition Measures in Weight-Stable Adults Using GE iDXA: Implications for Research and Practice
Reprinted from: *nutrients* **2018**, *10*, 1484, doi:10.3390/educsci10101484 60

Maria del Mar Bibiloni, Joanne Karam, Cristina Bouzas, Raquel Aparicio-Ugarriza, Raquel Pedrero-Chamizo, Antoni Sureda, Marcela González-Gross and Josep A. Tur
Association between Physical Condition and Body Composition, Nutrient Intake, Sociodemographic Characteristics, and Lifestyle Habits in Older Spanish Adults
Reprinted from: *nutrients* **2018**, *10*, 1608, doi:10.3390/educsci10111608 74

Ibiza Aguilar-Morales, Eloisa Colin-Ramirez, Susana Rivera-Mancía, Maite Vallejo and Clara Vázquez-Antona
Performance of Waist-To-Height Ratio, Waist Circumference, and Body Mass Index in Discriminating Cardio-Metabolic Risk Factors in a Sample of School-Aged Mexican Children
Reprinted from: *nutrients* **2018**, *10*, 1850, doi:10.3390/educsci10121850 90

Enza D'Auria, Valentina Fabiano, Simona Bertoli, Giorgio Bedogni, Alessandra Bosetti, Erica Pendezza, Marco Ugo Andrea Sartorio, Alessandro Leone, Angela Spadafranca, Barbara Borsani, Francesco Stucchi, Alberto Battezzati and Gian Vincenzo Zuccotti
Growth Pattern, Resting Energy Expenditure, and Nutrient Intake of Children with Food Allergies
Reprinted from: *nutrients* **2019**, *11*, 212, doi:10.3390/educsci11020212 104

Francisco J. Amaro-Gahete, Guillermo Sanchez-Delgado, Juan M.A. Alcantara, Borja Martinez-Tellez, Victoria Muñoz-Hernandez, Elisa Merchan-Ramirez, Marie Löf, Idoia Labayen and Jonatan R. Ruiz
Congruent Validity of Resting Energy Expenditure Predictive Equations in Young Adults
Reprinted from: *nutrients* **2019**, *11*, 223, doi:10.3390/educsci11020223 113

Maria del Mar Bibiloni, Alicia Julibert, Cristina Bouzas, Miguel A. Martínez-González, Dolores Corella, Jordi Salas-Salvadó, M. Dolors Zomeño, Jesús Vioque, Dora Romaguera, J. Alfredo Martínez, Julia Wärnberg, José López-Miranda, Ramón Estruch, Aurora Bueno-Cavanillas, Fernando Arós, Francisco Tinahones, Lluis Serra-Majem, Vicente Martín, José Lapetra, Clotilde Vázquez, Xavier Pintó, Josep Vidal, Lidia Daimiel, Miguel Delgado-Rodríguez, Pilar Matía, Emilio Ros, Rebeca Fernández-Carrión, Antonio Garcia-Rios, M. Angeles Zulet, Domingo Orozco-Beltrán, Helmut Schröder, Montserrat Fitó, Mónica Bulló, Josep Basora, Juan Carlos Cenoz, Javier Diez-Espino, Estefanía Toledo and Josep A. Tur
Nut Consumptions as a Marker of Higher Diet Quality in a Mediterranean Population at High Cardiovascular Risk
Reprinted from: *nutrients* **2019**, *11*, 754, doi:10.3390/educsci11040754 126

Hiba Bawadi, Merna Abouwatfa, Sara Alsaeed, Abdelhamid Kerkadi and Zumin Shi
Body Shape Index Is a Stronger Predictor of Diabetes
Reprinted from: *nutrients* **2019**, *11*, 1018, doi:10.3390/educsci11051018 144

About the Special Issue Editors

Josep A. Tur is a Professor of Physiology, University of the Balearic Islands (UIB) and Director of the Research Group on Community Nutrition and Oxidative Stress (NUCOX) at UIB, built-in CIBEROBN (Physiopathology of Obesity and Nutrition) of the Institute of Health Carlos III and Foundation of Health Research Institute of the Balearic Islands (IdISBa), Spain. Academic Founder of the Spanish Academy of Nutrition and Food Sciences and Corresponding Academic of the Royal Academy of Pharmacy of Catalonia. Member of the Scientific Committee of the Spanish Agency of Consumption, Food Safety and Nutrition (2014–2019). Member of the Scientific Committee of the Food and Nutrition Secretariat, Spanish Council of Pharmaceutical Colleges. Author of 65 books and book chapters, 320 papers, and 8 patents. Supervisor of 26 doctoral theses. Editorial Board member of *Nutrients*; *Antioxidants*; *Nutrition, Metabolism & Cardiovascular Diseases*; *Current Nutraceuticals*.

Maria del Mar Bibiloni is an Assistant Professor of Physiology, University of the Balearic Islands (UIB) and Member of the Research Group on Community Nutrition and Oxidative Stress (NUCOX) at UIB, built-in CIBEROBN (Physiopathology of Obesity and Nutrition) of the Institute of Health Carlos III and Foundation of Health Research Institute of the Balearic Islands (IdISBa), Spain. Author of 20 books and book chapters and 85 papers. Supervisor of 8 doctoral theses.

Editorial

Anthropometry, Body Composition and Resting Energy Expenditure in Human

Josep A. Tur * and Maria del Mar Bibiloni

Research Group on Community Nutrition and Oxidative Stress, University of Balearic Islands, IDISBA & CIBEROBN (Physiopathology of Obesity and Nutrition), 07122 Palma de Mallorca, Spain
* Correspondence: pep.tur@uib.es; Tel.: +34-971-173146

Received: 7 August 2019; Accepted: 12 August 2019; Published: 14 August 2019

Keywords: anthropometry; body composition; body mass index; free fat mass; body fat; nutritional status; dietary influences; lifestyle outcomes

---

Anthropometry (from the Greek *anthropos*: human, and *metron*: measure) refers to the systematic collection and correlation of measurements of human individuals, including the systematic measurement of the physical characteristics of the human body, primarily body weight, body size, and shape. Today, anthropometry includes single, portable, easily applicable, non-invasive, and inexpensive techniques to assess size and composition of the human body, reflecting health and nutritional status [1]. Today, anthropometric and body composition indicators are useful to predict the development of noncommunicable diseases, like diabetesor cardiovascular diseases [2,3], but it is also useful to assess relationships with physical condition and an active/inactive lifestyle, as well as thedecline of physical ability and sarcopenia incidence [4]. Therefore, anthropometric measurements are needed as part of methods to develop strategies for early identification of decline in physical condition and appropriate interventions to avoid physical impairments, and to promote quality of life.

Resting energy expenditure (REE) is the energy expenditure of an individual who is not fasting and is the number of calories required for a 24 h period by the body during a non-active period [5]. REE usually accounts for more than 60% of the total energy expenditure and is directly related to the amount of fat-free mass, which is more active metabolically than fat mass [6].The REE is useful to avoid or prevent underfeeding and/or overfeeding of individuals, especially in clinical care, but it also crucial to establish reachable goals for dietary and exercise interventions. REE can be estimated by numerous published formulas. Since the most used Harris–Benedict equation in 1918 [7], nearly 200 published REE formulas have been published dealing with various conditions [8], and the body composition is relevant to assess the validity of REE equations, which mainly depends on gender, age, and weight status [9].

The reliability and precision of body compartment measurements over a range of BMIs have been examinedby means of several techniques. Dual X-ray absorptiometry (DXA) and bioelectrical impedance devices (BIA) are the most used and precise methods. However, BIA lightly underestimated fat mass and overestimated fat-free mass and visceral adipose tissue compared to DXA [10,11]. However, BIA proved to be useful to measure changes in fat mass, body fat, total and skeletal muscle mass, ratio of lower extremity muscle mass, and ratio of upper extremity muscle mass to body weight in gastrectomized patients [12]. Simple anthropometric measurements, like waist circumference [10,13], are also useful and very informative, and BMI and body weight are still the most used parameters, in both clinical and epidemiological studies. In this way, studies on dietary and lifestyle intervention have used anthropometric, body weight, and body composition parameters as the basis of their assessment [14–16].

Data on nutritional status of human populations are periodically needed, as well as their relationships with anthropometry, body composition, body image, and energy expenditure, and also with healthy lifestyle outcomes. All these parameters contribute jointly to give a complete knowledge on dietary and lifestyle habits, and hence how to proceed to improve it in order to enjoy an optimal healthy status. Therefore, this Special Issue of *Nutrients* was designed and developed.

Author Contributions: J.A.T. and M.d.M.B. wrote the editorial.

Funding: By the official funding agency for biomedical research of the Spanish government, Institute of Health Carlos III (ISCIII) through the Fondo de Investigación para la Salud (FIS), which is co-funded by the European Regional Development Fund (Projects PI11/01791, PI14/00636 and PI17/01827, Red Predimed-RETIC RD06/0045/1004, and CIBEROBN CB12/03/30038), Grant of support to research groups no. 35/2011 (Balearic Islands Gov.), Fundació La Marató TV3 (Spain) project ref. 201630.10, and EU COST Action CA16112. The funders had no role in study design, data collection and analysis, decision to publish, or preparation of the manuscript.

Conflicts of Interest: The authors declare no conflict of interest.

References

1. World Health Organization. *Physical Status: The Use and Interpretation of Anthropometry, Report of a WHO Expert Committee*; World Health Organization: Geneva, Switzerland, 1995.
2. Britton, K.A.; Massaro, J.M.; Murabito, J.M.; Kreger, B.E.; Hoffmann, U.; Fox, C.S. Body Fat Distribution, Incident Cardiovascular Disease, Cancer, and All-cause Mortality. *J. Am. Coll. Cardiol.* **2013**, *62*, 921–925. [CrossRef] [PubMed]
3. Bawadi, H.; Abouwatfa, M.; Alsaeed, S.; Kerkadi, A.; Shi, Z. Body Shape Index is a Stronger Predictor of Diabetes. *Nutrients* **2019**, *11*, 1018. [CrossRef] [PubMed]
4. Bibiloni, M.M.; Karam, J.; Bouzas, C.; Aparicio-Ugarriza, R.; Pedrero-Chamizo, R.; Sureda, A.; González-Gross, M.; Tur, J.A. Association between Physical Condition and Body Composition, Nutrient Intake, Sociodemographic Characteristics, and Lifestyle Habits in Older Spanish Adults. *Nutrients* **2019**, *10*, 1608. [CrossRef] [PubMed]
5. Barton, R.G. Nutrition support. In *Critical Care Method: Principles of Diagnosis and Management in the Adult*, 3rd ed.; Parrillo, J.E., Dellinger, P., Eds.; Mosby: St. Louis, MO, USA, 2008; Chapter 83; pp. 1709–1727.
6. Jamy, A.D. Obesity. In *Handbook of Clinical Nutrition*, 4th ed.; Heimburger, D.C., Ard, A.D., Eds.; Mosby: St. Louis, MO, USA, 2006; Chapter 17; pp. 371–400.
7. Harris, J.A.; Benedict, F.G. A Biometric Study of Human Basal Metabolism. *Proc. Natl. Acad. Sci. USA* **1918**, *4*, 370–373. [CrossRef] [PubMed]
8. Frankenfield, D.C.; Muth, E.R.; Rowe, W.A. The Harris-Benedict Studies of Human Basal Metabolism: History and Limitations. *J. Am. Diet. Assoc.* **1998**, *98*, 439–445. [CrossRef]
9. Amaro-Gahete, F.J.; Sanchez-Delgado, G.; Alcantara, J.M.A.; Martinez-Tellez, B.; Muñoz-Hernandez, V.; Merchan-Ramirez, E.; Löf, M.; Labayen, I.; Ruiz, J.R. Congruent Validity of Resting Energy Expenditure Predictive Equations in Young Adults. *Nutrients* **2019**, *11*, 223. [CrossRef] [PubMed]
10. Dordevic, A.L.; Bonham, M.; Ghasem-Zadeh, A.; Evans, A.; Barber, E.; Day, A.; Kwok, A.; Truby, H. Reliability of Compartmental Body Composition Measures in Weight-Stable Adults Using GE iDXA: Implications for Research and Practice. *Nutrients* **2018**, *10*, 14. [CrossRef] [PubMed]
11. Day, K.; Kwok, A.; Evans, A.; Mata, F.; Verdejo-Garcia, A.; Hart, K.; Ward, L.C.; Truby, H. Comparison of a Bioelectrical Impedance Device against the Reference Method Dual Energy X-Ray Absorptiometry and Anthropometry for the Evaluation of Body Composition in Adults. *Nutrients* **2018**, *10*, 1469. [CrossRef] [PubMed]
12. Ozeki, Y.; Masaki, T.; Yoshida, Y.; Okamoto, M.; Anai, M.; Gotoh, K.; Endo, Y.; Ohta, M.; Inomata, M.; Shibata, H. Bioelectrical Impedance Analysis Results for Estimating Body Composition Are Associated with Glucose Metabolism Following Laparoscopic Sleeve Gastrectomy in Obese Japanese Patients. *Nutrients* **2018**, *10*, 1456. [CrossRef] [PubMed]
13. Flint, A.J.; Rexrode, K.M.; Hu, F.B.; Glynn, R.J.; Caspard, H.; Manson, J.E.; Willett, W.C.; Rimm, E.B. Body Mass Index, Waist Circumference, and Risk of Coronary Heart Disease: A Prospective Study among Men and Women. *Obes. Res. Clin. Pract.* **2010**, *4*, e171–e181. [CrossRef] [PubMed]
14. Albert Pérez, E.; Mateu Olivares, V.; Martínez-Espinosa, R.M.; Molina Vila, M.D.; Reig García-Galbis, M. New Insights about How to Make an Intervention in Children and Adolescents with Metabolic Syndrome: Diet,

Exercise vs. Changes in Body Composition. A Systematic Review of RCT. *Nutrients* **2018**, *10*, 878. [CrossRef] [PubMed]
15. Bitok, E.; Rajaram, S.; Jaceldo-Siegl, K.; Oda, K.; Sala-Vila, A.; Serra-Mir, M.; Ros, E.; Sabaté, J. Effects of Long-Term Walnut Supplementation on Body Weight in Free-Living Elderly: Results of a Randomized Controlled Trial. *Nutrients* **2018**, *10*, 1317. [CrossRef] [PubMed]
16. Bibiloni, M.M.; Julibert, A.; Bouzas, C.; Martínez-González, M.A.; Corella, D.; Salas-Salvadó, J.; Zomeño, M.D.; Vioque, J.; Romaguera, D.; Martínez, J.A.; et al. Nut Consumptions as a Marker of Higher Diet Quality in a Mediterranean Population at High Cardiovascular Risk. *Nutrients* **2019**, *11*, 754. [CrossRef] [PubMed]

© 2019 by the authors. Licensee MDPI, Basel, Switzerland. This article is an open access article distributed under the terms and conditions of the Creative Commons Attribution (CC BY) license (http://creativecommons.org/licenses/by/4.0/).

Review

New Insights about How to Make an Intervention in Children and Adolescents with Metabolic Syndrome: Diet, Exercise vs. Changes in Body Composition. A Systematic Review of RCT

Enrique Albert Pérez [1], Victoria Mateu Olivares [1], Rosa María Martínez-Espinosa [2,3], Mariola D Molina Vila [3,4] and Manuel Reig García-Galbis [3,5,*]

1. Faculty of Health Sciences, University of Alicante, 03690 Alicante, Spain; ejalbertperez@gmail.com (E.A.P.); victoriamateu94@hotmail.es (V.M.O.)
2. Division of Biochemistry and Molecular Biology, Department of Agrochemistry and Biochemistry, Faculty of Sciences, University of Alicante, 03690 Alicante, Spain; rosa.martinez@ua.es
3. Members of the Research Group of Applied Biochemistry (AppBiochem), Faculty of Sciences, University of Alicante, 03690 Alicante, Spain; mariola.molina@ua.es
4. Department of Mathematics, Faculty of Sciences, University of Alicante, 03690 Alicante, Spain
5. Department of Nutrition and Dietetics, Faculty of Health Sciences, University of Atacama, Avda Copayapu 2862, III Region, Copiapo 1530000, Chile
* Correspondence: manuel.reig@uda.cl; Tel.: +56-9-7534-7350

Received: 24 May 2018; Accepted: 2 July 2018; Published: 6 July 2018

Abstract: Objective: To record which interventions produce the greatest variations in body composition in patients ≤19 years old with metabolic syndrome (MS). Method: search dates between 2005 and 2017 in peer reviewed journals, following the PRISMA method (Preferred Reporting Items for Systematic reviews and Meta-Analyses). The selection criteria were: diagnostic for MS or at least a criterion for diagnosis; randomized clinical trials, ≤19 years of age; intervention programs that use diet and/or exercise as a tool (interventions showing an interest in body composition). Results: 1781 clinical trials were identified under these criteria but only 0.51% were included. The most frequent characteristics of the selected clinical trials were that they used multidisciplinary interventions and were carried out in America. The most utilized parameters were BMI (body mass index) in kg/m^2 and BW (body weight) in kg. Conclusions: Most of the clinical trials included had been diagnosed through at least 2 diagnostic criteria for MS. Multidisciplinary interventions obtained greater changes in body composition in patients with MS. This change was especially prevalent in the combinations of dietary interventions and physical exercise. It is proposed to follow the guidelines proposed for patients who are overweight, obese, or have diabetes type 2, and extrapolate these strategies as recommendations for future clinical trials designed for patients with MS.

Keywords: metabolic syndrome; children; adolescents; diet; exercise; body composition; weight and fat

1. Introduction

1.1. Definitions

Diabetes (Diabetes mellitus: DM): serious medical condition in which body cannot control the amount of sugar in your blood.

Insulin resistance: is a pathology in which cells fail to respond normally to the hormone insulin. Insulin controls the concentrations of glucose in blood and it is produced by the pancreas when glucose starts to be released into the bloodstream from the digestion of carbohydrates (primarily) in the diet.

Under normal conditions of insulin reactivity, this insulin response triggers glucose being taken into body cells, to be used for energy, and inhibits the body from using fat for energy, thereby causing the concentration of glucose in the blood to decrease. This, glucose concentration stays within the normal range even when a large amount of carbohydrates is consumed. During insulin resistance, excess glucose is not sufficiently absorbed by cells even in the presence of insulin, thereby causing an increase in the level of blood sugar. The insulin resistance syndrome (metabolic syndrome or syndrome X), and prediabetes are closely related and the show overlapping aspects.

Prediabetes (or "Pre-diabetic state): precursor stage before diabetes mellitus in which blood sugar is abnormally high. This stage is not a disease itself. Prediabetes is associated with obesity (especially abdominal or visceral obesity), dyslipidemia with high triglycerides and/or low HDL cholesterol, and hypertension. Thus, it is considered a metabolic diathesis or syndrome. Impaired fasting blood sugar and impaired glucose tolerance are two forms of prediabetes that are similar in clinical definition but are physiologically distinct.

Impaired glucose intolerance (IGT): pre-diabetic state of hyperglycemia that is associated with insulin resistance and increased risk of cardiovascular pathology. IGT may precede type 2 diabetes mellitus by many years

Isolated impaired fasting glucose (IFG): pre-diabetic state in which the concentrations of sugar in blood during fasting are consistently above the normal range, but below the diagnostic cut-off for a formal diagnosis of diabetes mellitus. Together with impaired glucose tolerance, it is a sign of insulin resistance. In this manner, it is also one of the conditions associated with Metabolic Syndrome.

1.2. Noncommunicable Diseases (NCDs)

Cardiovascular pathologies, cancers, chronic respiratory illnesses and diabetes are the primary causes of death around the world. More than 36 million people die annually from NCDs, which account for 63% of all deaths worldwide. These deaths are caused by poor diet, physical inactivity and the harmful use of alcohol and tobacco [1,2].

To prevent the development of these NCDs, the "Global Action Plan for the Prevention and Control of NCDs 2013–2020" was put into place by WHO (World Health Organization) and by the European health policy framework, Health 2020; thus, indicating a forward path for government and society. Among the voluntary global objectives, the following stand out: the reduction of widespread insufficient physical activity and the prevention of diabetes and obesity [1,2].

1.3. Metabolic Syndrome (MS): Concept and Prevalence (Tables 1 and 2)

Metabolic syndrome, also known as "Insulin Resistance Syndrome", can be defined as a series of physiological, biochemical and metabolic factors that increase the risk for cardiovascular disease and type 2 diabetes (T2DM). These factors include insulin resistance, T2DM or glucose intolerance, hypertension and central obesity [3–12].

The concept of MS in the pediatric population is difficult to define due to the physiological changes throughout their growth and development, racial differences, and the lack of cardiovascular events [11,13]. The amount of clinical trials available on this age group is scarce, and therefore, a universal definition for children and adolescents does not exist thus far [11,13–15]. Since 2001, adaptations of the standardized adult MS definitions have been applied to the juvenile clinical trials [11,13,15,16].

These adaptations lead to excessive variety in diagnosis of MS. For example, the prevalence of MS in adolescents in the United States has been greater than 10% (2000–2010) [17]. However, depending on which diagnostic criteria is used, the prevalence can vary between 0.9, 3.8, 4.1, 10.5 and 11.4%. This wide variation can be directly attributed to the inconsistent terms and definition of MS in children and adolescents (Tables 1 and 2) [18,19].

The diagnosis of obesity has evolved over time. The current definition of obesity based on weight and height cannot accurately identify all causes obesity-related risk of CVD (cardiovascular disease). People with a normal BMI (body mass index) and high content of BF (body fat) are at greater risk of metabolic disturbance, systemic inflammation and mortality. Thus, the metabolic alteration observed in individuals with normal weight metabolic obese can be only due to the increase of body adiposity not detected by the BMI [20].

1.4. Strategies for Intervention in Overweight, Obesity and T2DM

Thus far, specific guidelines for the treatments of MS have not been detailed. Therefore, evaluation and intervention guidelines on overweight, obesity and T2DM are presented (Tables 3 and 4).

Table 1. Diagnosis of metabolic syndrome in children and adolescents.

	AHA Criteria [21]	IDF Criteria			WHO Criteria	NCEP ATP III Criteria
Necessary components for the MS diagnosis	3 of the 5 must be present	Central obesity and 2 of 4 other components must be present [21]			At least 3 or hyperinsulinemia and at least 2 must be present [22]	At least 3 must be present [23]
Age (years)	12–19	6–9 [21]	10–15 [21] 10–16 [23]	>15 [21] ≥16 [24]	ND	ND
Essential criteria	ND	ND	WC ≥ 90th percentile [23] or adult cut-off if lower [21]	ND	Insulin resistance [23]	None [23]
Waist circumference	WC ≥ 90th percentile for age, sex and race/ethnicity	WC ≥ 90th percentile for age (MS as entity is not diagnosed) [21]		WC ≥ 90 cm in boys and ≥80 cm in girls [24] WC ≥ 94 cm in boys and ≥80 cm in girls [21]	Waist-to-hip ratio > 0.9 in boys and >0.85 in girls [23] BMI ≥ 75/85/95th percentile by age, sex [22]	WC ≥102 cm in boys and ≥88 cm in girls [23] WC > 90th percentile or BMI ≥ 97th percentile [22] WC > 75th percentile for age and sex [24]
BMI	ND	ND	ND	ND	>30 kg/m² [23]	ND
Blood pressure	≥90th percentile for age, sex, and height	ND	SBP ≥ 130 mmHg [23] SBP ≥ 130 mmHg or DBP ≥ 85 mmHg [24]	SBP ≥ 130 mmHg or DBP ≥85 mmHg [24] or treatment of previously diagnosed hypertension [21]	SBP ≥ 140 mmHg [23]	SBP ≥ 130 mmHg [23] SBP > 90th percentile for age and sex [24]
Dyslipidemia — Triglyceride	≥1.23 mmol/L (≥110 mg/dL)	ND	≥1.7 mmol/L (≥150 mg/dL) [23]	≥1.7 mmol/L (≥150 mg/dL) [24] or specific treatment for high triglycerides [21]	≥1.7 mmol/L (≥150 mg/dL) [23]	≥1.7 mmol/L (≥150 mg/dL) [23] ≥100 mg/dL [24]
Dyslipidemia — HDL-C	≤10th percentile for race and sex [21]	ND	<1.03 mmol/L (<40 mg/dL) [23]	<1.03 mmol/L (<40 mg/dL) in boys and <1.29 mmol/L (<50 mg/dL) in girls [24] or specific treatment for low HDL-C [21]	<0.91 mmol/L in boys <1.0 mmol/L in girls [23]	<1.0 mmol/L [23] 500 mg/dL, except boys from 15 to 18 years, whose cutoff point was <45 mg/dL [24]
Glucose	Fasting glucose ≥5.6 mmol/L (≥100 mg/dL) [21]	ND	Fasting glucose ≥5.6 mmol/L (≥100 mg/dL) [23]	Fasting glucose ≥5.6 mmol/L (≥100 mg/dL) [24] or known T2DM [21]	Insulin resistance or diabetes [23] Fasting glucose ≥ 6.1 mmol/L (≥110 mg/dL) or ≥80/90th percentile by age, sex or diabetes [22]	Fasting glucose >6.1 mmol/L (≥110 mg/dL) [23] Fasting glucose ≥5.6 or 6.1 mmol/L (≥100 or 110 mg/dL) or 2 h glucose ≥140 mg/dL [22]
Insulin	ND	ND	ND	ND	Insulin resistance [23]	ND

AHA: American Heart Association; BMI: body mass index; cm: centimeters; DBP: diastolic blood pressure; HDL-C: high-density lipoprotein cholesterol (lipoproteins that carry cholesterol from the tissues of the body to the liver); IDF: International Diabetes Federation; MS: metabolic syndrome; NCEP ATP III: National Cholesterol Education Program's Adult Treatment Panel; ND: not declared; SBP: systolic blood pressure; T2DM: type 2 diabetes mellitus (type of glycerol that belongs to the family of lipids, in mammals it is transported throughout the body while supplying energy or is stored as fat, for long periods; WC: waist circumference; WHO: World Health Organization.

Table 2. Diagnostic criteria for prediabetes, impaired glucose tolerance and type 2 diabetes mellitus in children and adolescents.

			WHO Criteria	ADA Criteria
Prediabetes [25]	Glucose	Fasting plasma glucose	110–125 mg/dL (6.1–6.9 mmol/L)	100–125 mg/dL (5.6–6.9 mmol/L)
		Random Plasma Glucose	ND	Not applicable
		2-h plasma glucose (OGTT)	140–200 mg/dL (7.8–11.0 mmol/L)	140–200 mg/dL (7.8–11.0 mmol/L)
	Hemoglobin A1c		ND	5.7–6.4%
Impaired glucose tolerance [26]	Glucose	2-h plasma glucose (OGTT)	ND	140–199 mg/dL (7.8–11.0 mmol/L)
Type 2 Diabetes Mellitus [25,26]	Glucose	Fasting plasma glucose	ND	≥126 mg/dL (7.0 mmol/L)
		Random Plasma Glucose	ND	≥200 mg/dL (11.1 mmol/L)
		2-h plasma glucose (OGTT)	ND	≥200 mg/dL (11.1 mmol/L)
	Hemoglobin A1c		ND	≥6.5%

ADA: American Diabetes Association; Fasting plasma glucose: fasting for at least 8 h with no calorie intake; OGTT (2-h plasma glucose): OGTT using a load of glucose 1.75 g/kg of body weight, with a maximum of 75 g; Random plasma glucose: In patients with hyperglycemic crises or classic symptoms of hyperglycemia (e.g., polyuria, polydipsia); diabetes: In the absence of unequivocal hyperglycemia, diagnosis is confirmed if two different tests are above threshold or a single test is above threshold twice; A1c: glycosylated hemoglobin; OGTT: Oral Glucose Tolerance Test; ND: Not Declared; WHO: World Health Organization.

Table 3. Guidelines and consensus on the treatment of overweight and obesity: children and adolescents *.

	Author	Recommendations in Dietary Intervention and Exercise
Overweight and obesity	AND [27]	**Intervention:** divided into three levels: primary, secondary and tertiary prevention Evidence: 2009 Academy of Nutrition and Dietetics (Figure 1) [28]
	ICSI [29]	**Intervention:** during the day, diet and physical activity. It identifies 4 levels of intervention in patients with BMI ≥ 85th percentile: prevention, structures weight management, integral multidisciplinary intervention, tertiary intervention **Dietary intervention:** the consumption of a diet with very low energy density BW: age, 2–11 years = 1 lb or 0.45 kg mo^{-1}; age, 12–18 years = 2 lb or 0.91 kg wk^{-1} Evidence: [29]
T2DM	[30]	**Dietary intervention:** 1. Interventions to reduce pediatric obesity should be multicomponent and include diet, physical activity, nutritional consulting and require participation of the parents or guardians. 2. A nutritional prescription should be formulated as part of the dietary intervention in a multi component pediatric weight control program. 3. The dietary factors that can be associated with the greatest risk for obesity are increasing the total amount of fats in diet as well as increasing the intake of beverages. 4. The dietary factors that can be associated with the least risk for obesity is the increase of fruits and vegetables. 5. The familiar dietary behaviors that are associated with the greatest risk for pediatric obesity are the parental restriction of healthy foods, the consumption of food outside the house (e.g., fast food), the large portion sizes of meals and the skipping of breakfast. Evidence: does not use the system of degrees of evidence

* Extensive information is given in Table 4; AND: Academy of Nutrition and Dietetics; ICSI: Health Care Guideline; VLCD: very low energy density diets; day (d); kilograms (Kg); minutes (min); month (mo); week (wk); pounds (lb).

Table 4. Intervention strategies for the reduction of body composition in overweight, obesity and T2DM: children and adolescents.

		Dietary Intervention
Energy restriction	Overweight and obesity	1000 a 2000 Kcal day^{-1} [27]
	T2DM	$\geq$1200 Kcal day^{-1} in ages between 6 and 12 years old [30]
VLCD	Overweight and obesity	$\leq$1,000 Kcal day^{-1} ó 600 a 800 Kcal day^{-1} (PSMF) [27]
	T2DM	$\geq$900 Kcal day^{-1} in ages between 6 and 12 years old [30]
Macronutrients and diets		Different quantities of macronutrients (carbohydrates, proteins and fats) and different types of diets; PSMF (10–20 weeks), proteins (1.5 to 2.0 g kg^{-1} to reach the optimum body weight), carbohydrates (20–25 g day^{-1}), water and other liquids without calories (2 L day^{-1}), daily multivitamin supplements, balanced diet (for 10 weeks) [27]
		Physical exercise
Overweight and obesity		$\leq$2 years old should not watch television, supervised free play is encouraged; 4 to 6 years old, up to 120 min of moderate to rigorous physical activity (MVPA) each day, 60 min in structured activity and 60 min of free play; $\geq$10 years old, at least $\geq$60 min day^{-1} of physical activity which should consist primarily of MVPA. In adolescents, promote and incorporate more complex and personalized activities [29]
T2DM		Children and adolescents with T2DM should practice moderate to vigorous physical activity for at least 60 min day^{-1} a day [27,31] Limited television time, to less than 2 h per day [27] Evidence grade D: expert opinions and evidence from metabolic syndrome and obesity studies. Prevalence of benefits over the harms.

T1DM: Diabetes mellitus type 1; PSMF: high protein diet.

Guides and/or algorithms for the management of the treatment of overweight, obesity and diabetes are technical reports supported by evidence. They contain an outline of interventions, indicating what must be done on these pathologies. Tables 3 and 4 summarize some guidelines, however, there are other guides not mentioned in this work [32–37]. Most of these guides are revised to evaluate the degree of evidence for each recommendation (Table 3). Thus, these guides show a consensus in the evidence regarding dietary techniques and physical exercise (Table 3). However, there are differences between the consensus established between these guides in terms of energy restriction and the recommendations related to the percentage of intake of macronutrients (Table 4). The consensus was obtained from clinical trials where the authors observed a decrease of BMI and/or body weight. Probably, this controversy could disappear if guides and/or algorithms record those clinical trials that consider the BMI and/or weight along with other anthropometric parameters, such as body fat and fat-free mass [38–41].

1.5. Changes in Body Composition Andmetabolic Abnormalities

At present the metabolic changes are being considered as a cardiometabolic syndrome, which is a set of various risk factors such as abdominal obesity, hypertension or hypertension, dyslipidemia, and prediabetes [42,43]. In response to this syndrome or metabolic alterations, the need has emerged to use better tools to monitor the patterns of individual growth, assess body composition in risk and identify those who are at increased risk of developing metabolic components of the disease. The risk assessment of this pathology should be evaluated beyond the capacity of the BMI and/or body weight, hence the need arises for other anthropometric parameters, such as the percentage of body fat, fat-free mass and/or skeletal muscle mass [40,41].

Current evidence suggests that the intervention of physical exercise in adolescents with overweight and obesity improves body composition, changes body fat, and therefore could improve some cardio-metabolic factors [44]. In the lifestyle interventions, the authors of these studies relate the changes in body weight with the cardio-metabolic results [45]. The most traditional dietary patterns, including the Mediterranean diet, are associated with better metabolic profiles [46].

1.6. Use of Pharmacology in the Interventions of Changes Body Composition

The advantage of using medication in interventions for the management of weight loss in patients aged 2 to 18 years is not yet clear [32,47]. In relation to the use of drugs in children and adolescents with prediabetes in 2017, clinical guidelines from the Endocrine Society recommend that pediatricians abstain from prescribing pharmacotherapy, including metformin [48]. However, there are other bibliographic sources that recommend its use [30,49]. The American Diabetes Association recognizes insulin and metformin as treatment for T2DM [50].

1.7. Theoretical Framework and Purpose of the Review

The interest and novelty of this systematic review are justified by the following premises:

1. Due to the prevalence observed in children and adolescents with MS [17–19].
2. The search for which dietary intervention and physical exercise obtains greater changes in body composition in children and adolescents with MS, as described by the overweight, obesity and T2DM guidelines [27,29,30].
3. The relationship between the changes in body composition and cardio-metabolic factors [44,45].
4. Adhering to the WHO Global Action Plan in the reduction [1,2], which is focused on the factors related to the diagnosis of MS [3,4].

The principal objective is to record which interventions produce the greatest variations in body composition in patients ≤19 years old with MS.

The secondary objectives are: (a) to identify which interventions, produce the greatest changes in body composition in patients ≤19 years of age with MS, either exclusive or multidisciplinary;

(b) to indicate which anthropometric parameters and units of measurement were the most used to record changes in body composition in patients ≤19 years old with MS.

2. Method

2.1. Selection Criteria of the Clinical Trials and Search Strategy

The selection criteria were: randomized clinical trials in humans; patients ≤19 years old [51] that had been diagnosed with MS and otherwise, should have been diagnosed using at least two diagnostic criteria (T2DM, high blood pressure, insulin resistance, hyperinsulinemia, hyperinsulinism, hyperglycemia, dislipemia, glucose intolerance and/or prediabetes) (Tables 1 and 2); intervention programs including diet, physical exercise and/or modifications in the style of life as treatment as well as the magnitude of changes in body composition; clinical trials published between 2005 and 2017 in scientific journals and in Spanish and English (Table 6). The exclusion criteria are detailed in the flowchart, Figure 1.

This observational investigation was based upon a systematic review following the recommended guidelines of PRISMA (Preferred Reporting Items for Systematic reviews and Meta-Analyses, Table S1) [52–54] and it used the information retrieval system "the Boolean Model" [55]. All data used were collected from the following databases: PubMed, EBSCOhost, ProQuest and Web of Science in articles of original clinical trials. The key words were: metabolic syndrome, children, teens, pediatrics, diet and exercise; the database "MeSH" (Medical Subject Headings) (Table 5 and Figure 1).

Using EBSCOhost, all of the databases that included the following options were selected: "AB Summary" and "academic publications" in types of publications; in PubMed an advanced search was used and the following options were selected: "Title/Abstract" and type of article was "Clinical Trial"; in ProQuest an advanced search was used and the following options were selected: "scientific journals" in type of source, "Primary article" in type of document and "Abstract"; in Web of Science a basic search was used and the following options were selected: "Clinical Trial" in types of documents and "theme".

The primary research question was: which are the clinical trials reporting the greatest variations in body composition, in patients <19 years old with MS?

2.2. Data Extraction, Synthesis of Results and Risk of Information Loss

Six tables and 3 figures were designed to execute this systematic review. Tables 1–4 identify the most relevant background information for the design of the theoretical framework. The flowchart displays the selection process of the clinical trials included (Figure 1).

Table 5 reflects which strategies and databases were utilized. Table 6 records the most relevant details about the clinical trials included and was ordered from the simplest intervention techniques (exclusive) to the most difficult (multidisciplinary). The searches were made independently (one for each of the authors). Therefore, there were five versions of Table 6, all of them including as much information as possible from the trials included. The rest of the tables were performed jointly.

As for the risk of information loss, only one clinical trial was found where the authors diagnosed MS (Table 6) [56]. Heterogeneous designs were identified in the selected clinical trials. The variations found were: the use of great diversity in the MS diagnostic criteria (Table 1), signs and/or pathologies prior to having MS (Table 2); disparity in the number of patients and their age; temporal duration; diversity in the intervention strategies used; diversity in the anthropometric parameters and units with which the changes of body composition are expressed (Table 6).

Table 5. Search strategies of identified and included clinical trials, dates: 2005–2017.

Search strategy	EBSCOhost Identified/Included	ProQuest Identified/Included	PubMed Identified/Included	Web of Science Identified/Included
"metabolic syndrome" AND "children" OR "teens" OR "pediatrics" AND "diet" OR "dietary treatment" OR "feeding" AND "nutrition" OR "nutritional counseling" OR "lifestyle"	12/0	25/0	3/0	32/1
"metabolic syndrome" AND "children" OR "teens" OR "pediatrics" AND "exercise" OR "physical activity" OR "sport" OR "weightlifting"	54/0	90/0	13/0	44/2
"metabolic syndrome" AND "children" OR "teens" OR "pediatrics" AND "weight loss" OR "weight reduction" OR "fat loss" OR "fat reduction"	12/0	27/0	8/0	277/3
"type II diabetes" OR "insulin resistance" OR "hyperinsulinism" OR "hyperinsulinaemia" OR "hyperglycemia" OR "dyslipidemia" OR "prediabetes" AND "children" OR "teens" OR "pediatrics" AND "weight loss" OR "weight reduction" OR "fat loss" OR "fat reduction"	29/1	75/1	25/2	88/7
"type II diabetes" OR "insulin resistance" OR "hyperinsulinism" OR "hyperinsulinaemia" OR "hyperglycemia" OR "dyslipidemia" OR "prediabetes" AND "children" OR "teens" OR "pediatrics" AND "diet" OR "dietary treatment" OR "feeding" AND "nutrition" OR "nutritional counseling" OR "lifestyle"	23/0	55/0	13/1	78/2
"type II diabetes" OR "insulin resistance" OR "hyperinsulinism" OR "hyperinsulinaemia" OR "hyperglycemia" OR "dyslipidemia" OR "prediabetes" AND "children" OR "teens" OR "pediatrics" AND "exercise" OR "physical activity" OR "sport" OR "weightlifting"	114/0	200/0	65/1	135/6
"metabolic syndrome" AND "hypertension" OR "high blood pressure" AND "children" OR "teens" OR "pediatrics" AND "weight loss" OR "weight reduction" OR "fat loss" OR "fat reduction"	3/0	6/0	0/0	45/0
"metabolic syndrome" AND "hypertension" OR "high blood pressure" AND "children" OR "teens" OR "pediatrics" AND "diet" OR "dietary treatment" OR "feeding" AND "nutrition" OR "nutritional counseling" OR "lifestyle"	4/0	13/0	0/0	40/0
"metabolic syndrome" AND "hypertension" OR "high blood pressure" AND "children" OR "teens" OR "pediatrics" AND "exercise" OR "physical activity" OR "sport" OR "weightlifting"	11/0	25/0	1/0	136/0

Table 6. Characteristics of included randomized trials in children and adolescents.

Author	Sample/Diagnostic Criteria	Duration (Months)	Intervention and Comparative Statistical Analysis of the Body Composition	BW (kg or z-Score/%)	BF (kg or % of BW)	FFM (kg)	LM (kg)	BMI (kg/m² or % of 95th Percentile or z-Score)	WC (cm)	Changes in Body Composition Mean ± sd or Mean ± (SE) or Mean (CI, 95%)
Armeno et al., 2011 [57]	n = 86 IG1: 47 IG2: 39 Girls: 58% Age: 11–19 years old Population: South America (Argentina) Obesity and Insulin Resistance, source of diagnostic criteria: 95th Percentile /NE	4	Dietary intervention	YES (kg and z-score)	YES (kg)	NO	NO	YES (kg/m² and z-score)	YES	BW: IG1: 8.9 kg IG2: −6.4 kg IG1: −0.53 ± 0.5 (z-score) IG2: −0.54 ± 0.4 (z-score) BF: IG1: −5.12 kg IG2: NE BMI: IG1: −3.9 kg/m² IG2: −2.9 kg/m² IG1: −0.35 ± 0.2 (z-score) IG2: −0.36 ± 0.2 (z-score) WC: IG1: −9.1 ± 4.8 cm IG2: −6.6 ± 4.6 cm
			Within groups: IG1 (low insulin response diet) IG2 (conventional diet)					NE	NE	
			Between groups	NE	NE			NE	NE	
				NS	NE			NS	$p < 0.05$	
Van der Aa et al., 2016 [58]	n = 42 IG1: 23 IG2: 19 Girls: 66% Age: 10–16 years old Population: Europe (The Netherlands) Obesity and Insulin Resistance, source of diagnostic criteria: NE/NE	18	Physical exercise intervention, pharmacology	YES (kg)	YES (kg and % of BW)	YES	NO	YES (kg/m²)	YES	BW [3]: IG1: 1.6 kg (−4.2, 5.9) IG2: 12 kg (2.7, 17) BF [3]: IG1: −0.2 kg (−5.2, 2.1) IG2: 2 kg (1.2, 6.4) IG1: −3.1% (−4.8, 0.3) IG2: −0.8% (−3.2, 1.6) FFM [3]: IG1: 2.0 kg (−0.1, 4) IG2: 4.5 kg (1.3, 11.6) BMI [3]: IG1: 0.2 kg/m² (−2.9, +1.3) IG2: 1.2 kg/m² (−0.3, 2.4) WC [3]: IG1 and IG2 NE (cm)
			Within groups: IG1 (metformin) IG2 (placebo)	NE	NE	NE		NE	NE	
				NE	NE	NE		NE	NE	
			Between groups	NE	$p < 0.05$/NS	$p < 0.05$		$p < 0.05$	NE	

Table 6. Cont.

Author	Sample/Diagnostic Criteria	Duration (Months)	Intervention and Comparative Statistical Analysis of the Body Composition	BW (kg or z-Score%)	BF (kg or % of BW)	FFM (kg/)	LM (kg)	BMI (kg/m² or % of 95th Percentile or z-Score)	WC (cm)	Changes in Body Composition Mean ± sd or Mean ± (SE) or Mean (CI, 95%)
Garnett et al., 2013 [59]	n = 111 IG1: 55 IG2: 56 Girls: 61% Age: 10-17 years old Population: Oceania (Australia) Overweight and Obesity/Prediabetes and/or Insulin Resistance, source of diagnostic criteria: International Obesity Task Force/ADA/NE	6	Dietary and physical exercise intervention, pharmacology Within groups: IG1 (high CH diet) IG2 (low CH diet) Between groups	YES (kg) NE NE NE	NO	NO	NO	YES (% of 95th percentile) $p < 0.05$ $p < 0.05$ NS	NO	BW: Total: −3.7 kg (median) BMI: Total NE % 95th percentile
Gómez-Díaz et al., 2012 [60]	n = 52 IG1: 28 IG2: 24 Girls: 56% Age: 4-17 years old Population: North America (Mexico) Glucose Intolerance, source of diagnostic criteria: ADA	3	Dietary intervention, physical exercise education, pharmacology Within groups: IG1 (metformin) IG2 (placebo) Between groups	YES (kg)/YES $p < 0.05$ $p < 0.05$ NS/ $p < 0.05$	NO	NO	NO	YES (kg/m²) $p < 0.05$ $p < 0.05$ NS	YES $p < 0.05$ $p < 0.05$ NS	BW: IG1: −2.7 kg IG1: −5.86% IG2: −1.6 kg IG2: −2.75% BMI: IG1: −4.3 kg/m² IG2: −1.0 kg/m² WC: IG1: −9.3 cm IG2: −5.7 cm

Table 6. Cont.

Author [59–64]	Sample/Diagnostic Criteria	Duration (Months)	Intervention and Comparative Statistical Analysis of the Body Composition	BW (kg or z-Score/%)	BF (kg or % of BW)	FFM (kg/)	LM (kg)	BMI (kg/m² or % of 95th Percentile or z-Score)	WC (cm)	Changes in Body Composition Mean ± sd or Mean ± (SE) or Mean (CI, 95%)
de Mello et al., 2011 [59]	$n = 30$ IG1: 15 IG2: 15 Boys: 67% Age: 15–19 years old Population: South America (Brazil) Metabolic Syndrome/ Obesity, source of diagnostic criteria: IDF/>95th Percentile	12	Physical exercise, dietary and psychological intervention, clinical therapy	YES (kg)	YES (kg and % of BW)	NO	YES	YES (kg/m²)/NO	YES	**BW:** IG1: −7.91 ± 7.48 kg IG2: −15.45 ± 6.95 kg **BF:** IG1: −5.67 ± 8.05 kg IG1: −2.87 ± 6.01%IG2: −17.34 ± 6.5 kg IG2: −11.42 ± 6.10% **LM:** IG1: −2.29 ± 4.01 kg IG2: 2.31 ± 5.22 kg **BMI:** IG1: −2.62 ± 2.35 kg/m² IG2: −5.54 ± 2.41 kg/m² **WC:** IG1: −5.7 ± 6.37 cm IG2: −17.06 ± 11.38 cm
	Within groups: IG1 (aerobic training) IG2 (aerobic plus resistance training)				$p < 0.05$		NS	$p < 0.05$	$p < 0.05$	
	Between groups			$p < 0.05$ $p < 0.05$	$p < 0.05$ $p < 0.05$		NS $p < 0.05$	$p < 0.05$ $p < 0.05$	$p < 0.05$ $p < 0.05$	
Yanovski et al., 2011 [61]	$n = 100$ IG1: 53 IG2: 47 Girls: 60% Age: 6–12 years old Population: North America (USA) Obesity/ Insulin resistance, source of diagnostic criteria: ≥ 95th Percentile /NE	6	Dietary and physical exercise intervention, pharmacology	YES (kg)	YES (kg)	NO	NO	YES (kg/m² and z-score)/NO	YES	**BW:** IG1: 1.47 kg (−0.31, 3.24) IG2: 4.85 kg (2.84, 6.85) **BF:** IG1: −0.48 kg (−0.8, 1.76) [1] IG2: −1.88 kg (0.44, 3.31) [1] IG1: −1.51 kg (−4.56, 1.54) [2] IG2: 1.81 kg (−1.64, 5.25) [2] **BMI:** IG1: −0.78 kg/m² (−1.54, −0.01) IG2: 0.32 kg/m² (−0.54, 1.18) IG1: −0.11 (−0.16, −0.05) (z-score) IG2: −0.04 (−0.1, 0.02) (z-score) **WC:** IG1: 1.84 cm (−1, 4.69) IG2: 4.38 cm (1.23, 7.53)
	Within groups: IG1 (metformin) IG2 (placebo)			NS $p < 0.05$	NS $p < 0.05$ [1] NS [2]			$p < 0.05$ NS	NS $p < 0.05$	
	Between groups			$p < 0.001$	$p < 0.05$			$p < 0.05$	$p < 0.05$	

Table 6. Cont.

Author	Sample/Diagnostic Criteria	Duration (Months)	Intervention and Comparative Statistical Analysis of the Body Composition	BW (kg or z-Score/%)	BF (kg or % of BW)	FFM (kg)	LM (kg)	BMI (kg/m² or % of 95th Percentile or z-Score)	WC (cm)	Changes in Body Composition Mean ± sd or Mean ± (SE) or Mean (CI, 95%)
Atabek et al., 2008 [56]	n = 120 IG1: 90 IG2: 30 Girls: 50% Age: 9–17 years old Population: Europe (Turkey) Obesity/Hyperinsulinemia, source of diagnostic criteria: >95th Percentile /NE	6	Dietary and physical exercise intervention pharmacology Within groups: IG1 (metformin) IG2 (placebo) Between groups	YES (kg) $p < 0.001$ NS NE	NO	NO	NO	YES (kg/m²) $p < 0.001$ NS $p < 0.01$	NO	BW: IG1: −3.4 kg IG2: 3.6 kg BMI: IG1: −2.08 ± 2.32 kg/m² IG2: 0.65 ± 2.5 kg/m²
Love-Osborne et al., 2008 [64]	n = 64 IG1: 48 IG2: 16 Girls: 71% Age: 12–19 years old Population: North America (USA) Obesity/Insulin Resistance, source of diagnostic criteria: >95th Percentile /NE	6	Dietary and physical exercise intervention, pharmacology Within groups: IG1 (metformin) IG2 (placebo) Between groups	YES (kg) NE NE NS	NO	NO	NO	YES (kg/m²) NE NE NS	NO	BW: IG1 and IG2: NE (kg) BMI: IG1: −0.16 ± 1.89 kg/m² IG2: 0.63 ± 1.29 kg/m²

Intervention groups (IG); kilograms (kg); centimeters (cm); body weight (BW); body fat (BF); Fat-free mass (FFM); lean mass (LM); Body Mass Index (BMI); medical Subject Heading (MeSH); metabolic syndrome (MS); study of the analyzed anthropometric parameter (YES); The article does not include its study (NO); not significant (NS); there is a variation of the anthropometric parameter, but this information is not available in the clinical trial evaluated (NE); percentage (%); waist circumference (WC); [1] BF by air displacement plethysmography (kg); [2] BF by DEXA (kg); [3] Median (IQR).

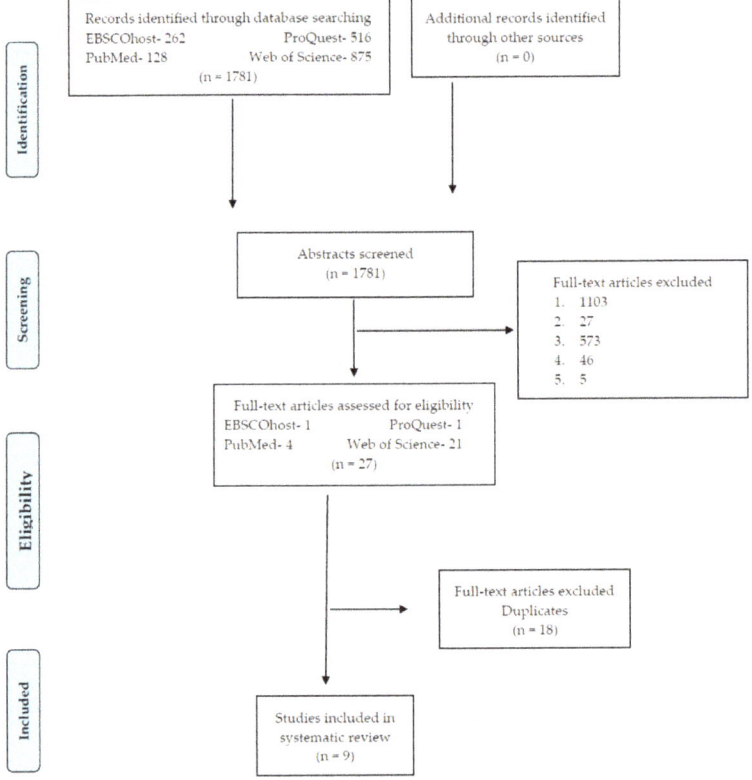

Figure 1. Flow chart of the screening process for the selection of included clinical trials [52–54].

3. Results

3.1. Search Characteristics and Types of Identified Interventions

Of the 1781 clinical trials identified, only 0.51% were included (Figure 1 and Table 5). The most useful search engine was Web of Science and the most effective search strategy was the fourth (Table 5).

From the most frequently observed characteristics in the randomized clinical trials (Table 6), we can highlight: completed intervention programs, 55.56% of which had a duration of 6 months (3 to 18-month range). Six of the studies had a female presence that was slightly larger than the male. The places of origin were: America (66.67%), Oceania (11.11%) and Europe (22.22%). The age of participants ranged from 4 to 19 years of age, while the simple size included between 25 to 150 participants (Median, 58 individuals). The pathology with the most incidence was insulin resistance (66.66%).

All the studies show two intervention groups. The observed intervention modalities were: diet, physical exercise, psychology, and pharmacology; Multidisciplinary interventions were the most frequent at 88.89% (Table 6).

Legend of exclusion criteria (Figure 1):

1. Include a part or a sample without the objective pathology of the systematic revision
2. Dietary and physical exercise interventions or education to changes body composition not defined
3. No comparison or analysis of the anthropometric parameter of interest, before or after intervention
4. Include adult sample (older than 18 years old)
5. Sample not human

3.2. Variations in Body Composition; Exclusive vs. Multidisciplinary Intervention (Table 6)

In response to the principal objective and research question of this systematic review, the greatest changes in body composition from the following clinical trials were reported. The Mello MT clinical trial showed the greatest changes in body composition, in BW (15.45 ± 6.95 kg, which represents a change with respect to the medium base weight 14.27%), in BF, in kg and in % of BW, of 17.34 ± 6.5 kg and 11.42 ± 6.10%, respectively in BMI of 5.54 ± 2.41 kg/m^2 and in WC of 17.06 ± 11.38 cm. It was a multidisciplinary intervention of 30 total patients (15 per group) without the use of medication that combines dietary intervention, physical exercise, and both group and individual psychology from a medical professional. The intervention that provokes these changes is based on a balanced diet with energy expenditure of low physical activity, despite the completed physical exercise (which includes both aerobic and resistance exercises), one hour of group psychology, and monthly medical follow-ups. This clinical trial is also the only one to present data close to the lean mass (LM). The group which performed both aerobic and resistance exercises demonstrated greater growth in the body composition of LM (2.31 ± 5.22 kg) [56].

The Gomez-Diaz clinical trial was the only trial to perform the statistical study of the percentage changes of BW, obtaining a change of 5.86% in the group treated with metformin (with a range of 2.0–19%). This trial was treated as a multidisciplinary intervention based on the use of a balanced diet, a normocaloric diet, the inclusion of moderate physical exercise and the use of metformin [60]. None of the trials perform a study on the percent changes of other parameters.

The Van der Aa. MP clinical trial is the only one which reports information close to the variation in body composition in FFM. It was a multidisciplinary intervention based on the inclusion of physical exercise, carried out twice a week with supervision of a physical therapist, and with training courses. It is the second intervention group to not use metformin [58]. The median range of growth was 4.5 kg with an interquartile range from 1.3 to 11.6 kg in the group that did not use metformin, versus the group that did.

In response to the secondary objective of this review, the multidisciplinary interventions are the ones with the most variation in body composition, especially with the combination of dietary intervention and physical exercise [56,58,60].

3.3. Anthropometric Parameters and Units of Measurement to Express the Changes in Body Composition

Regarding the final secondary objective of this review, the anthropometric parameters and units of measurement were BMI in kg/m^2 (analyzed by all articles) and BW in kg (8 out of 9 articles). The percentage of use of the rest of the parameters and units that appear in Table 6, are reflected in Figure 2.

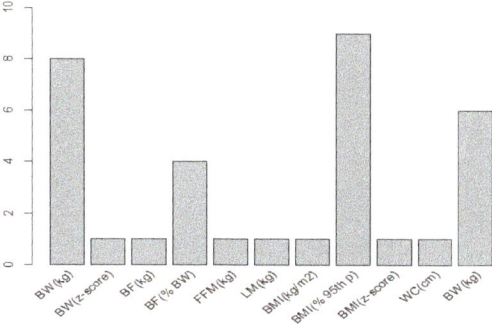

Figure 2. Number of articles within the study of the corresponding parameter and unit.

In Table 6, the variations of body composition are compiled from each of the 2 intervention groups for each studied variable. It shows if significant differences are present in the changes within each intervention group, as well as between them.

With respect to the sole article using exclusive interventions, it studies BW, BF, BMI and WC, but only reports a statistically significant (p-value < 0.05) change in WC between the intervention groups (-9.1 ± 4.8 cm in the group with a low insulin response diet versus -6.6 ± 4.6 cm in the group with conventional diet). It does not report information about differences within groups [57].

Concerning the multidisciplinary intervention trials, 87.5% of them included the study of BW changes in kg, in z-score and/or relative units. Three of them do not report any information about the differences within intervention groups (final vs. baseline levels). Regarding the differences in BW between intervention groups, five present the differences and are statistically significant in four of the cases.

Regarding BMI, all the papers include the variable for their study in some of the units. All of them study the parameter in absolute units, but only five report significant differences between the intervention groups.

The loss in WC is collected in five of the eight works, registering a statistically significant change between intervention groups in two of them.

As for the rest of the units and parameters, in each case there is only one work that presents its study.

Figure 3 represents the forest plot of the four works that present data for the calculation of the variable BMI in kg/m^2. All of them are studies where the difference between the two intervention groups lies on the use or nonuse of metformin. However, it should be noted that they present a high degree of heterogeneity ($I^2 = 70.46\%$).

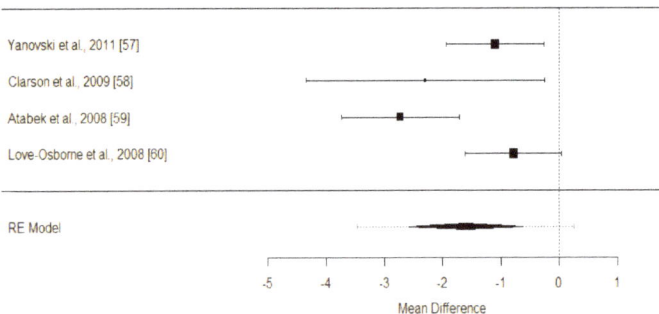

Figure 3. Confidence interval (95%) of the difference in BMI (kg/m^2) between intervention groups.

4. Discussion

4.1. Changes in Body Composition. Comparison between This Work and Other Reviews and/or Meta-Analyses

The most important variations in the parameters and units used to analyze body composition are discussed in the following. Comparisons between the main conclusion from this work, as well as from other reviews, are also included (Table 6).

Until now, reviews and/or meta-analyses that analyze the parameters and units for expressing body composition in patients with MS or T2DM have not been found. Thus, the comparisons were made with the reviews and/or meta-analyses of children and adolescents with overweight, obesity, insulin-resistance or prediabetes.

In this literary search, it has not been possible to find reviews or meta-analyses that present a clinical trial with a greater variation in body composition that the clinical trials analyzed in this systematic review [44,65–69].

Most reviews and/or meta-analyses that have been analyzed do not consider the variation in body composition that occurs when diet and physical exercise are used as treatment tools in these patients [7,25,70]. It has been demonstrated that the changes in body composition produce favorable changes in the metabolic illness risk factors in children, adolescents and adults [71], which is why further research in this area is recommended.

4.2. Practical Recommendations for the Design of Future Clinical Trials of Patients with Overweight, Obesity, T2DM and MS (Tables 3 and 4)

Anthropometric parameters and units of measurement express the changes in body composition through the changes of some parameters (BW, BF, BMI and WC) and increase of other parameters (FFM and LM). Due to the heterogeneity in the design of clinical trials analyzed here, and considering the main conclusion from this research, the authors propose the following indications for future trials:

1. Follow the guidelines for the design of randomized trial reports [72] and other randomized guides [73].
2. The use of the percentage in both the BW as in BF is recommended (in parameters as well as in the units used), especially when the sample is composed of individuals of different ages and/or genders [38,41,74–76].
3. The BF is an indicator of the quality of the changes obtained in body composition [38,74,75,77].
4. Set the limit at 5% changes of BF to evaluate the effectiveness of the intervention [38,68,74,78].
5. The changes in body composition (BW, BF and BMI) not only occurs with the assistance of the patient, but also the consultation as can be seen in Table 4 [74].
6. Based on the lifestyle changes in weight loss programs, the following results were obtained [32]: (6a) One contact with the patient in ≥ 26 h, demonstrating small reductions in weight excess in overweight and obese patients, without evidence of harm. (6b) One contact with the patient in ≥ 52 h, demonstrating an improved blood pressure and other cardio-metabolic improvements.
7. In the dietary intervention, at the stage of changes in body composition, the type of energy restriction must be selected depending on the degree of excess weight (Tables 3 and 4). Besides, the following recommendations must also be considered: (7a) an adaptation in the daily planning of the energy density and macronutrients if the patient completes the physical exercises regularly, especially the intake of complex carbohydrates [79]. (7b) be especially cautious regarding the planning of the carbohydrate intake guidelines for the days where physical exercise is completed [80].
8. In dietary interventions a period of treatment up to 6 months is recommended, because this is the time required to reach the maximum average WL and the BF (%) [38,74,81]. Recommendations for the reduction of body composition are in Table 3 of this review.
9. Tables 3 and 4 summarize the strategies that must be shown by an intervention of physical exercise in patients looking for changes of body composition (BW, BF, BMI and WC). In addition, according to the American College of Sports Medicine (ACSM) in clinical trials including physical exercise, the following aspects should be recorded [82]: (9a) Cardiorespiratory fitness exercise of resistance: the frequency (days per week), intensity (mild, moderate or vigorous), time (duration), type, volume (the distance travelled or the expenditure of energy that causes), pattern (one or more than one session for day) and progression (in volume of exercise adjusted to the duration, the frequency and/or intensity). (9b) Resistance exercise: frequency (each muscle group should be trained 2–3 times per week), intensity (mild, moderate or vigorous in function of the maximum repetitions and on the weight lifted), time (to be determined), the type (depending on the muscle group involved and the weight lifted); repetitions, session or patterns (rest intervals of 2–3 min between each set of repetitions; it is recommended ≥ 48 h between sessions for any muscle group) and progression (gradual increase of greater resistance, and/or more replicates per set).

10. In the article by Pieles GE and colleagues (Table 1 and Figure 1), it is shown that progress has been made in the recommendations for children and adolescents. However, a more accurate vision should be taken as indicated by ACSM both theoretically and practically to be able to prove effectiveness [82,83]. For example, in the maintenance and/or reduction of body composition in patients with overweight, obesity, T2DM and MS, the amount of time they can be seated in front of the television, must be limited and relative to their ages (Table 4). However, occasionally this recommendation is not met [84].
11. Mark the objective of the changes in body composition, around a 5, 10 or 15% changes of body weight or body fat, without necessity to set an ideal BMI [85,86]. One should be cautious when it comes to not regaining the weight and/or fat [87] and be more tolerant of variations in body composition [85].
12. Dietician-nutritionists must be involved in the design of the dietary intervention [81,88–90].
13. A healthcare professional must have a role as manager who informs and educates about the most effective options in the process of decreasing body composition [90,91].

Therefore, it is recommended to follow the recommendations for the design of future clinical trials of patients with MS. In addition, these recommendations may also be used for patients with overweight, obesity, pre-diabetes, insulin resistance and T2DM.

4.3. Limitations and Strength of the Systematic Review

The strengths of this systematic review are:

1. The range of search dates of this systematic review, having found 1781 clinical trials from 2005–2017.
2. The following contributions to the review of this subject: (2a) The MS definitions and diagnostic criteria (Tables 1 and 2). (2b) A synthesis of guides about the treatment of overweight, obesity, and T2DM (Tables 3 and 4) together with the development of practical recommendations for the design of future clinical trials related to MS in children and adolescents. This is due to the lack of guidelines and consensus on MS in children and adolescents.
3. The trial has been carried out and overseen by professionals versed in dietary intervention and physical exercise for patients with overweight, obesity, and T2DM [38,39,74,77,90,92,93].

The limitations of this systematic review were previously discussed in the theoretical framework and in the section on risk methodology of information loss.

5. Conclusions

With the increasing prevalence of MS, the lack of unification in the accepted diagnostic criteria of MS makes it difficult to determine the prevalence of this syndrome and its use as a diagnostic criterion.

In this systematic review, most of the included clinical trials with children and adolescents have been diagnosed by at least one MS diagnostic criterion, which implies the lack of use of the MS definitions.

The relationship between the changes in body composition (changes of some parameters such as BW, BF, BMI and WC; increase of other parameters such as FFM and LM) and metabolic abnormalities of the MS, make it advisable to increase the research in this area.

The parameters and units showing the highest changes in body composition were BW (kg) and BMI (kg/m^2).

The evidence is still not clear as to the use of medication in the intervention programs for the changes of body weight in children and adolescents.

It is proposed to follow the guidelines proposed for patients with overweight, obesity and T2DM (Tables 3 and 4) and extrapolate these strategies as recommendations to the future clinical trials designed in patients with MS.

Supplementary Materials: The following are available online at http://www.mdpi.com/2072-6643/10/7/878/s1, Table S1: PRISMA 2009 Checklist [63].

Author Contributions: E.A.P.: collaborated in the selection of included clinical trials; elaboration of the tables and the flow diagram. ORCID: https://orcid.org/0000-0001-6575-3503. V.M.O.: collaborated in the selection of included clinical trials; elaboration of the tables and the flow diagram. ORCID: https://orcid.org/0000-0002-9438-2008. R.M.M.-E.: selection of the information of interest in the tables; information analysis using the PRISMA methodology; writing, translation and revision of the manuscript. ORCID: https://orcid.org/0000-0003-2679-135X. M.D.M.V.: selection of information of interest displayed in the tables; information analysis using the PRISMA methodology; writing, translation and revision of the manuscript. ORCID: https://orcid.org/0000-0002-1767-2714. M.R.G.-G.: collaborated in the selection of the included clinical trials; elaboration and design of the tables; information analysis using the PRISMA methodology; writing of the manuscript draft. ORCID: https://orcid.org/0000-0002-4428-0652.

Funding: This research is partially supported by Generalitat Valenciana, Grant GV/2017/177.

Conflicts of Interest: The authors report no conflict of interest.

References

1. Diem, G.; Brownson, R.C.; Grabauskas, V.; Shatchkute, A.; Stachenko, S.; Diem, G.; Brownson, R.C.; Grabauskas, V.; Shatchkute, A.; Stachenko, S. Prevention and control of noncommunicable diseases through evidence-based public health: Implementing the NCD 2020 Action Plan. *Glob. Health Promot.* **2016**, *23*, 5–13. [CrossRef] [PubMed]
2. Riley, L.; Guthold, R.; Cowan, M.; Savin, S.; Bhatti, L.; Timothy Armstrong, T.; Bonita, R. The World Health Organization STEPwise Approach to Noncommunicable Disease Risk-Factor Surveillance: Methods, Challenges, and Opportunities. *Am. J. Public Health* **2016**, *106*, 74–78. [CrossRef] [PubMed]
3. Rodríguez-Monforte, M.; Sánchez, E.; Barrio, F.; Costa, B.; Flores-Mateo, G. Metabolic syndrome and dietary patterns: A systematic review and meta-analysis of observational studies. *Eur. J. Nutr.* **2016**, *56*, 925–947. [CrossRef] [PubMed]
4. Yamaoka, K.; Tango, T. Effects of lifestyle modification on metabolic syndrome: A systematic review and meta-analysis. *BMC Med.* **2012**, *10*, 138. [CrossRef] [PubMed]
5. Grundy, S.M. Metabolic syndrome update. *Trends Cardiovasc. Med.* **2016**, *26*, 364–373. [CrossRef] [PubMed]
6. Han, T.S.; Lean, M.E. A clinical perspective of obesity, metabolic syndrome and cardiovascular disease. *JRSM Cardiovasc. Dis.* **2016**, *5*. [CrossRef] [PubMed]
7. Dulloo, A.G.; Montani, J.P. Pathways from dieting to weight regain, to obesity and to the metabolic syndrome: An overview. *Obes. Rev.* **2015**, *16*, 1–6. [CrossRef] [PubMed]
8. Hong, A.R.; Lim, S. Clinical characteristics of metabolic syndrome in Korea, and its comparison with other Asian countries. *J. Diabetes Investig.* **2015**, *6*, 508–515. [CrossRef] [PubMed]
9. Calton, E.K.; James, A.P.; Pannu, P.K.; Soares, M.J. Certain dietary patterns are beneficial for the metabolic syndrome: Reviewing the evidence. *Nutr. Res.* **2014**, *34*, 559–568. [CrossRef] [PubMed]
10. Kaur, J. A Comprehensive Review on Metabolic Syndrome. *Cardiol. Res. Pract.* **2014**, *2014*, 943162. [CrossRef] [PubMed]
11. Weiss, R.; Bremer, A.A.; Lustig, R.H. What is metabolic syndrome, and why are children getting it? *Ann. N. Y. Acad. Sci.* **2013**, *1281*, 123–140. [CrossRef] [PubMed]
12. Jain, V.K.; Badjatya, V.; Nema, R.K. A review on the metabolic syndrome: Plethora of disease. *Adv. Pharmacol. Toxicol.* **2013**, *14*, 29–42.
13. Nelson, R.A.; Bremer, A.A. Insulin Resistance and Metabolic Syndrome in the Pediatric Population. *Metab. Syndr. Relat. Disord.* **2010**, *8*, 1–14. [CrossRef] [PubMed]
14. Halpern, A.; Mancini, M.C.; Magalhães, M.E.C.; Fisberg, M.; Radominski, R.; Bertolami, M.C.; Adriana Bertolami, A.; de Melo, M.E.; Zanella, M.T.; Queiroz, M.S. Metabolic syndrome, dyslipidemia, hypertension and type 2 diabetes in youth: From diagnosis to treatment. *Diabetol. Metab. Syndr.* **2010**, *2*, 55–75. [CrossRef] [PubMed]
15. Fleischman, A.; Rhodes, E.T. Management of obesity, insulin resistance and type 2 diabetes in children: Consensus and controversy. *Diabetes Metab. Syndr. Obes.* **2009**, *2*, 185–202. [PubMed]
16. Hanefeld, M.; Pistrosch, F.; Bornstein, S.R.; Birkenfeld, A.L. The metabolic vascular syndrome—Guide to an individualized treatment. *Rev. Endocr. Metab. Disord.* **2016**, *17*, 5–17. [CrossRef] [PubMed]

17. Pucci, G.; Alcidi, R.; Tap, L.; Battista, F.; Mattace-Raso, F.; Schillaci, G. Sex-and gender-related prevalence, cardiovascular risk and therapeutic approach in metabolic syndrome: A review of the literature. *Pharmacol. Res.* **2017**, *120*, 34–42. [CrossRef] [PubMed]
18. Graf, C.; Ferrari, N. Metabolic Syndrome in Children and Adolescents. *Visc. Med.* **2016**, *32*, 357–362. [CrossRef] [PubMed]
19. Kelishadi, R.; Hovsepian, S.; Djalalinia, S.; Qorbani, M. A systematic review on the prevalence of metabolic syndrome in Iranian children and adolescents. *J. Res. Med. Sci.* **2016**, *21*, 90. [PubMed]
20. Oliveros, E.; Somers, V.K.; Sochor, O.; Goel, K.; Lopez-Jimenez, F. The concept of normal weight obesity. *Prog. Cardiovasc. Dis.* **2014**, *56*, 426–433. [CrossRef] [PubMed]
21. Pacifico, L.; Anania, C.; Martino, F.; Poggiogalle, E.; Chiarelli, F.; Arca, M.; Chiesa, C. Management of metabolic syndrome in children and adolescents. *Nutr. Metab. Cardiovasc. Dis.* **2011**, *21*, 455–466. [CrossRef] [PubMed]
22. Huang, T.T.K.; Ball, G.D.C.; Franks, P.W. Metabolic syndrome in youth: Current issues and Challenges. *Appl. Physiol. Nutr. Metab.* **2007**, *32*, 13–22. [CrossRef] [PubMed]
23. Titmuss, A.T.; Srinivasan, S. Metabolic syndrome in children and adolescents: Old concepts in a young population. *J. Paediatr. Child Health* **2016**, *52*, 928–934. [CrossRef] [PubMed]
24. Tavares Giannini, D.; Caetano Kuschnir, M.C.; Szklo, M. Metabolic Syndrome in Overweight and Obese Adolescents: A Comparison of Two Different Diagnostic Criteria. *Ann. Nutr. Metab.* **2014**, *64*, 71–79. [CrossRef] [PubMed]
25. Haemer, M.A.; Grow, H.M.; Fernandez, C.; Lukasiewicz, G.J.; Rhodes, E.T.; Shaffer, L.A.; Sweeney, B.; Woolford, S.J.; Estrada, E. Addressing prediabetes in childhood obesity treatment programs: Support from research and current practice. *Child. Obes.* **2014**, *10*, 292–303. [CrossRef] [PubMed]
26. American Diabetes Association (ADA). Diagnosis and Classification of Diabetes Mellitus. *Diabetes Care.* **2014**, *37*, S81–S90.
27. Hoelscher, D.M.; Kirk, S.; Ritchie, L.; Cunningham-Sabo, L. Academy Positions Committee. Position of the Academy of Nutrition and Dietetics: Interventions for the Prevention and Treatment of Pediatric Overweight and Obesity. *J. Acad. Nutr. Dietet.* **2013**, *113*, 1375–1394. [CrossRef] [PubMed]
28. Seagle, H.M.; Strain, G.W.; Makris, A.; Reeves, R.S. American Dietetic Association. Position of the American Dietetic Association: Weight management. *J. Am. Dietet. Assoc.* **2009**, *109*, 330–346.
29. Fitch, A.; Fox, C.; Bauerly, K.; Gross, A.; Heim, C.; Judge-Dietz, J.; Kaufman, T.; Krych, E.; Kumar, S.; Landin, D.; et al. Prevention and Management of Obesity for Children and Adolescents. Institute for Clinical Systems Improvement. Available online: https://www.ohcoop.org/wp-content/uploads/Clinical-Guidelines-Prevention-and-Management-Obesity-in-Children-and-Adolscent.pdf (accessed on 1 February 2018).
30. Copeland, K.C.; Silverstein, J.; Moore, K.R.; Prazar, G.E.; Raymer, T.; Shiffman, R.N.; Springer, S.C.; Thaker, V.V.; Anderson, M.; Spann, S.J.; et al. Management of newly diagnosed type 2 Diabetes Mellitus (T2DM) in children and adolescents. *Pediatrics* **2013**, *131*, 364–382. [CrossRef] [PubMed]
31. American Diabetes Association (ADA). 4. Lifestyle Management. *Diabetes Care* **2017**, *40*, 33–43.
32. O'Connor, E.A.; Evans, C.V.; Burda, B.U.; Walsh, E.S.; Eder, M.; Lozano, P. Screening for obesity and intervention for weight management in children and adolescents: Evidence report and systematic review for the US Preventive Services Task Force. *JAMA* **2017**, *317*, 2427–2444. [CrossRef] [PubMed]
33. Consideration of the Evidence on Childhood Obesity for the Commission on Ending Childhood Obesity: Report of the ad Hoc Working Group on Science and Evidence for Ending Childhood Obesity, Geneva, Switzerland. 2016. Available online: http://apps.who.int/iris/bitstream/10665/206549/1/9789241565332_eng.pdf?ua=1 (accessed on 1 February 2017).
34. Onge, E.S.; Miller, S.A.; Motycka, C.; DeBerry, A. A review of the treatment of type 2 diabetes in children. *J. Pediatr. Pharmacol. Ther.* **2015**, *20*, 4–16. [PubMed]
35. National Health and Medical Research Council (NHMRC). Clinical Practice Guidelines for the Management of Overweight and Obesity in Adults, Adolescents and Children in Australia. Available online: https://www.nhmrc.gov.au/guidelines-publications/n57 (accessed on 3 July 2018).
36. Logue, J. *Management of Obesity. A National Clinical Guideline*; NHS Quality Improvement Scotland: Edinburgh, UK, 2010.

37. August, G.P.; Caprio, S.; Fennoy, I.; Freemark, M.; Kaufman, F.R.; Lustig, R.H.; Silverstein, J.H.; Speiser, P.W.; Styne, D.M.; Montori, V.M. Prevention and treatment of pediatric obesity: An endocrine society clinical practice guideline based on expert opinion. *J. Clin. Endocrinol. Metab.* **2008**, *93*, 4576–4599. [CrossRef] [PubMed]
38. Reig, M.; Rizo, M.M.; Cortés, E. Predictors of weight loss and fat in the dietary management: Sex, age, BMI and consultin assistance. *Nutr. Hosp.* **2015**, *32*, 1028–1035.
39. Gutiérrez, A.; Reig, M.; Rizo, M.; Cortés, E.; Mur, N.; Aguilar, M.I. Measurement units used in treatments to reduce weight and obesity. Systematic review. *Nutr. Hosp.* **2014**, *30*, 478–485.
40. McCarthy, H.D.; Samani-Radia, D.; Jebb, S.A.; Prentice, A.M. Skeletal muscle mass reference curves for children and adolescents. *Ped. Obes.* **2014**, *9*, 249–259. [CrossRef] [PubMed]
41. McCarthy, H.D. Measuring growth and obesity across childhood and adolescence. *Proc. Nutr. Soc.* **2014**, *73*, 210–217. [CrossRef] [PubMed]
42. Oguoma, V.M.; Nwose, E.U.; Richards, R.S. Prevalence of cardio-metabolic syndrome in Nigeria: A systematic review. *Public Health* **2015**, *129*, 413–423. [CrossRef] [PubMed]
43. Duprez, D.; Toleuova, A. Prehypertension and the cardiometabolic syndrome: Pathological and clinical consequences. *Expert Rev. Cardiovasc. Ther.* **2013**, *11*, 1725–1733. [CrossRef] [PubMed]
44. Stoner, L.; Rowlands, D.; Morrison, A.; Credeur, D.; Hamlin, M.; Gaffney, K.; Lambrick, D.; Matheson, A. Efficacy of Exercise Intervention for Weight Loss in Overweight and Obese Adolescents: Meta-Analysis and Implications. *Sports Med.* **2016**, *46*, 1737–1751. [CrossRef] [PubMed]
45. Ho, M.; Garnett, S.P.; Baur, L.; Burrows, T.; Stewart, L.; Neve, M.; Collins, C. Effectiveness of lifestyle interventions in child obesity: Systematic review with meta-analysis. *Pediatrics* **2012**, *130*, e1647–e1671. [CrossRef] [PubMed]
46. Martínez-González, M.Á.; Martín-Calvo, N. The major European dietary patterns and metabolic syndrome. *Rev. Endocr. Metab. Disord.* **2013**, *14*, 265–271. [CrossRef] [PubMed]
47. Quinn, S.M.; Baur, L.A.; Garnett, S.P.; Cowell, C.T. Treatment of clinical insulin resistance in children: A systematic review. *Obes. Rev.* **2010**, *11*, 722–730. [CrossRef] [PubMed]
48. Khokhar, A.; Umpaichitra, V.; Chin, V.L.; Perez-Colon, S. Metformin Use in Children and Adolescents with Prediabetes. *Pediatr. Clin. N. Am.* **2017**, *64*, 1341–1353. [CrossRef] [PubMed]
49. Ho, M.; Garnett, S.P.; Baur, L.A. Childhood Obesity and Insulin Resistance: How Should It Be Managed? *Curr. Treat. Opt. Cardiovasc. Med.* **2014**, *16*, 351. [CrossRef] [PubMed]
50. American Diabetes Association (ADA). 12. Children and Adolescents. *Diabetes Care* **2017**, *40*, S105–S113.
51. Rodd, C.; Metzger, D.L.; Sharma, A. Canadian Pediatric Endocrine Group (CPEG) Working Committee for National Growth Charts. Extending World Health Organization weight-for-age reference curves to older children. *BMC Pediatr.* **2014**, *14*, 32. [CrossRef] [PubMed]
52. Moher, D.; Liberati, A.; Tetzlaff, J.; Altman, D.G. Preferred reporting items for systematic reviews and meta-analyses: The PRISMA statement. *Ann. Inter. Med.* **2009**, *151*, 264–269. [CrossRef]
53. Hutton, B.; Salanti, G.; Caldwell, D.M.; Chaimani, A.; Schmid, C.H.; Cameron, C.; Ioannidis, J.P.A.; Straus, S.; Thorlund, K.; Jansen, J.P.; et al. The PRISMA Extension Statement for Reporting of Systematic Reviews Incorporating Network Meta-analyses of Health Care Interventions: Checklist and Explanations. *Ann. Intern. Med.* **2015**, *162*, 777–784. [CrossRef] [PubMed]
54. Liberati, A.; Altman, D.G.; Tetzlaff, J.; Mulrow, C.; Gøtzsche, P.C.; Ioannidis, J.P.A.; Clarke, M.; Devereaux, P.J.; Kleijnen, J.; Moher, D. The PRISMA statement for reporting systematic reviews and meta-analyses of studies that evaluate health care interventions: Explanation and elaboration. *PLoS Med.* **2009**, *6*, e1000100. [CrossRef] [PubMed]
55. Wiesman, F.; Hasman, A.; van den Herik, H.J. Information retrieval: An overview of system characteristics. *Int. J. Med. Inform.* **1997**, *47*, 5–26. [CrossRef]
56. de Mello, M.T.; de Piano, A.; Carnier, J.; Sanches, P.D.L.; Corrêa, F.A.; Tock, L.; Ernandes, R.M.Y.; Tufik, S.; Dâmaso, A.R. Long-term effects of aerobic plus resistance training on the metabolic syndrome and adiponectinemia in obese adolescents. *J. Clin. Hypertens.* **2011**, *13*, 343–350. [CrossRef] [PubMed]
57. Armeno, M.L.; Krochik, A.G.; Mazza, C.S. Evaluation of two dietary treatments in obese hyperinsulinemic adolescents. *J. Pediatr. Endocrinol. Metab.* **2011**, *24*, 715–722. [CrossRef] [PubMed]
58. Van der Aa, M.P.; Elst, M.A.J.; Van De Garde, E.M.W.; Van Mil, E.G.A.H.; Knibbe, C.A.J.; Van der Vorst, M.M.J. Long-term treatment with metformin in obese, insulin-resistant adolescents: Results of a randomized double-blinded placebo controlled trial. *Nutr. Diabetes* **2016**, *6*, e228. [CrossRef] [PubMed]

59. Garnett, S.P.; Gow, M.; Ho, M.; Baur, L.A.; Noakes, M.; Woodhead, H.J.; Broderick, C.R.; Burrell, S.; Chisholm, K.; Halim, J.; et al. Optimal macronutrient content of the diet for adolescents with prediabetes; RESIST a randomised control trial. *J. Clin. Endocrinol. Metab.* **2013**, *98*, 2116–2125. [CrossRef] [PubMed]
60. Gómez-Díaz, R.A.; Talavera, J.O.; Pool, E.C.; Ortiz-Navarrete, F.V.; Solórzano-Santos, F.; Mondragón-González, R.; Valladares-Salgado, A.; Cruz, M.; Aguilar-Salinas, C.A.; Wacher, N.H. Metformin decreases plasma resistin concentrations in pediatric patients with impaired glucose tolerance: A placebo-controlled randomized clinical trial. *Metabolism* **2012**, *61*, 1247–1255. [CrossRef] [PubMed]
61. Yanovski, J.A.; Krakoff, J.; Salaita, C.G.; McDuffie, J.R.; Kozlosky, M.; Sebring, N.G.; Reynolds, J.C.; Brady, S.M.; Calis, K.A. Effects of metformin on body weight and body composition in obese insulin-resistant children: A randomized clinical trial. *Diabetes* **2011**, *60*, 477–485. [CrossRef] [PubMed]
62. Clarson, C.L.; Mahmud, F.H.; Baker, J.E.; Clark, H.E.; Mckay, W.M.; Schauteet, V.D.; Hill, D.J. Metformin in combination with structured lifestyle intervention improved body mass index in obese adolescents, but did not improve insulin resistance. *Endocrine* **2009**, *36*, 141–146. [CrossRef] [PubMed]
63. Atabek, M.E.; Pirgon, O. Use of metformin in obese adolescents with hyperinsulinemia: A 6-month, randomized, double-blind, placebo-controlled clinical trial. *J. Pediatr. Endocrinol. Metab.* **2008**, *21*, 339–348. [CrossRef] [PubMed]
64. Love-Osborne, K.; Sheeder, J.; Zeitler, P. Addition of metformin to a lifestyle modification program in adolescents with insulin resistance. *J. Pediatr.* **2008**, *152*, 817–822. [CrossRef] [PubMed]
65. Mead, E.; Brown, T.; Rees, K.; Azevedo, L.B.; Whittaker, V.; Jones, D.; Olajide, J.; Mainardi, G.M.; Corpeleijn, E.; O'Malley, C.; et al. Diet, physical activity and behavioural interventions for the treatment of overweight or obese children from the age of 6 to 11 years. *Cochrane Database Syst. Rev.* **2017**, *6*, CD012651. [CrossRef] [PubMed]
66. García-Hermoso, A.; Sánchez-López, M.; Martínez-Vizcaíno, V. Effects of Aerobic Plus Resistance Exercise on Body Composition Related Variables in Pediatric Obesity: A Systematic Review and Meta-Analysis of Randomized Controlled Trials. *Pediatr. Exerc. Sci.* **2015**, *27*, 431–440. [CrossRef] [PubMed]
67. Ho, M.; Garnett, S.P.; Baur, L.A.; Burrows, T.; Stewart, L.; Neve, M.; Collins, C. Impact of dietary and exercise interventions on weight change and metabolic outcomes in obese children and adolescents: A systematic review and meta-analysis of randomized trials. *JAMA Pediatr.* **2013**, *167*, 759–768. [CrossRef] [PubMed]
68. Larsen, T.M.; Dalskov, S.; Van Baak, M.; Jebb, S.; Kafatos, A.; Pfeiffer, A.; Martinez, J.A.; Handjieva-Darlenska, T.; Kunešová, M.; Holst, C.; et al. The Diet, Obesity and Genes (Diogenes) Dietary Study in eight European countries – a comprehensive design for long-term intervention. *Obes. Rev.* **2010**, *11*, 76–91. [CrossRef] [PubMed]
69. Whitlock, E.P.; O'Connor, E.A.; Williams, S.B.; Beil, T.L.; Lutz, K.W. Effectiveness of Weight Management Interventions in Children: A Targeted Systematic Review for the USPSTF. *Pediatrics* **2010**, *125*, e396–e418. [CrossRef] [PubMed]
70. Gow, M.L.; Garnett, S.P.; Baur, L.A.; Lister, N.B. The Effectiveness of Different Diet Strategies to Reduce Type 2 Diabetes Risk in Youth. *Nutrients* **2016**, *8*, 486. [CrossRef] [PubMed]
71. Kroeger, C.M.; Hoddy, K.K.; Varady, K.A. Impact of weight regain on metabolic disease risk: A review of human trials. *J. Obes.* **2014**. [CrossRef] [PubMed]
72. Moher, D.; Hopewell, S.; Schulz, K.F.; Montori, V.; Gøtzsche, P.C.; Devereaux, P.J.; Elbourne, D.; Egger, M.; Altman, D.G. CONSORT 2010 explanation and elaboration: Updated guidelines for reporting parallel group randomised trials. *Int. J. Surg.* **2012**, *10*, 28–55. [CrossRef] [PubMed]
73. Argimon, J.M.; Jimenéz, J. Métodos de investigación clínica y epidemiológica. *Elsevier* **2013**, *27*, 109–112. (In Spanish)
74. Reig, M.; Rizo, M.M.; Cortés, E. Indicators of success in the dietary management of overweight and obesity: Weight, body fat loss and quality. *Nutr. Hosp.* **2015**, *32*, 1009–1016.
75. Millstein, R.A. Measuring Outcomes in Adult Weight Loss Studies That Include Diet and Physical Activity: A Systematic Review. *J. Nutr. Metab.* **2014**, *2014*, 421423. [CrossRef] [PubMed]
76. McCarthy, H.D.; Cole, T.J.; Fry, T.; Jebb, S.A.; Prentice, A.M. Body fat reference curves for children. *Int. J. Obes. (Lond.)* **2006**, *30*, 598–602. [CrossRef] [PubMed]
77. Reig, M.R.; Castell, E.C.; Baeza, M.R.; Hervás, A.G. The variability in adherence to dietary treatment and quality of weight loss: Overweight and obesity. *Nutr. Hosp.* **2015**, *31*, 2017–2024.

78. Stubbs, J.; Whybrow, S.; Teixeira, P.; Blundell, J.; Lawton, C.; Westenhoefer, J.; Engel, D.; Shepherd, R.; Mcconnon, Á.; Gilbert, P.; et al. Problems in identifying predictors and correlates of weight loss and maintenance: Implications for weight control therapies based on behaviour change. *Obes. Rev.* **2011**, *12*, 688–708. [CrossRef] [PubMed]
79. Desbrow, B.; McCormack, J.; Burke, L.M.; Cox, G.R.; Fallon, K.; Hislop, M.; Logan, R.; Marino, N.; Sawyer, S.M.; Shaw, G.; et al. Sports Dietitians Australia Position Statement: Sports Nutrition for the Adolescent Athlete. *Int. J. Sport Nutr. Exerc. Metab.* **2014**, *24*, 570–584. [CrossRef] [PubMed]
80. Jeukendrup, A.E. Nutrition for endurance sports: Marathon, triathlon, and road cycling. *J. Sports Sci.* **2011**, *29*, S91–S99. [CrossRef] [PubMed]
81. Jensen, M.D.; Ryan, D.H. 2013 AHA/ACC/TOS. Guideline for management of overweight and obesity in adults. *J. Am. Coll. Cardiol.* **2014**, *63*, 2994–3000. [CrossRef] [PubMed]
82. Garber, C.E.; Blissmer, B.; Deschenes, M.R.; Franklin, B.A.; Lamonte, M.J.; Lee, I.M.; Nieman, D.C.; Swain, D.P. American College of Sports Medicine position stand (ACSM). Quantity and quality of exercise for developing and maintaining cardiorespiratory, musculoskeletal, and neuromotor fitness in apparently healthy adults: Guidance for prescribing exercise. *Med. Sci. Sports Exerc.* **2011**, *43*, 1334–1359. [CrossRef] [PubMed]
83. Pieles, G.E.; Horn, R.; Williams, C.A.; Stuart, A.G. Paediatric exercise training in prevention and treatment. *Arch. Dis. Child.* **2014**, *99*, 380–385. [CrossRef] [PubMed]
84. Mielgo-Ayuso, J.; Aparicio-Ugarriza, R.; Castillo, A.; Ruiz, E.; Avila, J.M.; Aranceta-Bartrina, J.; Angel Gil, A.; Ortega, R.M.; Serra-Majem, L.; Varela-Moreiras, G.; et al. Sedentary behavior among Spanish children and adolescents: Findings from the ANIBES study. *BMC Public Health* **2017**, *17*, 94. [CrossRef] [PubMed]
85. Ravussin, E.; Ryan, D. Energy Expenditure and Weight Control: Is the Biggest Loser the Best Loser? *Obesity* **2016**, *24*, 1607–1608. [CrossRef] [PubMed]
86. Ryan, D.; Heaner, M. Guidelines (2013) for managing overweight and obesity in adults: Preface to the full report. *Obesity (Silver Spring)* **2014**, *22*, S1–S3. [CrossRef] [PubMed]
87. Cefalu, W.T.; Bray, G.A.; Home, P.D.; Garvey, W.T.; Klein, S.; Pi-Sunyer, F.X.; Hu, F.B.; Raz, I.; Gaal, V.L.; Wolfe, B.M.; et al. Advances in the Science, Treatment, and Prevention of the Disease of Obesity: Reflections From a Diabetes Care Editors' Expert Forum. *Diabetes Care* **2015**, *38*, 1567–1582. [CrossRef] [PubMed]
88. Delahanty, L.M. An expanded role for dietitians in maximising retention in nutrition and lifestyle intervention trials: Implications for clinical practice. *J. Hum. Nutr. Diet.* **2010**, *23*, 336–343. [CrossRef] [PubMed]
89. Spear, B.A.; Barlow, S.E.; Ervin, C.; Ludwig, D.S.; Saelens, B.E.; Schetzina, K.E.; Taveras, E.M. Recommendations for Treatment of Child and Adolescent Overweight and Obesity. *Pediatrics* **2007**, *120*, 254–288. [CrossRef] [PubMed]
90. Reig, M. The management of qualitative and quantitative dietary treatment for overweight and obesity: Methodology and a new perspective on individualised assessment. *Nutr. Hosp.* **2015**, *32*, 2019–2029.
91. Apovian, C.M.; Garvey, W.T.; Ryan, D.H. Challenging Obesity: Patient, Provider, and Expert Perspectives on the Roles of Available and Emerging Nonsurgical Therapies. *Obesity* **2015**, *23*, S1–S26. [CrossRef] [PubMed]
92. Quiles, P.; Reig, M. Glycemic control through physical exercise in type 2 diabetes systematic review. *Nutr. Hosp.* **2015**, *31*, 1465–1472.
93. Albert Pérez, E.J.; Reig García-Galbis, M. Effects of green tea on the nutritional status of the exercise. *Nutr. Hosp.* **2015**, *32*, 1417–1431. [PubMed]

© 2018 by the authors. Licensee MDPI, Basel, Switzerland. This article is an open access article distributed under the terms and conditions of the Creative Commons Attribution (CC BY) license (http://creativecommons.org/licenses/by/4.0/).

Article

Effects of Long-Term Walnut Supplementation on Body Weight in Free-Living Elderly: Results of a Randomized Controlled Trial

Edward Bitok [1,2,*], Sujatha Rajaram [1], Karen Jaceldo-Siegl [1], Keiji Oda [1], Aleix Sala-Vila [3,4], Mercè Serra-Mir [3], Emilio Ros [3,4] and Joan Sabaté [1]

1. Center for Nutrition, Healthy Lifestyle and Disease Prevention, School of Public Health, Loma Linda University, Loma Linda, CA 92350, USA; srajaram@llu.edu (S.R.); kjaceldo@llu.edu (K.J.-S.); koda@llu.edu (K.O.); jsabate@llu.edu (J.S.)
2. Department of Nutrition & Dietetics, School of Allied Health Professions, Loma Linda University, Loma Linda, CA 92350, USA
3. Lipid Clinic, Endocrinology and Nutrition Service, Institut d'Investigacions Biomèdiques August Pi Sunyer (IDIBAPS), Hospital Clínic, Barcelona 08036, Spain; asala@clinic.cat (A.S.-V.); SERRAMIR@clinic.cat (M.S.-M.); EROS@clinic.cat (E.R.)
4. Ciber Fisiopatología de la Obesidad y Nutrición (CIBEROBN), Instituto de Salud Carlos III (ISCIII), Madrid 28029, Spain
* Correspondence: ebitok@llu.edu; Tel.: +1-909-558-1000 (ext. 59820)

Received: 25 August 2018; Accepted: 16 September 2018; Published: 18 September 2018

Abstract: *Objective*: To assess the effects of chronic walnut consumption on body weight and adiposity in elderly individuals. *Methods*: The Walnuts and Healthy Aging study is a dual-center (Barcelona, Spain and Loma Linda University (LLU)), 2-year randomized parallel trial. This report concerns only the LLU cohort. Healthy elders (mean age 69 year, 67% women) were randomly assigned to walnut (n = 183) or control diets (n = 173). Subjects in the walnut group received packaged walnuts (28–56 g/day), equivalent to ≈15% of daily energy requirements, to incorporate into their habitual diet, while those in the control group abstained from walnuts. Adiposity was measured periodically, and data were adjusted for in-trial changes in self-reported physical activity. *Results*: After 2 years, body weight significantly decreased (p = 0.031), while body fat significantly increased (p = 0.0001). However, no significant differences were observed between the control and walnut groups regarding body weight (−0.6 kg and −0.4 kg, respectively, p = 0.67) or body fat (+0.9% and +1.3%, respectively, p = 0.53). Lean body mass, waist circumference, and waist-to-hip ratio remained essentially unchanged. Sensitivity analyses were consistent with the findings of primary analysis. *Conclusion*: Our findings indicate that walnuts can be incorporated into the daily diet of healthy elders without concern for adverse effects on body weight or body composition.

Keywords: nuts; walnuts; body weight; adiposity; obesity; elderly; energy

1. Introduction

Obesity in older adults continues to be a major public health challenge in the United States (U.S.) and around the world [1,2]. More than a third of U.S. adults aged 60 years and over are considered as being obese [1,2], a trend that will continue to rise in parallel with the pace of population aging [3]. Excess body fat is an important risk factor for morbidity and mortality from heart disease, diabetes mellitus, dyslipidemia, and metabolic syndrome [4]. In older adults, obesity imposes further functional limitations on top of declining physical function and adversely affects quality of life [5].

Over the years, mounting scientific evidence has shown that consuming nuts in moderate amounts is associated with reduced risk of coronary heart disease [6]. Nuts have a high total fat content (mostly as mono- and polyunsaturated fat), ranging from 46% in cashews and pistachios to 76% in macadamia nuts, and provide 20–30 kJ per gram [7]. They are also rich in protein, fiber, vitamins, minerals, phytosterols, and polyphenols [8]. Following the approval of a qualified health claim by the Food and Drug Association (FDA) supporting the inclusion of 1.5 ounces (42 g) walnuts in the daily diet [9], several agencies including the American Heart Association (AHA) and the Academy of Nutrition and Dietetics (AND) recommend the inclusion of nuts in the daily diet to further heart health [10,11]. Notwithstanding the recommendations, there is a common perception that consuming nuts on a regular basis may lead to unwanted increase in body weight and a higher risk of developing overweight or obesity. However, a meta-analysis of 33 clinical trials assessing the effects of nut-enriched diets compared with various control diets on changes in body weight, body mass index (BMI), and waist circumference indicates that nut-enriched diets do not increase adiposity [12]. In fact, including nuts as part of a weight loss regimen can lead to greater weight loss than simply following a low-fat diet [13]. It is worth noting that many of the trials included in the meta-analysis were conducted over a relatively short period of time (≤ 6 m) and with mostly young and middle-age adults. Thus, whether long-term inclusion of nuts in the daily, self-selected, unrestricted-calorie diets of elderly subjects results in weight gain remains unclear.

We had a unique opportunity to clarify this issue within the framework of a 2-year trial testing the effects of walnuts on age-related cognitive decline and macular degeneration in healthy elderly subjects. We were primarily interested in determining if daily consumption of walnuts for an extended period of time induced weight gain in free-living elderly subjects when compared to a similar concurrent group of individuals with low nut consumption.

2. Materials and Methods

2.1. Study Design and Population

Details of the Walnuts and Healthy Aging (WAHA) study have been published [14]. In brief, it was a randomized dual-center trial, conducted at Loma Linda University (California) and Hospital Clínic (Barcelona, Spain). This opportunistic sub-study concerns data from participants recruited at the Loma Linda site between October 2012 and May 2014. Recruitment for the WAHA study was multi-pronged, and included direct mailings, brochures, flyers, web, and newspaper advertisements. Candidates were pre-screened and excluded from participation if they had morbid obesity, uncontrolled diabetes or hypertension, impaired cognitive function, or bilateral eye conditions preventing visualization of the retina. The present study was conducted according to guidelines laid down in the Declaration of Helsinki. The Institutional Review Board at Loma Linda University approved the study protocol. Written informed consent was obtained from each participant prior to enrollment into the study.

2.2. Intervention

With a parallel design, candidates who met eligibility criteria were randomly assigned to either a walnut (experimental) or control group using a web-based, computerized random number table with stratification by sex and age. Couples entering the study were treated as one number and were randomized into the same group to facilitate compliance. We then utilized the World Health Organization (WHO) formula for energy needs for adults >60 years [15] to estimate individual energy requirements, following which participants received 28, 42, or 56 g (1, 1.5, or 2.0 oz.) of packaged walnuts per day providing ≈15% of their estimated daily energy needs. No advice on food replacement was given and no recipes were provided. Participants in the control group simply continued their habitual diet with no supplementation and with instructions to refrain from eating walnuts or excessive intake of other nuts (>2 servings/week). Simply being in a research study can cause individuals to alter their lifestyle or behavior due to the awareness that they are being watched. This observation is particularly common among studies that collect body measurements. Consequently, we asked participants not to alter their usual lifestyle habits, including physical activity level, while in the study. Participants were largely unaware that adiposity measurements were outcomes of interest in the study.

2.3. Assessment of Diet

We collected 1490 unannounced 24-h telephone diet recalls from study participants during the 2-year period (752 in walnut group and 738 in control group). The diet recalls were obtained at regular intervals to capture variability and seasonality in food intake. Dietary intake data were collected by trained research dietitians and nutrient data obtained using the Nutrition Data System for Research (NDSR) software version 2013 developed by the Nutrition Coordinating Center (NCC), University of Minnesota, Minneapolis, MN [16]. Portion sizes were estimated using common household items; for example, a fist for one baked potato, a deck of cards for a 3-oz serving of meat, or two handfuls for 1-oz of chips or pretzels, as previously described [17]. The dietary recalls were used to determine if subjects in the walnut group consumed their allotted amounts of walnuts and if their counterparts in the control group refrained from deliberate consumption of walnuts. For the walnut group, consumption of walnuts 6–7 days/week (85–100%) was considered excellent compliance and 4–5 days/week (57–71%), as good compliance. Those who consumed walnuts ≤3 days/week were classified as non-compliant. In the control group, participants were considered fully compliant if they refrained from eating walnuts in any of the recalls, or if they consumed no more than 15 g of walnuts on any given day. We also used the red blood cell (RBC) proportion of alpha-linolenic acid (ALA), a nutrient enriched in walnuts, as an objective biomarker [18] to assess adherence to the intervention.

2.4. Anthropometry, Body Composition, and Physical Activity

We measured participants' body weight to the nearest 0.1 kg at baseline and bimonthly. Body fat and lean body mass were measured at baseline, 1-year, and end of study. Body measurements were obtained without shoes or heavy clothing using Tanita® TBF 300A Bioelectrical Impedance Analysis scale (Tanita Corporation of America, Arlington Heights, IL, USA). Participants were asked to avoid exercise or heavy hydration prior to visiting the clinic for body measurements. Height was measured to the nearest 0.1 cm using a wall-mounted stadiometer (Holtain Ltd., Crymych, Dyfed, UK). Waist circumference was measured to the nearest 0.1 cm an inch (2.54 cm) above the umbilicus using a tape measure. Hip circumference was measured to the nearest 0.1 cm at the outermost part of the greater trochanters. The waist-to-hip ratio (WtHR) was computed as the ratio of these circumferences. All measurements were obtained following the Centers for Disease Control (CDC) guidelines for the National Health and Nutrition Examination Survey (NHANES III) anthropometric measurements [19]. We also asked participants to fill in a validated short version of the Minnesota physical activity questionnaire for adult populations [19] at baseline, 1-year, and end of the study. We then applied CDC and American College of Sports Medicine guidelines [20] to compute metabolic equivalent (MET)-hours per week and to categorize general physical activities according to level of intensity (low/sedentary, moderate, and vigorous).

2.5. Biomarker Analyses

Detailed procedures for blood collection and analyses in the WAHA study are published [14]. Fasting blood samples were obtained from all participants at baseline and end of the study. To reduce assay variability, all samples were stored and run together in the same laboratory at the end of the study. The RBC proportion of ALA was assessed as described [21] in a random subset of participants (n = 105, 51 in the control group and 54 in the walnut group). In brief, cells contained in a 100-µL aliquot of EDTA-collected blood were hemolyzed and spun. The pellet (>99% RBC membranes) was dried, dissolved in 1 mL BF_3 methanol solution and heated to hydrolyze and methylate glycerophospholipid fatty acids. The fatty acid methyl esters were isolated by adding n-hexane and were separated by gas chromatography using an Agilent HP 7890 Gas Chromatograph equipped with a 30 m × 0.25 µm × 0.25 mm SupraWAX-280 capillary column (Teknokroma, Barcelona,

Spain), an autosampler, and a flame ionization detector. The amount of ALA was expressed as a percentage of total identified fatty acids in the RBC sample.

2.6. Statistical Analyses

Per protocol analysis was utilized to estimate changes in body measurements. To reduce intra-individual variation, measurements taken in duplicate were averaged and analyses performed on the average. Descriptive statistics are reported as proportions (%) or means ± standard deviations. When appropriate, the ANOVA or chi-square tests were used to assess whether the completers were comparable to non-completers in terms of age, sex, ethnicity, and baseline BMI. Baseline imbalances in demographic, anthropometric, and lifestyle variables between treatment groups were assessed by Chi-square test for independence, two-sample *t*-test, and Fisher's exact test, as appropriate. The independent samples *t*-test was used to test between group difference in energy and nutrient intake. Changes in body weight and adiposity measures were estimated using linear mixed models with random intercepts and random slopes. Analyses were performed adjusting for in-trial changes in physical activity. The main outcome was change in body weight from baseline to 2 years, with five repeated measurements obtained in between. We also examined changes in body fat, waist circumference, lean body mass, and WtHR at 1-year and end of the study. The predictors for the model were time (as a continuous variable) and intervention (walnut or control group). In the models we included interaction terms for time and intervention (group) by time effects. Three-way interactions between time, intervention, and either age ($\leq$70 years vs. $\geq$71 years), sex, or ethnicity (white vs. non-white) were also assessed. Changes in ALA as proportion of total identified fatty acids were determined by use of ANOVA, and the relationship between changes in self-reported walnut intake and changes in RBC ALA assessed using Pearson correlation. Assuming a standard deviation of 4 kg, the sample size of 356 participants provided >95% power (with $p = 0.05$) to detect a mean difference of 1 kg between groups. All analyses were performed using Statistical Analysis System (SAS Version 9.4).

3. Results

3.1. Participants

Baseline characteristics of 356 subjects who began the study are detailed in Table 1. Overall, the walnut supplement was well accepted and well tolerated by study participants. Forty-nine participants (24 in the walnut group and 25 in the control group) dropped out due to health-related concerns, intolerance to walnuts, loss to follow-up, or undisclosed personal reasons. One death due to esophageal cancer early in the study (unrelated to treatment) occurred in the walnut group. The dropouts did not differ significantly from completers regarding age, sex, ethnicity, or baseline BMI (data not shown). Nine incident cases of constipation and eight of diarrhea were reported in the walnut group during the 2-year study period. Figure 1 is the study flowchart. Data presented are for participants who completed the study (159 from the walnut group and 148 from the control group).

Table 1. Baseline characteristics of participants by intervention group.

Variable		Walnut	Control	p-Value
n (%)		183 (51.4)	173 (48.6)	–
Age—year. (mean ± SD)		69.7 (4.1)	69.1 (3.7)	0.137 [a]
Sex—no. (%)	Women	119 (65.0)	118 (68.2)	0.525 [b]
	Men	64 (35.0)	55 (31.8)	
Ethnicity—no. (%)	White	144 (78.7)	131 (75.7)	0.221 [a]
	Non-white	39 (21.3)	42 (24.3)	
Height—cm		167.2 (9.8)	165.9 (8.8)	0.176 [a]
Weight—kg		77.1 (17.2)	75.6 (16.1)	0.348 [a]
Body mass index (BMI)—kg/m^2		27.5 (4.8)	27.4 (4.8)	0.833 [a]
Waist circumference—cm		99.2 (14.1)	98.4 (13.4)	0.615 [a]
Smoking—no. (%)	Never	174 (95.1)	169 (97.7)	0.503 [c]
	Former	7 (3.8)	3 (1.7)	
	Current	2 (1.1)	1 (0.6)	
Physical activity—METs-h/week		3.54 (3.5)	3.70 (3.4)	0.840 [a]

Data are expressed as mean (SD), except for qualitative variables, expressed as n (%). [a] Two-sample t-test; [b] Chi-square test for independence; [c] Fisher's exact test.

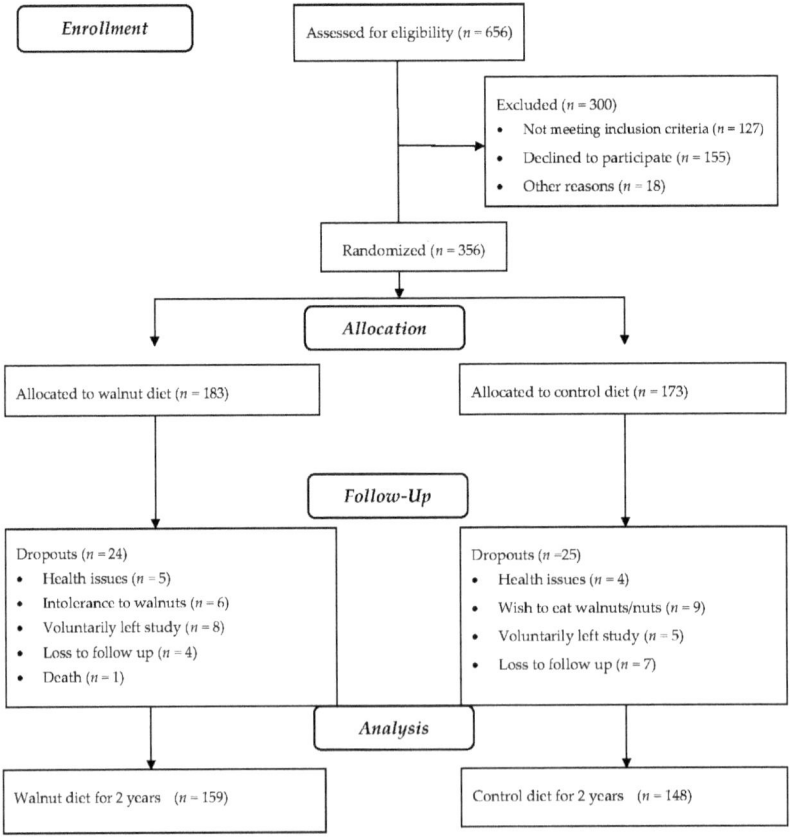

Figure 1. Study flowchart.

3.2. Compliance with Treatment

Only 1% of dietary recalls from the control group showed intake of trivial amounts of walnuts (<15 g), mostly as an ingredient in recipes and commercially prepared foods such as walnut bread, cookies, or salads. We therefore considered the subjects in the control group to have been 100% compliant with instructions not to consume walnuts. Similarly, 99% of dietary recalls in the walnut group reported consumption of the prescribed amount of walnuts (between 28 and 56 g/day, average 43 g/day). Table 2 shows data of macronutrients based on self-reported intake at two years. On average, energy, total polyunsaturated fatty acids, protein and fiber intake was significantly higher in the walnut group compared to control. The walnut supplement contributed approximately 15% of estimated daily energy needs.

Table 2. Average daily intake of macronutrients at 2 years by intervention group in participants completing the trial.

Variable	Walnut (n = 159) Mean * (SD)	Control (n = 148) Mean * (SD)	p-Value [d]
Energy (kcal)	1821 (503)	1593 (423)	<0.0001
Total carbohydrate (g)	204 (76)	192 (64)	0.199
Total protein (g)	70 (18)	65 (19)	0.011
Vegetable protein (g)	30 (11)	24 (11)	<0.0001
Total fat (g)	84 (24)	63 (20)	<0.0001
Saturated fat (g)	22 (9)	21 (9)	0.185
Monounsaturated fat (g)	25 (8)	22 (7)	0.001
Polyunsaturated fat (g)	31 (8)	14 (5)	<0.0001
Dietary cholesterol (mg)	202 (102)	218 (114)	0.308
Total dietary fiber (g)	24 (10)	20 (8)	<0.0001
Total carbohydrate (% E)	42.8 (10.2)	47.3 (11.4)	<0.0001
Total protein (% E)	15.5 (5)	16.6 (5.6)	0.01
Total fat (% E)	40.2 (8.7)	33.6 (9.7)	<0.0001
Saturated fat (% E)	10 (3.9)	11 (4.9)	0.01
Monounsaturated fat (% E)	11.8 (3.7)	11.9 (4.4)	0.662
Polyunsaturated fat (% E)	15.1 (4.7)	7.8 (3.7)	<0.0001

* Mean values for five 24-h diet recalls per individual; [d] Two sample t-test for group differences; % E denotes macronutrient intake as percent of total energy.

Analysis of baseline RBC fatty acids in a random sub-set of 105 study participants showed similar baseline levels of ALA (mean, 0.30% for the walnut group and 0.28% for the control group; $p = 0.830$). By the end of the study, the mean RBC ALA had increased by 33% in the walnut group and by 14% in the control group ($p < 0.001$). The correlation between 2-year changes in self-reported walnut intake and changes in RBC ALA was significant ($r = 0.49$, $p < 0.001$).

3.3. Changes in Physical Activity and Anthropometric Measurements

Table 3 shows the results of anthropometric measurements. Overall, body weight decreased significantly over time in all study participants ($p = 0.031$). Figure 2 is a plot of the average body weight of participants obtained periodically during clinic visits. Participants in the walnut group lost an average of 0.4 kg compared to 0.6 kg in the control group, with no between group differences ($p = 0.671$).

Table 3. Adiposity and physical activity during the 2-year follow-up by intervention group.

Variable	Timepoint	Walnut (n = 159) Mean (95% CI)	Control (n = 148) Mean (95% CI)	p-Value [e] Time Effect	p-Value [e] Group × Time Interaction Effect
Weight—kg	Baseline	77.1 (74.5, 79.6)	75.6 (73.0, 78.2)	0.031	0.671
	Year 1	76.9 (74.4, 79.4)	75.3 (72.7, 77.9)		
	Year 2	76.7 (74.1, 79.2)	75.0 (72.4, 77.6)		
Body fat—kg	Baseline	25.5 (24.4, 26.7)	25.5 (24.3, 26.2)	0.0001	0.528
	Year 1	25.9 (24.9, 27.0)	25.7 (24.6, 26.8)		
	Year 2	26.4 (25.3, 27.4)	26.0 (24.8, 27.1)		
Lean body mass—kg	Baseline	51.2 (49.4, 53.0)	49.5 (47.6, 51.3)	0.220	0.740
	Year 1	51.0 (49.2, 52.7)	49.4 (47.6, 51.2)		
	Year 2	50.8 (49.0, 52.6)	49.3 (47.4, 51.1)		
Waist circumference—cm	Baseline	99.4 (97.3, 101.6)	98.6 (96.4, 100.8)	0.680	0.651
	Year 1	99.6 (97.5, 101.7)	98.6 (96.5, 100.8)		
	Year 2	99.7 (97.6, 101.8)	98.6 (96.4, 100.8)		
Waist-to-hip ratio	Baseline	0.93 (0.91, 0.94)	0.92 (0.91, 0.94)	0.697	0.160
	Year 1	0.93 (0.92, 0.94)	0.92 (0.90, 0.93)		
	Year 2	0.93 (0.92, 0.95)	0.91 (0.90, 0.93)		
PA-METS—h/week	Baseline	3.54 (3.06, 4.02)	3.70 (3.21, 4.19)	<0.001	0.841
	Year 1	3.83 (3.40, 4.25)	4.02 (3.58, 4.46)		
	Year 2	4.11 (3.62, 4.61)	4.34 (3.83, 4.85)		

PA denotes physical activity; METS, metabolic equivalents. [e] Linear mixed models with three timepoints (baseline, year 1, and year 2). Model includes time, intervention, and their interaction. Results are adjusted for in-trial changes in PA.

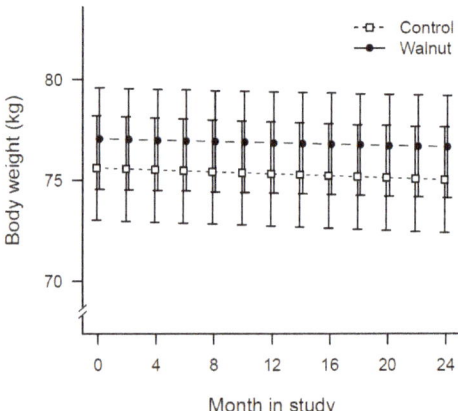

Figure 2. Plot of changes in mean body weight of participants over time by treatment allocation.

Figure 3A is a plot of the average waist circumference of participants at baseline, 1-year, and end of the study. The increase in waist circumference over time was not significant ($p = 0.680$) and there were no between group difference ($p = 0.651$). Figure 3B is a plot of the average body fat at baseline, 1-year, and end of the study. Mean body fat increased significantly in both groups ($p < 0.001$). Participants in the walnut group gained ≈0.9 kg (1.8%) body fat compared to 0.5 kg (0.9%) in the control group ($p = 0.528$ for between group differences).

Lean body mass decreased by 0.4 kg (0.8%) in the walnut group and by 0.2 kg (0.4%) in the control group. The change in lean body mass over time was not significant ($p = 0.220$) and did not differ between the two groups ($p = 0.740$) (Figure 3C). The change in WtHR over time (Figure 3D) was negligible, −0.009 in the control and +0.005 in the walnut group. Self-reported physical activity increased significantly over time in the two groups ($p = 0.0007$) without significant between group differences ($p = 0.841$).

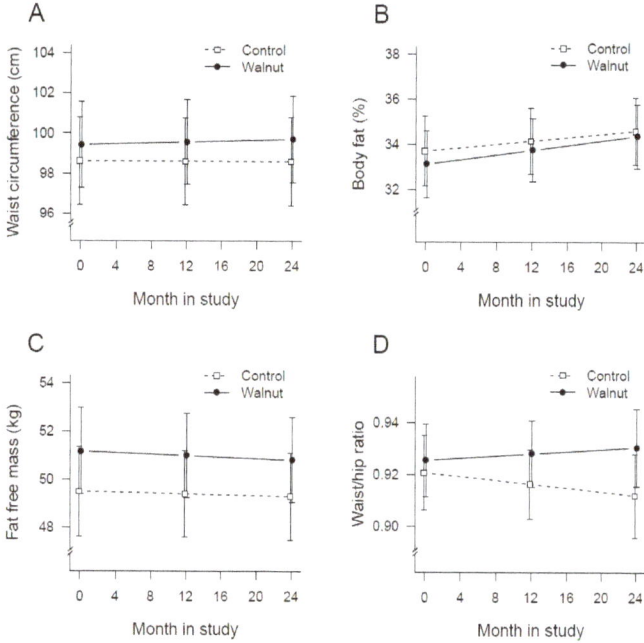

Figure 3. Plot of changes in mean waist circumference (**A**), body fat (**B**), lean body mass (**C**), and waist-to-hip ratio (**D**) over time by intervention group.

We considered potential differences in adiposity changes based on age at baseline, sex, and ethnicity. However, the inclusion of these variables into the models did not significantly affect adiposity measures.

4. Discussion

This opportunistic study within a randomized controlled trial sought to investigate adiposity changes after walnut supplementation for 2 years in an independently living, predominantly healthy, elderly cohort. The increase in RBC ALA content in the walnut group is a reliable indicator that participants adhered to the intervention. We previously reported a decrease in RBC ALA in the control group at one year [22], which we speculated was the result of restricting the use of ALA-rich flax. It is possible that some control group participants may have reverted to consuming these products in the second year of the study, perhaps due to perceived benefits, hence the increase in RBC ALA.

Overall, our data indicate that ingesting an average of nearly 300 kcal from walnuts daily for 2 years (without advice on foods to be replaced when adding walnuts to the diet) does not promote weight gain or cause significant changes in body composition. Sensitivity analyses showed that weight and adiposity trends were proportionally similar for men and women.

A tendency towards loss of lean body mass and fat gain over time has previously been reported in studies that have longitudinally assessed spontaneous adiposity changes in healthy, weight-stable elders [23,24]. One such study on free-living elderly persons of comparable mean age followed for the same period of time as our study participants reported a 0.32 kg and 0.16 kg loss in lean body mass and a concurrent 0.4% and 0.5% increase in body fat in men and women, respectively [25]. The self-reported increase in physical activity might have been due to participants' awareness that they were being monitored and the general tendency to over-report physical activity. Superior methods of assessing physical activity such as the use of accelerometers can help validate physical activity in future long-term nut trials in free-living individuals.

Notwithstanding the high energy density of walnuts, the lack of body weight increase might be explained by several mechanisms. We have previously reported that the energy contained in walnuts was offset in part by ≈19% spontaneous reduction in caloric intake from other food sources [22], although the compensatory response of our study subjects was lower than previously reported [26,27]. Other possible mechanisms include increased satiety following nut intake [28], energy regulation by nuts [29,30], and inefficient energy absorption from nuts [31] leading to increased fecal fat excretion [30,32–34]. Concerning increased fecal fat, it has been demonstrated that as much as 10–20% of the total energy from nuts is lost due to limited bioavailability in the gut [35]. In confirmation, recent findings show that the metabolizable energy content of walnuts is approximately 5.22 kcal/g (146 kcal/serving) as compared to the Atwater-calculated amount of 6.61 kcal/g (185 kcal/serving). Thus, Atwater factors overestimate by 21% the metabolizable energy content of walnuts [36]. Food compensation, increased satiety and reduced available energy are the most likely factors accounting for a stable weight during chronic nut consumption.

Our study has limitations. The original study was designed to assess changes in cognitive function and retinal health [14] and our results derive from a post hoc analysis. Also, three different clinical investigators obtained body measurements, suggesting that the data collected may be subject to interobserver variability despite the use of standardized protocols. Our study also has strengths. To the best of our knowledge, this study is the longest and largest randomized controlled trial to examine body weight change in relation to nut consumption in free-living healthy elders. Our parallel design is best suited for assessing weight changes since it disallows the potential for carry-over effects commonly seen in crossover feeding studies. Also, compliance with walnut consumption was corroborated with objective biomarkers. Future studies should consider examining whether walnuts contribute to energy regulation by increasing resting energy expenditure. Objective assessment of physical activity, i.e., using accelerometers, should assist in determining precisely the extent to which physical activity influences changes in body weight and adiposity measures in the context of chronic nut consumption.

5. Conclusions

In conclusion, our findings indicate that walnuts can be incorporated into the daily diet of healthy elders without concern for adverse effects on body weight or body composition. Even so, we recognize that individual differences in energy utilization and nutrient absorption and metabolism do exist, a reason why results may vary from person to person.

Author Contributions: Conceptualization, J.S. and E.B.; methodology, E.R., J.S., S.R., E.B.; formal analysis, K.O.; investigation, E.B., J.S., S.R.; writing—original draft preparation, E.B.; writing—review and editing, J.S., E.R., K.J.-S., A.S.-V., M.S.-M., K.O., S.R.; supervision, J.S.; funding acquisition, J.S. and E.R.

Funding: This work was supported by a grant from the California Walnut Commission, Folsom, CA, USA. The funding agency had no input in the study design, data collection, analyses or writing, and submission of the manuscript. An external overseeing committee monitors the study to ensure quality control data, integrity, and participants' safety. A.S.-V. is recipient of the Instituto de Salud Carlos III Miguel Servet fellowship (CP12/03299) and Fondo de Investigación Sanitaria grant—FEDER funds (PI15/01014).

Acknowledgments: We thank Natalie Kazzi and Lynnley Huey for their assistance in data collection, Ahmed Al Abdrabalnabi for his help with data cleaning, and Rawiwan Sirirat for her assistance with quality control on 24-h telephone diet recalls. CIBEROBN is an initiative of ISCIII, Spain.

Conflicts of Interest: A.S.-V., E.R., and J.S. have received grants for research through their respective institutions from the California Walnut Commission; E.R. and J.S. have also received personal money for preparing scientific presentations and are nonpaid members of its Scientific Advisory Committee. The funders had no role in the design of the study; in the collection, analyses, or interpretation of data; in the writing of the manuscript, or in the decision to publish the results.

References

1. Ogden, C.L.; Carroll, M.D.; Fryar, C.D.; Flegal, K.M. *Prevalence of Obesity among Adults and Youth: United States, 2011–2014*; US Department of Health and Human Services, Centers for Disease Control and Prevention, National Center for Health Statistics: Washington, DC, USA, 2015.

2. Hales, C.M.; Carroll, M.D.; Fryar, C.D.; Ogden, C.L. *Prevalence of Obesity among Adults and Youth: United States, 2015–2016*; US Department of Health and Human Services, Centers for Disease Control and Prevention, National Center for Health Statistics: Washington, DC, USA, 2017.
3. King, D.E.; Matheson, E.; Chirina, S.; Shankar, A.; Broman-Fulks, J. The status of baby boomers' health in the United States: The healthiest generation? *JAMA Intern. Med.* **2013**, *173*, 385–386. [CrossRef] [PubMed]
4. Aune, D.; Keum, N.; Giovannucci, E.; Fadnes, L.T.; Boffetta, P.; Greenwood, D.C.; Tonstad, S.; Vatten, L.J.; Riboli, E.; Norat, T. Nut consumption and risk of cardiovascular disease, total cancer, all-cause and cause-specific mortality: A systematic review and dose-response meta-analysis of prospective studies. *BMC Med.* **2016**, *14*, 207. [CrossRef] [PubMed]
5. Villareal, D.T.; Chode, S.; Parimi, N.; Sinacore, D.R.; Hilton, T.; Armamento-Villareal, R.; Napoli, N.; Qualls, C.; Shah, K. Weight loss, exercise, or both and physical function in obese older adults. *N. Engl. J. Med.* **2011**, *364*, 1218–1229. [CrossRef] [PubMed]
6. Ros, E. Nuts and CVD. *Br. J. Nutr.* **2015**, *113*, S111–S120. [CrossRef] [PubMed]
7. Ros, E.; Mataix, J. Fatty acid composition of nuts–implications for cardiovascular health. *Br. J. Nutr.* **2006**, *96*, S29–S35. [CrossRef] [PubMed]
8. Ros, E. Health benefits of nut consumption. *Nutrients* **2010**, *2*, 652–682. [CrossRef] [PubMed]
9. Taylor, S.E. *Qualified Health Claims: Letter of Enforcement Discretion-Walnuts and Coronary Heart Disease (Docket No 02P-0292)*; US Food and Drug Administration: Silver Spring, MD, USA, 2004.
10. Krauss, R.M.; Eckel, R.H.; Howard, B.; Appel, L.J.; Daniels, S.R.; Deckelbaum, R.J.; Erdman, J.W., Jr.; Kris-Etherton, P.; Goldberg, I.J.; Kotchen, T.A.; et al. AHA dietary guidelines revision 2000: A statement for healthcare professionals from the Nutrition Committee of the American Heart Association. *Circulation* **2000**, *102*, 2284–2299. [CrossRef] [PubMed]
11. Vannice, G.; Rasmussen, H. Position of the academy of nutrition and dietetics: Dietary fatty acids for healthy adults. *J. Acad. Nutr. Diet.* **2014**, *114*, 136–153. [CrossRef] [PubMed]
12. Flores-Mateo, G.; Rojas-Rueda, D.; Basora, J.; Ros, E.; Salas-Salvadó, J. Nut intake and adiposity: Meta-analysis of clinical trials. *Am. J. Clin. Nutr.* **2013**, *97*, 1346–1355. [CrossRef] [PubMed]
13. Mattes, R.D.; Kris-Etherton, P.M.; Foster, G.D. Impact of peanuts and tree nuts on body weight and healthy weight loss in adults. *J. Nutr.* **2008**, *138*, 1741S–1745S. [CrossRef] [PubMed]
14. Rajaram, S.; Valls-Pedret, C.; Cofán, M.; Sabaté, J.; Serra-Mir, M.; Pérez-Heras, A.M.; Arechiga, A.; Casaroli-Marano, R.P.; Alforja, S.; Sala-Vila, A.; Doménech, M. The Walnuts and Healthy Aging Study (WAHA): Protocol for a Nutritional Intervention Trial with Walnuts on Brain Aging. *Front. Aging Neurosci.* **2017**, *8*, 333. [CrossRef] [PubMed]
15. Volp, A.C.P.; Oliveira, F.C.E.; Alves, R.D.M.; Esteves, E.; Bressan, J. Energy expenditure: Components and evaluation methods. *Nutr. Hosp.* **2011**, *26*, 430–440.
16. Nutrition Coordinating Center. *Nutrition Data System for Research*; University of Minnesota: Minneapolis, MN, USA, 2011.
17. Fraser, G.E.; Bennett, H.W.; Jaceldo, K.B.; Sabaté, J. Effect on body weight of a free 76 kilojoule (320 calorie) daily supplement of almonds for six months. *J. Am. Coll. Nutr.* **2002**, *21*, 275–283. [CrossRef] [PubMed]
18. Sabate, J.; Fraser, G.E.; Burke, K.; Knutsen, S.F.; Bennett, H.; Lindsted, K.D. Effects of walnuts on serum lipid levels and blood pressure in normal men. *N. Engl. J. Med.* **1993**, *328*, 603–607. [CrossRef] [PubMed]
19. National Center for Health Statistics. *Anthropometry Procedures Manual—National Health and Nutrition Examination Survey (NHANES)*; NCHS: Hyattsville, MD, USA, 2013.
20. Haskell, W.L.; Lee, I.M.; Pate, R.R.; Powell, K.E.; Blair, S.N.; Franklin, B.A.; Macera, C.A.; Heath, G.W.; Thompson, P.D.; Bauman, A. Physical activity and public health: Updated recommendation for adults from the American College of Sports Medicine and the American Heart Association. *Circulation* **2007**, *116*, 1081. [CrossRef] [PubMed]
21. Sala-Vila, A.; Harris, W.S.; Cofán, M.; Pérez-Heras, A.M.; Pintó, X.; Lamuela-Raventós, R.M.; Covas, M.I.; Estruch, R.; Ros, E. Determinants of the omega-3 index in a Mediterranean population at increased risk for CHD. *Br. J. Nutr.* **2011**, *106*, 425–431. [CrossRef] [PubMed]
22. Bitok, E.; Jaceldo-Siegl, K.; Rajaram, S.; Serra-Mir, M.; Roth, I.; Feitas-Simoes, T.; Ros, E.; Sabaté, J. Favourable nutrient intake and displacement with long-term walnut supplementation among elderly: Results of a randomised trial. *Br. J. Nutr.* **2017**, *118*, 201. [CrossRef] [PubMed]

23. Gallagher, D.; Ruts, E.; Visser, M.; Heshka, S.; Baumgartner, R.N.; Wang, J.; Pierson, R.N.; Pi-Sunyer, F.X.; Heymsfield, S.B. Weight stability masks sarcopenia in elderly men and women. *Am. J. Physiol.-Endocrinol. Metab.* **2000**, *279*, E366–E375. [CrossRef] [PubMed]
24. Forbes, G.B. Longitudinal changes in adult fat-free mass: Influence of body weight. *Am. J. Clin. Nutr.* **1999**, *70*, 1025–1031. [CrossRef] [PubMed]
25. Zamboni, M.; Zoico, E.; Scartezzini, T.; Mazzali, G.; Tosoni, P.; Zivelonghi, A.; Gallagher, D.; De Pergola, G.; Di Francesco, V.; Bosello, O. Body composition changes in stable-weight elderly subjects: The effect of sex. *Aging Clin. Exp. Res.* **2003**, *15*, 321–327. [CrossRef] [PubMed]
26. Sabaté, J.; Cordero-MacIntyre, Z.; Siapco, G.; Torabian, S.; Haddad, E. Does regular walnut consumption lead to weight gain? *Br. J. Nutr.* **2005**, *94*, 859–864. [CrossRef] [PubMed]
27. Kirkmeyer, S.; Mattes, R.D. Effects of food attributes on hunger and food intake. International journal of obesity and related metabolic disorders. *J. Int. Assoc. Study Obes.* **2000**, *24*, 1167–1175. [CrossRef]
28. Mattes, R.D.; Dreher, M.L. Nuts and healthy body weight maintenance mechanisms. *Asia Pac. J. Clin. Nutr.* **2010**, *19*, 137–141. [PubMed]
29. Alper, C.; Mattes, R.D. Effects of chronic peanut consumption on energy balance and hedonics. International journal of obesity and related metabolic disorders. *J. Int. Assoc. Study Obes.* **2002**, *26*, 1129–1137. [CrossRef] [PubMed]
30. Hollis, J.; Mattes, R.D. Effect of chronic consumption of almonds on body weight in healthy humans. *Br. J. Nutr.* **2007**, *98*, 651–656. [CrossRef] [PubMed]
31. Levine, A.S.; Silvis, S.E. Absorption of whole peanuts, peanut oil, and peanut butter. *N. Engl. J. Med.* **1980**, *303*, 917–918. [CrossRef] [PubMed]
32. Haddad, E.; Sabate, J. (Eds.) Effect of pecan consumption on stool fat. *FASEB J.* **2000**, *14*, A294.
33. Kris-Etherton, P.M.; Hu, F.B.; Ros, E.; Sabaté, J. The role of tree nuts and peanuts in the prevention of coronary heart disease: Multiple potential mechanisms. *J. Nutr.* **2008**, *138*, 1746S–1751S. [CrossRef] [PubMed]
34. Zemaitis, J.; Sabaté, J. (Eds.) Effect of almond consumption on stool weight and stool fat. *FASEB J.* **2001**, *15*, A602.
35. Ellis, P.R.; Kendall, C.W.; Ren, Y.; Parker, C.; Pacy, J.F.; Waldron, K.W.; Jenkins, D.J. Role of cell walls in the bioaccessibility of lipids in almond seeds. *Am. J. Clin. Nutr.* **2004**, *80*, 604–613. [CrossRef] [PubMed]
36. Baer, D.; Gebauer, S.; Novotny, J. Atwater factors overestimate the calorie content of walnuts (371.1). *FASEB J.* **2014**, *28* (Suppl. 1), 371.

© 2018 by the authors. Licensee MDPI, Basel, Switzerland. This article is an open access article distributed under the terms and conditions of the Creative Commons Attribution (CC BY) license (http://creativecommons.org/licenses/by/4.0/).

Article

Bioelectrical Impedance Analysis Results for Estimating Body Composition Are Associated with Glucose Metabolism Following Laparoscopic Sleeve Gastrectomy in Obese Japanese Patients

Yoshinori Ozeki [1], Takayuki Masaki [1,*], Yuichi Yoshida [1], Mitsuhiro Okamoto [1], Manabu Anai [1], Koro Gotoh [1], Yuichi Endo [2], Masayuki Ohta [2], Masafumi Inomata [2] and Hirotaka Shibata [1]

1. Department of Endocrinology, Metabolism, Rheumatology and Nephrology, Faculty of Medicine, Oita University, Yufu City, Oita 879-5593, Japan; ozeki23@oita-u.ac.jp (Y.O.); y-yoshida@oita-u.ac.jp (Y.Y.); mokamoto@oita-u.ac.jp (M.O.); manabua@oita-u.ac.jp (M.A.); gotokoro@oita-u.ac.jp (K.G.); hiro-405@oita-u.ac.jp (H.S.)
2. Department of Gastroenterological and Pediatric Surgery, Oita University, Yufu City, Oita 879-5593, Japan; endo@oita-u.ac.jp (Y.E.); ohta@oita-u.ac.jp (M.O.); inomata@oita-u.ac.jp (M.I.)
* Correspondence: masaki@oita-u.ac.jp; Tel.: +81-975-86-5793

Received: 16 August 2018; Accepted: 5 October 2018; Published: 8 October 2018

Abstract: We investigated the association between body composition and changes in glucose metabolism following laparoscopic sleeve gastrectomy (LSG) in obese Japanese patients. Thirty-two Class III obese patients were assessed before LSG and 3, 6, and 12 months postoperatively. Variables including fat mass (FM), % body fat (%FM), total and skeletal muscle mass (MM), the ratio of lower extremity MM to body weight (BW) (L/W), and the ratio of upper extremity MM to BW (U/W) were measured while using bioelectrical impedance analysis (BIA). LSG significantly decreased BW, FM, and %FM in all time periods observed after surgery with concomitant improvements in metabolic markers. MM was decreased at three months but maintained from 3–12 months post-surgery. Importantly, %MM, U/W, and the L/W ratio increased after LSG. Furthermore, change in FM was positively correlated with change in BW 12 months after LSG, whereas changes in %MM were negatively correlated with fasting plasma glucose (FPG) and hemoglobin A1c (HbA1c). Finally, multivariable stepwise regression analyses showed that changes in % total MM was an independent determinant of FPG and change in % skeletal MM was a significant independent determinant of HbA1c in Class III obese Japanese patients after LSG.

Keywords: obesity; sleeve gastrectomy; body composition; fat mass

1. Introduction

Bariatric surgery is one of the most effective treatments for Class III obese patients. It significantly reduces obesity and lessens comorbid conditions, such as type-2 diabetes [1]. Among the surgical techniques utilized to promote weight loss, laparoscopic sleeve gastrectomy (LSG) is the most popular bariatric surgery and it is covered by health insurance in Japan [2,3]. LSG-associated body weight loss is also effective for improving type-2 diabetes [2,3].

Body composition assessments have an important role in clinical evaluation as well as in the monitoring of absolute and relative changes in fat mass (FM) and lean body mass during specific therapeutic regimens. Various assessment techniques have been evaluated in previous studies and different patterns have been reported [4–6]. Dual-energy X-ray absorptiometry (DXA) is traditionally used to assess body composition and it is considered to be valid and reliable [4].

However, the widespread application of this method is limited because it requires expensive equipment, trained technicians, and dedicated facilities.

Bioelectrical impedance analysis (BIA) represents a simple and noninvasive means of assessing body composition [7–9]. The method is based on the principle that electrical current moves more freely through hydrated tissue and extracellular water than through adipose tissue, providing reproducible and rapidly obtained results [8,9]. However, obese patients exhibit variable levels of soft tissue hydration, which may lead to errors in the results of this method. In addition, obese individuals experience changes in body composition, which are characterized by an increased amount of FM [9].

The loss of muscle mass (MM) via conditions such as sarcopenia is involved in type 2 diabetes and obesity [10–12]. A combination of skeletal MM decline and excess adiposity is termed sarcopenic obesity, which increases the risks for disability and mortality [13]. Several indices of sarcopenia have also been defined, including the ratio of lower extremity muscle mass to body weight (L/W ratio) and the ratio of lower extremity muscle mass to upper extremity muscle mass [11,14]. Although several studies have analyzed body composition in obese subjects after bariatric surgery, little is known about the relationships between body compositions, particularly MM, and glucose metabolism disorders. The objective of the study was to examine the relationships between glucose metabolism and body composition, as measured by BIA, particularly MM. Therefore, we investigated the association between MM, including total and skeletal MM, L/W, U/W ratio, and glucose metabolism disorders in Class III obese Japanese patients.

2. Materials and Methods

2.1. Subjects and Protocol

We retrospectively recruited 50 consecutive Class III obese patients (mean body mass index (BMI) 45.1 ± 9.7 kg/m^2, age 40.5 ± 9.1 years) undergoing LSG at Oita University Hospital from November 2013 to March 2018. Patients were selected for LSG according to the inclusion criteria standardized by the Ministry of Health, Labour, and Welfare of Japan. Eighteen subjects were excluded from the study between 0 months and 12 months after surgery. Inability to adhere to the testing schedule represented the key reason for exclusion. The final study cohort included 32 subjects, including 14 males and 18 females. In the present study, 10 of 17 patients with hypertension were taking hypertensive medication (Ca inhibitor, eight patients; ARB, nine patients; others, two patients). Three of 16 patients with hyperlipidemia were taking lipid-lowering medications (statins, one patient; fibrates, 0 patients; others, two patients). 18 patients did not have type-2 diabetes and eleven of 14 patients with type-2 diabetes were taking glucose-lowering medications (insulin, 0 patients; DPP-4 inhibitors, five patients; SGLT2 inhibitor, four patients; sulfonylureas, two patients; others, seven patients). None of the patients with type 2 diabetes was taking glucose-lowering medication to reduce glucose levels to the healthy range. In the present study, we examined time-course changes in obese patients with LSG; therefore, there was no control group (e.g., obese patients without LSG). Extensive clinical and hormonal endocrine evaluations were used to identify and exclude patients with endocrine diseases. The study design was in accordance with the Helsinki Declaration and was approved by the Ethical Committee of Oita University. The subjects gave their informed consent to participate in the study.

2.2. Biochemical Measurement and Blood Pressure

Blood was taken at 8:00 A.M. from the antecubital vein in patients in a recumbent position after an overnight fast. All of the patients underwent routine laboratory tests, including assays for plasma aspartate aminotransferase (AST), alanine transaminase (ALT), glutamic pyruvic transaminase (GTP), blood urea nitrogen (BUN), creatinine (Cr), low-density lipoprotein (LDL), triglycerides, high-density lipoprotein (HDL), glucose, and HbA1c. Fasting plasma glucose (FPG) was measured while using an enzymatic method (EIKEN, Tokyo, Japan). Hemoglobin A1c (HbA1c) was measured using high-performance liquid chromatography. BP was measured using the cuffoscillometric method between 8:00–10:00 A.M.

2.3. Anthropometry and Body Analyses

Body weight (BW), height, and BMI were measured for all subjects. BW was measured to the nearest 0.1 kg using digital scales; height was measured to the nearest 0.1 cm with the subjects wearing light indoor clothing. BMI was calculated from weight and height (kg/m^2). Ideal body weights were calculated as the body weight at a BMI of 25. The percent of total body weight loss (%TBWL) after surgery was calculated as (BW loss/BW) × 100. Excess body weight loss was BW—ideal body weight and percent of excess body weight loss (%EBWL) after surgery was (BW loss/EBW) × 100.

2.4. Bioelectrical Impedance Analysis

Body composition was analyzed using a BIA device (In-Body 770 Biospace Co., Ltd., Tokyo, Japan). The method is based on the principle that lean body mass contains higher levels of water and electrolytes than fat tissue, and so these tissues can be distinguished based on electrical impedance. Segmental body composition was estimated using a patented eight-point tactile electrode system. The device uses six frequencies (1, 5, 50, 250, 500, and 1000 kHz) and produces 30 impedance values for five body segments: right and left upper extremities, trunk, and right and left lower extremities [15]. A previous validation study showed that both fat mass (FM) and fat free mass (FFM) evaluated by this device were highly correlated with measurements using dual-energy X-ray absorptiometry (correlation coefficient = 0.832 and 0.899, respectively) [16].

Body composition was determined according to the standard technique, with the subject in a standing position and the electrodes placed on the right and left upper hand and foot. Patients were evaluated after overnight fasting and with an empty bladder. They were asked to refrain from strenuous exercise during the one-day preceding the measurements. Weight and height were recorded, and a clinical examination was performed. Body composition was calculated from bioelectrical measurements and anthropometric data by applying the software that was provided by the manufacturer, which incorporated validated predictive equations for BW. FM, percent of fat mass (%FM), total MM, skeletal MM, bone mineral content, and total body fluid were assessed. %FM was calculated as the product of percent fat and weight. Lean mass was determined to be the difference between BW and fat weight. % total MM was calculated as total MM (kg)/weight (kg) × 100. % skeletal MM was calculated as skeletal MM (kg)/weight (kg) × 100. L/W was calculated as lower muscle per kg/BW. U/W was calculated as upper muscle per kg/BW, according to a previous study [11].

2.5. Statistical Analyses

The data are presented as means ± SDs and they were analyzed by commercial software (JMP13.2 SAS Institute, Cary, NC, USA). The data of time-course change for each parameter were statistically evaluated by one-way analysis of variance (ANOVA). In addition, the data of each time point were evaluated by a post-hoc multiple comparison. A p value of less than 0.05 was considered to be statistically significant. Simple (Spearman rank) correlation coefficients were calculated, and then multiple regression analyses were used to evaluate the independent associations of these variables. Multiple stepwise regression analyses were conducted to access the association between body composition and glycemic profiles after adjusting for potential confounders, including BW and body fluid. Body fluid was included as a covariate in the BW model, and BW and body fluid were included as covariates in the FPG and HbA1c models.

3. Results

3.1. Basal Clinical Characteristics of Obese Patients and Body Weight Changes after LSG

The descriptive characteristics of the subjects prior to surgery are shown in Table 1. BW and BMI were both decreased at 3, 6, and 12 months after LSG when compared to pre-surgery ($p < 0.01$ for each) (Table 1). There was no significant difference between 3 vs. 6, 6 vs. 12 or 3 vs. 12 months in BW and BMI. The levels of %TBWL and %EBWL at 6 and 12 months were both increased compared to them at 3 months (Table 1). At 12 months after LSG compared to pre-surgery, there was no significant difference between males and females in the change in BW (males -37.1 ± 14.1 kg vs. females -38.2 ± 10.6 kg: $p = 0.80$), FM (males -29.2 ± 15.5 kg vs. females -27.8 ± 12.1 kg: $p = 0.52$), and %FM (males -13.7 ± 8.2 kg vs. females -15.5 ± 7.8 kg: $p = 0.64$) after bariatric surgery. However, male and female patients significantly differed with regard to %TBW loss (male 27.9 ± 8.9% vs female -34.7 ± 7.0%: $p = 0.02$).

3.2. Changes in Fat Mass after LSG

Observed FM and %FM were dramatically decreased at the 3, 6, and 12 month time points as compared to pre-surgery ($p < 0.01$ for each) (Table 1). In addition, both FM and %FM at 12 months were significantly decreased compared to them at three months (Table 1). Bone mineral content did not significantly change throughout the study ($p > 0.1$).

3.3. Muscle Mass Changes after LSG

Data on the MM, L/W, and U/W ratio over time are given in Table 1. The MM at 3, 6, and 12 months was decreased when compared to pre-surgery values, and MM was preserved 3 to 12 months after LSG. L/W and U/W ratio were significantly increased 3 or 6 months after LSG, and L/W ratio at 12 months increased compared to L/W at 3 months ($p < 0.05$). U/W ratio was unchanged from 3 month to 12 months after LSG. Observed total and skeletal %MM were dramatically increased at the 3, 6, and 12 month time points as compared to pre-surgery. In addition, both total and skeletal %MM at 12 months increased compared to %MM at three months.

3.4. Time Course Changes in Plasma Metabolic Parameters

Levels of FPG, HbA1C, AST, ALT, GTP, and triglycerides were all significantly decreased after LSG at 3, 6, and 12 months compared to pre-surgery levels. Conversely, plasma HDL was increased after LSG at 6 and 12 months compared to pre-surgery levels. There was no significant difference between 3 vs. 6, 6 vs. 12, or 3 vs. 12 months in FPG, HbA1C, AST, ALT, GTP, and triglycerides (Table 1). Plasma LDL, BUN, and Cr did not significantly change throughout the time period.

3.5. Correlation between Changes in Body Compositions and Changes in Glycemic Metabolic Parameters 12 Months after LSG

Changes in BW were associated with changes in FM, %FM ($r = 0.58$; $p = 0.001$), total MM ($r = 0.43$; $p = 0.02$), skeletal MM ($r = 0.46$; $p = 0.01$), % total MM ($r = -0.57$; $p = 0.001$), % skeletal MM ($r = -0.55$; $p = 0.001$), U/W ($r = -0.52$; $p = 0.003$), and L/W ($r = -0.64$; $p < 0.001$). Changes in FPG were correlated with changes in %FM ($r = 0.42$; $p = 0.02$), %total MM, %skeletal MM ($r = -0.40$; $p = 0.03$), and L/W ($r = -0.38$; $p = 0.04$). Changes in HbA1c were correlated with changes in %FM ($r = 0.52$; $p = 0.003$), %MM, U/W ($r = -0.43$; $p = 0.02$), and L/W ($r = -0.41$; $p = 0.02$). Figure 1 shows the data on correlations between ΔBW-ΔFM, ΔFPG-Δ%total MM, and ΔHbA1c-Δ%MM.

Table 1. Time-course changes in body weight, plasma metabolic parameters, and body composition.

	pre-LSG	Three Months	Six Months	Twelve Months	f	F-Value	p-Value
Body weight (kg)	120.0 ± 25.9	91.9 ± 21.3 ***	85.7 ± 20.8 ***	82.3 ± 22.2 ***	3	18.4	<0.001
Total body weight loss (kg)		28.1 ± 8.7	34.3 ± 10.0 †	37.8 ± 12.1 *†††	2	7.16	0.001
%TBWL		23.4 ± 5.5	28.6 ± 6.0 †	31.7 ± 8.5 *†††	2	12.3	<0.001
%EBWL		51.9 ± 21.4	71.9 ± 24.3 †	79.6 ± 28.9 *††	2	5.51	0.006
BMI (kg/m^2)	45.1 ± 9.7	34.6 ± 7.9 ***	32.2 ± 7.7 ***	30.8 ± 8.1 ***	3	19.1	<0.001
Systolic blood pressure (mmHg)	136.1 ± 19.6	123.1 ± 18.2 **	121.4 ± 20.0 **	121.2 ± 16.5 **	3	4.74	0.004
Diastolic blood pressure (mmHg)	84.8 ± 14.5	79.8 ± 12.4	77.4 ± 12.3	77.1 ± 12.3	3	2.46	0.07
Fasting plasma glucose (mg/dL)	109.6 ± 21.0	91.8 ± 15.7 ***	89.1 ± 9.9 ***	91.1 ± 15.8 ***	3	10.8	<0.001
HbA1c (%)	6.4 ± 0.9	5.3 ± 0.4 ***	5.3 ± 0.3 ***	5.3 ± 0.3 ***	3	31.2	<0.001
Triglycerides (mg/dL)	163.9 ± 92.0	98.8 ± 33.8 ***	92.0 ± 30.6 ***	83.8 ± 39.7 ***	3	13.5	<0.001
HDL cholesterol (mg/dL)	45.7 ± 8.7	47.1 ± 9.6	53.8 ± 11.4 ***	59.1 ± 14.1 ****†††	3	9.45	<0.001
LDL cholesterol (mg/dL)	125.2 ± 28.7	122.9 ± 32.4	125.8 ± 28.0	122.9 ± 35.4	3	0.07	0.97
BUN (mg/dL)	12.5 ± 3.0	11.3 ± 4.0	12.3 ± 3.7	13.6 ± 3.7	3	2.32	0.08
Creatinine (mg/dL)	0.70 ± 0.21	0.69 ± 0.17	0.71 ± 0.15	0.72 ± 0.17	3	0.21	0.89
AST (IU/L)	37.7 ± 24.9	19.0 ± 5.7 ***	15.8 ± 3.2 ***	16.0 ± 4.2 ***	3	20.7	<0.001
ALT (IU/L)	55.4 ± 45.1	18.4 ± 10.2 ***	12.8 ± 4.1 ***	12.9 ± 5.5 ***	3	24.7	<0.001
GTP (IU/L)	45.3 ± 34.9	20.1 ± 16.4 ***	17.7 ± 17.2 ***	16.1 ± 10.1 ***	3	12.9	<0.001
FM (%)	48.1 ± 6.9	39.9 ± 10.2 ***	35.9 ± 9.8 ***	33.4 ± 10.5 ***††	3	14.8	<0.001
FM (kg)	56.5 ± 19.0	37.3 ± 16.3 ***	31.2 ± 14.8 ***	28.1 ± 15.3 ***†	3	19.7	<0.001
Total MM (kg)	56.7 ± 11.6	50.6 ± 10.3 *	50.6 ± 11.0 *	50.0 ± 10.7 *	3	2.67	0.05
Total MM/BW	0.49 ± 0.06	0.57 ± 0.10 **	0.61 ± 0.10 ***	0.63 ± 0.10 ***††	3	14.5	<0.001
Skeletal MM (kg)	33.4 ± 7.2	29.3 ± 6.4 *	29.2 ± 6.7 *	29.0 ± 6.7 **	3	3.18	0.03
Skeletal MM/BW	0.29 ± 0.04	0.33 ± 0.06 *	0.35 ± 0.06 ***	0.36 ± 0.06 ***†	3	10.9	<0.001
Upper Skeletal MM/BW	0.06 ± 0.01	0.07 ± 0.01	0.07 ± 0.01 **	0.07 ± 0.01 **	3	4.17	0.008
Lower Skeletal MM/BW	0.16 ± 0.02	0.19 ± 0.03 ***	0.20 ± 0.03 ***	0.21 ± 0.03 ***†	3	15.3	<0.001

LSG: laparoscopic sleeve gastrectomy; TBWL: total body weight loss; EBWL: excessive body weight loss; BMI: body mass index; BUN: blood urea nitrogen; HDL: high-density lipoprotein; LDL: low-density lipoprotein; AST: aspartate aminotransferase; ALT: alanine transaminase; GTP: glutamic pyruvic transaminase; HbA1c: hemoglobin A1c; FM: fat mass; MM: muscle mass; BW: body weight. f, degrees of freedom; F-value and p-value for each parameter are described in right columns (indicate significant time-course changes assessed by ANOVA analysis). * $p < 0.05$, ** $p < 0.01$, *** $p < 0.001$ vs. pre-surgery; † $p < 0.05$, †† $p < 0.01$, ††† $p < 0.001$ vs. 3 month (indicate significant changes between each time assessed by posthoc multiple comparison).

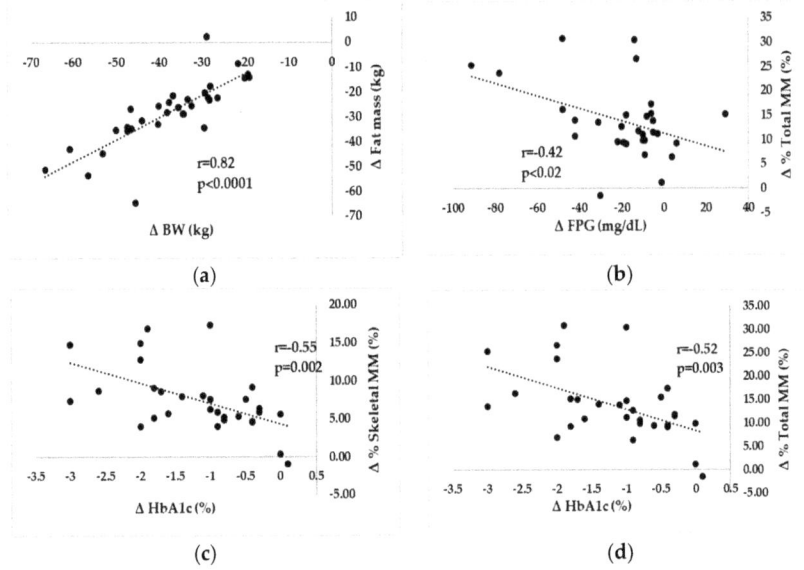

Figure 1. Correlation between changes in body compositions and changes in glycemic metabolic parameters. (**a**) relationship between BW and fat mass; (**b**) relationship between FPG and % total MM; (**c**) relationship between HbA1c and % skeletal MM; (**d**) relationship between HbA1c and % total MM, Variables: Δ (0–12 month) variables; BW: body weight, MM: muscle mass, FPG: fasting plasma glucose, HbA1c: hemoglobin A1c. Simple correlation coefficients were calculated. r = correlation coefficient. A p value of less than 0.05 was considered to be statistically significant.

3.6. Relationships among Changes in Body Weight, FPG, and HbA1c

Multiple stepwise regression analyses were conducted to assess the association between body composition and glycemic profiles after adjusting for potential confounders, including BW and body fluid (Table 2). Multiple stepwise regression analyses were carried out for changes in BW as a dependent variable, including changes in FM, %FM, MM, %MM, U/W, and L/W as independent variables. Only changes in FM were independently correlated with changes in BW.

Table 2. Multiple stepwise regression models with ΔBW, ΔFPG, and ΔHbA1c as dependent valuables.

Model	Independent Variables	F Value	p Value
BW	Fat mass (kg)	59.6	<0.001 **
FPG	% Total MM (%)	5.9	0.022 *
HbA1c	% Skeletal MM (%)	11.2	0.002 **

Independent variables: Δ (0–12 month) variables, BW: body weight, FPG: fasting plasma glucose; HbA1c: hemoglobin A1c, MM: muscle mass, Δ (0–12 month), The covariates in BW model is body; fluid and covariates in FPG and HbA1c model are BW and body fluid. * $p < 0.05$, ** $p < 0.01$.

To examine the contribution of changes in %FM, %MM, and L/W to changes in FPG, multivariate stepwise regression analyses were used. When changes in BW and changes in body fluid entered into the equation as covariates, only changes in %total MM remained as an independent determinant of changes in FPG. In addition, multiple stepwise regression analyses were carried out for changes in HbA1c as a dependent variable, including changes in %FM, %MM, L/W, U/W, body fluid, BW, and HbA1c as independent variables. Only changes in % skeletal MM were independently correlated with changes in HbA1c.

4. Discussion

The present study demonstrated that BW, FM, and %FM decreased, while % total MM and % skeletal MM increased after LSG. In addition, changes in FM and %MM were correlated with obesity, FPG, and HbA1c in Class III obese Japanese patients after LSG.

Bariatric surgery is used to treat obesity and comorbid conditions. In terms of weight loss, a sustained reduction of ≥50% excess weight is considered as a success. Recent meta-analyses and systematic reviews have reported a %EBWL close to 60% one year after a gastric bypass with ranges from 33% to 77% [17–19]. In the present study, LSG reduced BW in all time periods observed. %TBWL was 31.7 ± 8.5% and %EBWL was 79.6 ± 28.9% at 12 months compared to pre-surgery weights. The results are similar to previous studies [17–19]. In addition, several studies described the data in Japanese patients following bariatric surgery [20,21]. Japan nationwide surveys of bariatric surgery demonstrated the mean age of obese patients was 41 years, and mean BMI was 42 kg/m^2 [20]. After LSG with duodeno-jejunal bypass, %TBWL was 29% at one year in Japan [21]. The age and changes in weight are also almost comparable to data in the present study.

The great weight loss observed in our patients prompted concern regarding the impact of weight loss on body composition, including FM and MM. The excess weight in obese patients is mainly due to FM [19,22], and several studies have demonstrated a close correlation between the content of body fat and several cardiovascular and metabolic diseases. In our study, there was a significant loss of FM in all patients. One year after surgery, the %FM reached levels within 30%, a significant finding given that FM loss is important to improve glucose metabolism disorders.

Contrary to FM loss, a reduction of MM has undesirable effects on diabetic obese patients. Our data demonstrate the time course of several changes to muscle composition in obese Japanese patients. This study showed that MM are maintained in patients from 3 to 12 months after LSG. L/W ratio was increased three months after LSG, and L/W ratio also increased at 12 months compared to three months. Total and skeletal %MM were dramatically increased at the 3, 6, and 12 month time points as compared to pre-surgery. In addition, %MM was increased at 12 months compared to three months after LSG. This resulted in a positive change in body composition after LSG in obese patients.

There is question about the utility of the BIA method for examining body composition of Class III obese patients. Several studies have validated the accuracy of body composition determined by BIA in bariatric surgery patients. Parallel measurements of body composition using BIA and DXA in a homogeneous normo-hydrated group of obese subjects post-LAGB shows high agreement between the results obtained by BIA and DXA. These findings indicate that the BIA method might be useful as an alternative to DXA [16,23]. To avoid the influence of body fluids on MM, body compositions were adjusted for body fluid in the present study.

We also examined sex-specific changes in body composition after LSG. It is well recognized that women have more body fat than men at the same relative BMI. A previous study observed that obese female patients had higher body fat and lower muscle percentages than males [24]. Additionally, several studies have tested for gender differences in weight and fat loss after bariatric surgery [25,26]. One study found no significant differences in the BMIs of males and females after bariatric surgery, although male patients continued to weigh significantly more than females and lost significantly more pounds than did females after bariatric surgery [25]. Another study found that %EBWL differed significantly between male and female patients after LSG [26]. In the present study, changes in BW, FM, and %FM did not differ between the sexes. However, %BW loss differed significantly between male and female patients. This may be due to the difference between the absolute value and the % of BW. In this study, however, changes in BMI, body fat, and muscle weight percentage did not differ between the sexes. The results are difficult to explain. It appears that changes in individual body composition with weight loss are highly variable even within the same sex. Several studies have demonstrated a mechanistic link between menstruation and body composition, but it is clear that additional studies are needed to further clarify the potential sex differences in body composition measures after bariatric surgery.

A recent study described the effect of bariatric surgery on diabetes outcomes persists fifth year after surgery in non-Japanese individuals [27]. In the present study, we examined the relationships between changes in body composition and plasma glycemic parameters in Japanese patients for 12 months following LSG. FPG and HbA1c were dramatically improved after LSG. Changes in FM were correlated with changes in BW after LSG. In addition, changes in %MM were negatively correlated with changes in FPG and HbA1c up to 12 months after LSG. Multivariable regression analyses showed that changes in FM were independent and significant determinants of BW loss, changes in % total MM were significant independent determinants of FPG, and changes in % skeletal MM were significant independent determinants of HbA1c. The precise significance of differences between changes in %total MM and changes in % skeletal MM are unknown, however, our results show that changes in %MM are significant determinants of FPG and HbA1c in obese Japanese patients after LSG. In fact, enhanced skeletal muscle offers great benefits for glucose regulation via muscle-intrinsic mechanisms. Also, enhanced muscle growth has positive effects on fat metabolism and insulin resistance/sensitivity through several molecular mechanisms, such as increasing adiponectin expression [28].

Limitations to our study included statistical overfitting because of a small sample size and potential confounding factors. BIA is sensitive to hydration, and we did not measure hydration status or caffeine intake in this study. The study design did not allow us to examine a causal relationship, and future prospective studies including appropriate control patients would help to clarify some of the outcomes. Further studies are necessary to clarify the physiological mechanisms that contribute to changes in body composition. In addition, although almost all patients were medication-free after LSG, we cannot fully exclude a possible influence of several temporal medications. Finally, more detailed and longer studies are needed to validate the effects of LSG on muscle parameters, including muscle strength and quality.

Author Contributions: Y.O., T.M., Y.E., M.Ohta., M.I. and H.S. conceived and designed the study; Y.O., T.M., Y.Y., M.Okamoto. and M.A. contributed to the analysis; Y.O., T.M., and K.G. contributed to the interpretation of data for the work; Y.O., T.M., and H.S. wrote the paper.

Funding: This work was supported by JSPS KAKENHI grant number JP17K01854.

Acknowledgments: The authors thank RD Yuko Hirota and Kazuyo Adachi for excellent technical assistance.

Conflicts of Interest: The authors declare no conflict of interest.

Abbreviations

LSG	laparoscopic sleeve gastrectomy
BW	Body weight
BIA	bioelectrical impedance analysis
DX	Dual-energy X-ray absorptiometry
FM	fat mass
MM	muscle mass weight
%MM	% muscle mass
L/W	the ratio of lower extremity MM to BW
U/W	the ratio of upper extremity MM to BW
TBWL	total body weight loss
EBWL	excessive body weight loss
AST	aspartate aminotransferase
ALT	alanine transaminase
GTP	glutamic pyruvic transaminase
BUN	blood urea nitrogen
Cr	creatinine
LDL	low-density lipoprotein
HDL	high-density lipoprotein
FPG	fasting plasma glucose
HbA1c	Hemoglobin A1c

References

1. Shoar, S.; Mahmoudzadeh, H.; Naderan, M. Long-term outcome of bariatric surgery in morbidly obese adolescents: A systematic review and meta-analysis of 950 patients with a minimum of 3 years follow-up. *Obes. Surg.* **2017**, *27*, 3110–3117. [CrossRef] [PubMed]
2. Wang, Y.; Yi, X.; Li, Q. The effectiveness and safety of sleeve gastrectomy in the obese elderly patients: A systematic review and meta-analysis. *Obes. Surg.* **2016**, *26*, 3023–3030. [CrossRef] [PubMed]
3. Switzer, N.J.; Prasad, S.; Debru, E. Sleeve gastrectomy and type 2 diabetes mellitus: A systematic review of long-term outcomes. *Obes. Surg.* **2016**, *26*, 1616–1621. [CrossRef] [PubMed]
4. Ramírez-Vélez, R.; Correa-Bautista, J.E.; González-Ruíz, K. Predictive validity of the body adiposity index in overweight and obese adults using dual-energy x-ray absorptiometry. *Nutrients* **2016**, *8*, 737. [CrossRef] [PubMed]
5. Gómez-Ambrosi, J.; González-Crespo, I.; Catalán, V. Clinical usefulness of abdominal bioimpedance (ViScan) in the determination of visceral fat and its application in the diagnosis and management of obesity and its comorbidities. *Clin. Nutr.* **2018**, *37*, 580–589. [CrossRef] [PubMed]
6. Umemura, A.; Sasaki, A.; Nitta, H. Effects of changes in adipocyte hormones and visceral adipose tissue and the reduction of obesity-related comorbidities after laparoscopic sleeve gastrectomy in Japanese patients with severe obesity. *Endocr. J.* **2014**, *61*, 381–391. [CrossRef] [PubMed]
7. Widen, E.M.; Strain, G.; King, W.C. Validity of bioelectrical impedance analysis for measuring changes in body water and percent fat after bariatric surgery. *Obes. Surg.* **2014**, *24*, 847–854. [CrossRef] [PubMed]
8. Buffa, R.; Mereu, E.; Comandini, O. Bioelectrical impedance vector analysis (BIVA) for the assessment of two-compartment body composition. *Eur. J. Clin. Nutr.* **2014**, *68*, 1234–1240. [CrossRef] [PubMed]
9. Xiao, J.; Purcell, S.A.; Prado, C.M. Fat mass to fat-free mass ratio reference values from NHANES III using bioelectrical impedance analysis. *Clin. Nutr.* **2017**, *5614*, 31353–31355. [CrossRef] [PubMed]
10. Tanaka, K.I.; Kanazawa, I.; Sugimoto, T. Reduced muscle mass and accumulation of visceral fat are independently associated with increased arterial stiffness in postmenopausal women with type 2 diabetes mellitus. *Diabetes Res. Clin. Pract.* **2016**, *122*, 141–147. [CrossRef] [PubMed]
11. Hamasaki, H.; Kawashima, Y.; Adachi, H. Associations between lower extremity muscle mass and metabolic parameters related to obesity in Obese Japanese patients with type 2 diabetes. *Peer. J.* **2015**, *3*, e942. [CrossRef] [PubMed]
12. Wannamethee, S.G.; Atkins, J.L. Muscle loss and obesity: The health implications of sarcopenia and sarcopenic obesity. *Proc. Nutr. Soc.* **2015**, *74*, 405–412. [CrossRef] [PubMed]
13. Rossi, A.P.; Bianchi, L.; Volpato, S. Dynapenic abdominal obesity as a predictor of worsening disability, hospitalization, and mortality in older adults: Results from the In CHIANTI study. *J. Gerontol. Biol. Sci. Med. Sci.* **2017**, *72*, 1098–1104. [CrossRef] [PubMed]
14. Dixon, J.B.; Bhasker, A.G.; Lambert, G.W. Leg to leg bioelectrical impedance analysis of percentage fat mass in obese patients: Can it tell us more than we already know? *Surg. Obes. Relat. Dis.* **2016**, *12*, 1397–1402. [CrossRef] [PubMed]
15. Anderson, L.J.; Erceg, D.N.; Schroeder, E.T. Utility of multifrequency bioelectrical impedance compared with dual-energy X-ray absorptiometry for assessment of total and regional body composition varies between men and women. *Nutr. Res.* **2012**, *32*, 479–485. [CrossRef] [PubMed]
16. Faria, S.L.; Faria, O.P.; Cardeal, M.D. Validation study of multi-frequency bioelectrical impedance with dual-energy X-ray absorptiometry among obese patients. *Obes. Surg.* **2014**, *24*, 1476–1480. [CrossRef] [PubMed]
17. Kim, H.J.; Madan, A.; Fenton-Lee, D. Does patient compliance with follow-up influence weight loss after gastric bypass surgery? A systematic review and meta-analysis. *Obes. Surg.* **2014**, *24*, 647–651. [CrossRef] [PubMed]
18. Zhang, C.; Yuan, Y.; Qiu, C. A meta-analysis of 2-year effect after surgery: Laparoscopic Roux-en-Y gastric bypass versus laparoscopic sleeve gastrectomy for morbid obesity and diabetes mellitus. *Obes. Surg.* **2014**, *24*, 1528–1535. [CrossRef] [PubMed]
19. Qi, L.; Guo, Y.; Liu, C.Q. Effects of bariatric surgery on glycemic and lipid metabolism, surgical complication and quality of life in adolescents with obesity: A systematic review and meta-analysis. *Surg. Obes. Relat. Dis.* **2017**, *13*, 2037–2055. [CrossRef] [PubMed]

20. Haruta, H.; Kasama, K.; Ohta, M. Long-Term Outcomes of Bariatric and Metabolic Surgery in Japan: Results of a Multi-Institutional Survey. *Obes. Surg.* **2017**, *27*, 754–762. [CrossRef] [PubMed]
21. Seki, Y.; Kasama, K.; Haruta, H. Five-Year-Results of Laparoscopic Sleeve Gastrectomy with Duodenojejunal Bypass for Weight Loss and Type 2 Diabetes Mellitus. *Obes. Surg.* **2017**, *27*, 795–801. [CrossRef] [PubMed]
22. Rayner, J.J.; Banerjee, R.; Francis, J.M. Normalization of visceral fat and complete reversal of cardiovascular remodeling accompany gastric bypass, not banding. *J. Am. Coll. Cardiol.* **2015**, *66*, 2569–2570. [CrossRef] [PubMed]
23. Tewari, N.; Awad, S.; Macdonald, I.A. A comparison of three methods to assess body composition. *Nutrition* **2018**, *47*, 1–5. [CrossRef] [PubMed]
24. Van Caenegem, E.; Wierckx, K.; Taes, Y. Bone mass, bone geometry, and body composition in female-to-male transsexual persons after long-term cross-sex hormonal therapy. *J. Clin. Endocrinol. Metab.* **2012**, *97*, 2503–2511. [CrossRef] [PubMed]
25. Tymitz, K.; Kerlakian, G.; Engel, A. Gender differences in early outcomes following hand-assisted laparoscopic Roux-en-Y gastric bypass surgery: Gender differences in bariatric surgery. *Obes. Surg.* **2007**, *17*, 1588–1591. [CrossRef] [PubMed]
26. Perrone, F.; Bianciardi, E.; Benavoli, D. Gender Influence on Long-Term Weight Loss and Comorbidities after Laparoscopic Sleeve Gastrectomy and Roux-en-Y Gastric Bypass: A Prospective Study with a 5-Year Follow-up. *Obes. Surg.* **2016**, *26*, 276–281. [CrossRef] [PubMed]
27. Ikramuddin, S.; Korner, J.; Lee, W.J. Lifestyle Intervention and Medical Management with vs without Roux-en-Y Gastric Bypass and Control of Hemoglobin A1c, LDL Cholesterol, and Systolic Blood Pressure at 5 Years in the Diabetes Surgery Study. *JAMA* **2018**, *319*, 266–278. [CrossRef] [PubMed]
28. Yang, J. Enhanced skeletal muscle for effective glucose homeostasis. *Prog. Mol. Biol. Transl. Sci.* **2014**, *121*, 133–163. [PubMed]

© 2018 by the authors. Licensee MDPI, Basel, Switzerland. This article is an open access article distributed under the terms and conditions of the Creative Commons Attribution (CC BY) license (http://creativecommons.org/licenses/by/4.0/).

Article

Comparison of a Bioelectrical Impedance Device against the Reference Method Dual Energy X-Ray Absorptiometry and Anthropometry for the Evaluation of Body Composition in Adults

Kaitlin Day [1,*], Alastair Kwok [1], Alison Evans [1], Fernanda Mata [1,2], Antonio Verdejo-Garcia [2], Kathryn Hart [3], Leigh C. Ward [4] and Helen Truby [1]

1. Department of Nutrition, Dietetics and Food, Monash University, Notting Hill, VIC 3168, Australia; alastair.kwok@monash.edu (A.K.); Alison.evans@monash.edu (A.E.); fernandagmata@gmail.com (F.M.); helen.truby@monash.edu (H.T.)
2. School of Psychological Sciences, Monash University, Clayton, VIC 3168, Australia; Antonio.Verdejo@monash.edu
3. Department of Nutritional Sciences, University of Surrey, Guildford GU2 7XH, UK; k.hart@surrey.ac.uk
4. School of Chemistry and Molecular Biosciences, The University of Queensland, Brisbane, QLD 4072, Australia; l.ward@uq.edu.au
* Correspondence: kaitlin.day@monash.edu; Tel.: +61-3-9902-4261

Received: 31 July 2018; Accepted: 4 October 2018; Published: 10 October 2018

Abstract: This study aimed to compare the use of the bioelectrical impedance device (BIA) seca® mBCA 515 using dual X-ray absorptiometry (DXA) as a reference method, for body composition assessment in adults across the spectrum of body mass indices. It explores the utility of simple anthropometric measures (the waist height ratio (WHtR) and waist circumference (WC)) for the assessment of obesity. In the morning after an overnight fast (10 h), 30 participants underwent a body composition DXA (GE iDXA) scan, BIA (seca 515), and anthropometric measures. Compared to the DXA reference measure, the BIA underestimated fat mass (FM) by 0.32 kg (limits of agreement −3.8 kg, 4.4 kg); overestimated fat free mass (FFM) by 0.43 kg (limits of agreement −8.2 kg, 4.3 kg). Some of the variation was explained by body mass index (BMI), as for FM, the mean difference of the normal range BMI group was smaller than for the overweight/obese group (0.25 kg and 0.35 kg, respectively) with wider limits of agreement (−4.30 kg, 4.81 kg, and −3.61 kg, 4.30 kg, respectively). There were significant differences in visceral adipose tissue (VAT) volume measurements between methods with BIA systematically overestimating VAT compared to DXA. WC was more strongly correlated with DXA FM (rho = 0.90, $p < 0.001$) than WHtR (rho = 0.83, $p < 0.001$). BIA had some agreement with DXA; however, they are not equivalent measures for the range of BMIs explored, with DXA remaining the more informative tool. WC is a useful and simple assessment tool for obesity.

Keywords: body composition; dual X-ray absorptiometry; bioelectrical impedance; validation; anthropometry

1. Introduction

In Australia, 63.4% of adults are overweight or obese, according to their body mass index (kg/m^2, BMI), [1]. With growing obesity rates comes an increase in lifestyle diseases, such as type 2 diabetes mellitus and cardiovascular disease [2,3]. It is widely accepted that the risk of developing an obesity-related disease is more closely associated with body fat distribution than an individual's body fat percentage [4]. Central adiposity is of particular concern, which tends to be associated with excess subcutaneous adipose tissue and visceral adipose tissue (VAT) [5]. VAT is a highly metabolically active tissue which stimulates lipolytic activity, increasing circulating levels of free fatty acids. Through this and other mechanisms, it orchestrates a switch from an anti-inflammatory to a pro-inflammatory profile of cytokines in circulating plasma [6–8]. This drives metabolic dysregulation, and as such, those with a central deposition of VAT are at a higher risk of several obesity-related diseases which is often independent of overall obesity [9–13].

BMI is a widely used method for the assessment of obesity, with a cut-off of ≥ 25 kg/m^2 utilized to discriminate individuals of normal weight from overweight and obese individuals [14]. Although BMI is well-accepted at a group level for the assessment of metabolic risk and the risk of premature death, at an individual level, as a surrogate measure of body fatness, it is unable to provide an indication of body fat distribution. Optimal use of other body composition assessment tools depends upon whether the individual is of a normal weight or is overweight, as defined by BMI. Simple anthropometric measures, such as waist circumference (WC) and its ratio with height (WHtR) are used to determine risks associated with central adiposity. The development and validation of WHtR as a tool to identify those at risk of metabolic complications of obesity has been well-established for adults and children [15,16].

Assessment of body composition is used in a variety of settings, from weight management clinics to sports performance, and screening at a population level for risk of obesity complications [17]. Therefore, methods for body composition assessment must be able to detect clinically relevant changes quickly and robustly. Owing to the wide range of applications for body composition assessment, an instrument must be accurate and precise for a range of body sizes; or where such an instrument is not available, it must be determined which method of body composition is most suitable for a particular population, as defined by their body size. Consequently, establishing agreement and/or equivalence between different methods is necessary to understand the appropriate use and setting for each instrument.

Dual X-ray absorptiometry (DXA) is a commonly used method for the assessment of body composition, especially bone density and soft tissue [18]. The GE Lunar iDXA uses a fan beam system to measure bone density and total cell mass, and it can also estimate fat mass (FM) and fat-free mass (FFM). DXA is a well-accepted reference method of body composition assessment (FM and FFM) in adults and children and the GE Lunar iDXA, with its proprietary CoreScan software, also estimates VAT. This measure, although not directly measured, has shown good agreement with computer topography (CT) and magnetic resonance imaging (MRI) [18–20]. DXA machines are expensive, large, and are not readily portable. They require specialist staff, and present a radiation hazard, albeit a low one, to participants. This makes them unsuitable as a method for screening large numbers of potentially at-risk patients in the community.

Bioelectrical impedance devices (BIA) are smaller, some being hand-held, and faster, and require little training for their use. They use a harmless electrical current, rather than radiation, to assess body composition. BIA measures the opposition (impedance or resistance) to the flow of an electric current through the body, and uses this information to predict total body water (TBW). Predictions are made via the use of algorithms, often empirically derived and device-specific, in order to quantify FFM, calculated as TBW/0.732 where 0.732 is an assumed hydration fraction of the FFM. FM is obtained by subtracting FFM from total mass. The seca® mBCA 515 Analyser (seca®, Hamburg, Germany) offers the additional calculation of VAT volume through an in-house developed proprietary algorithm [21].

Current literature suggests that BIA could be a viable alternative to DXA for determining body composition, with BIA offering an inexpensive, faster, and less invasive option. However, to date, studies have not investigated its utility across a wide spectrum of body sizes (BMI) [22,23]. Shafer et al. (2009) found that BIA significantly overestimated FM and FFM compared to DXA. The magnitude of the overestimation was dependent on BMI [24]. Contrastingly, a study by Anderson et al. (2012) demonstrated good agreement between BIA and DXA for FM and lean body mass in a range of BMIs [25]. Other studies have reported small errors in FM measurements [23,26] and even smaller errors in FFM measurements [27,28] in various BIA analyzers. This highlights that the validity of BIA instruments varies across manufacturers and, as such, each new BIA model should be independently assessed against accepted reference methods, such as DXA.

There is a clear need for a better understanding of the strengths and weaknesses of different techniques of body composition instruments, which is particularly true when proprietary algorithms are incorporated into simple devices but with little explanation, such as with the seca 515 mBCA Analyzer. Often, BIA devices are used interchangeably with other body composition methods, and so there is a need to explore whether this is appropriate. Other simple measures include WHtR and WC, which are quick and simple anthropometric measures often used to assess central adiposity, and can be surrogate indicators of disease risk in both adults and children [16,29]. The BIA and DXA instruments tested here offer detailed body composition assessment, including the quantification of VAT. With multiple options for the assessment of body composition, it is important to be able to provide evidence for the optimal use of these tools, and to define their accuracy and inter-changeability in terms of body sizes.

There is a need to quantify VAT, as it is potentially a more precise screening measurement for identifying those at risk of metabolic disorders associated with obesity. The reference methods for the quantification of VAT is MRI or CT scanning. The GE iDXA with CoreScan technology is widely used for body composition assessment, and also reports the quantification of VAT; this has been confirmed against CT scanning [19]. Between BIA devices themselves, variability in agreement with the reference methods of either DXA or MRI have been observed. Few BIA devices give a quantified measurement of VAT, with many reporting risk scores [30,31]. Some BIA devices, such as the seca mBCA 515 Analyzer, offer the ability to measure VAT. In order to gain a greater understanding of the potential benefit of different body composition analyzers as a screening tool, they must be compared across a range of BMIs to assess their appropriate use and determine the strengths and weaknesses of different methods.

The aims of this study were: to compare the use of the seca mBCA 515 Analyzer for body composition (FM and FFM) against a body composition scan, using the GE Lunar iDXA as a reference method; to explore the VAT measures across both instruments; and to assess the utility of WHtR and WC as indicators of body fatness.

2. Materials and Methods

2.1. Participants

Thirty participants enrolled in this observational study. Recruitment commenced in October 2015 and concluded in September 2016. Participants were recruited through online staff and student forums and poster advertisements at Monash University, Melbourne, Australia. Inclusion criteria were: healthy adults, who were able to comprehend and consent to the study in English; being aged between 18 and 65 years; having a BMI between 18.5 kg/m^2 and 50 kg/m^2; and those who reported to have a stable weight and were not actively attempting to lose or gain weight. Exclusion criteria included: pregnant women; anyone who had exposure to radiation three months prior to study enrolment; and those with standard exclusions for DXA and/or BIA, such as those with implanted defibrillator devices or prostheses.

Participants were required to attend one three-hour session in the morning after an overnight fast. All subjects gave their full informed consent for inclusion before participation in the study. The study was conducted in accordance with the Declaration of Helsinki, and the protocol and supporting documents were approved by the Monash University Human Research Ethics Committee (CF15/2790-2015001139).

2.2. Anthropometric Measurements

Height was measured using a Holtain fixed stadiometer (Holtain Ltd., Crosswell, Wales, UK) to the nearest 0.1 cm [32]. Weight was measured using stand-on digital scales (seca, Hamburg, Germany) to the nearest 0.1 kg. Anatomical WC was measured at the mid-point between the top of the iliac crest and the bottom of the lowest rib, to the nearest 0.5 cm [33]. All measurements were repeated twice using standard operating procedures, and all assessors were trained by a single level 2 certified anthropometrist. WHtR was calculated as WC divided by height, and BMI was calculated as body weight (kg) divided by height, squared (m^2).

2.3. Dual-Energy X-Ray Absorptiometry

The DXA scan was conducted on a GE Lunar iDXA (GE Healthcare, Software Lunar DPX enCORE 2012 version 14.0, Madison, WI, USA). Each participant received a total body scan, conducted by a single qualified radiographer (AE) who was experienced in DXA scanning. Participants were scanned in the supine position and VAT was estimated using the android region (from the ribs to the iliac crest) via the inbuilt CoreScan software (GE Healthcare, Software Lunar DPX enCORE 2012 version 14.0, Madison, WI, USA). FFM was determined by the sum of bone mineral content and lean soft tissue values, and FM was also determined. The coefficient of the variations were 0.74% for FM, 0.48% for lean mass, and 11.84% for VAT volume.

2.4. Bioelectrical Impedance Analysis

The seca mBCA 515 (seca, Hamburg, Germany) uses multi-frequency 8-point stand-on bioelectrical impedance analysis to measure TBW by applying an electrical current of 100 µA to the body. The drop in voltage between sensor electrodes at the hands and feet is used to determine total body water. The manufacturer's operating instructions and proprietary software calculated FM, FFM, and VAT volume from total body water, weight, WC, height, age, and gender [21]. The BIA device measures at 20 frequencies, ranging from 1 kHz to 1000 kHz. Participants were scanned once in the standing position, with four electrodes at the feet and four electrodes at the hands. Participants were instructed to remain stationary for the duration of the scan, which lasted 60 s.

2.5. Statistical Analysis

All statistics were analyzed using IBM SPSS Statistics 24 (IBM, New York, NY, USA). The sample was analyzed as a whole group and then split into those with a weight within the normal range (BMI < 18.5 kg/m^2 and <25 kg/m^2) and those with a weight in the overweight or obese range (BMI ≥ 25 kg/m^2), as defined by BMI. Descriptive characteristics are displayed as means ± the standard deviation for the total sample, both males and females. For FM, FFM, and VAT, one-sample *t*-tests were performed to initially assess the variation from zero for the difference between methods. If the variation was not significantly different from zero, a Bland-Altman plot was created to assess the agreement between methods and determine the limits of agreement for each variable [34]. Linear regression was used to determine the proportional bias in differences between the methods. Two one-sided T tests (TOST) were used to determine clinically significant equivalence between BIA and DXA measures of body composition [35]. The delta was set to 5% of the average, as measured by DXA, the reference method in this instance. These data were not normally distributed; therefore, correlations between BIA, DXA, and WHtR were analyzed using Spearman's Rank correlation. Concordance between DXA and BIA measurements of FM, FMM, and VAT were assessed using Lin's concordance [36]. All graphs were created using GraphPad Prism 7.01 (GraphPad Software, La Jolla, CA, USA).

3. Results

Descriptive characteristics of the population are displayed in Table 1. The average age of the sample population was 29.9 ± 11.2 years, and the average BMI was 29.2 ± 7.3 kg/m^2 with a range from 18.8 kg/m^2 to 48.9 kg/m^2, where 73% were of Caucasian descent. Of the total sample, 33% had a BMI in the normal weight range (*n* = 10), 47% were classified as overweight (*n* = 14), and 20% were obese (*n* = 6), as defined by the World Health Organization's cutpoints for BMI. Height (cm) and weight (kg) were significantly different between males and females (Table 1).

Table 1. Participant characteristics (mean ± standard deviation).

	Male (n = 14)	Female (n = 16)	Total (n = 30)
Age (years)	32.3 ± 12.9	27.9 ± 9.4	29.9 ± 11.2
Height (cm)	177.7 ± 3.6 *	170.0 ± 8.9 *	173.6 ± 7.9
Weight (kg)	99.7 ± 26.9 **	79.9 ± 25.4 **	89.1 ± 27.6
BMI (kg/m^2)	31.6 ± 8.4	27.2 ± 5.8	29.2 ± 7.3
Range			18.8–48.9 [a]
Anatomical waist circumference (cm)	105.9 ± 23.4 (n = 13)	94.1 ± 26.4	99.4 ± 25.4
Waist to height ratio	0.6 ± 0.1	0.6 ± 0.1	0.6 ± 0.2

* $p < 0.05$, ** $p < 0.01$ for differences between males and females by independent samples t-test. [a] Body mass index (BMI) range, number of participants is stated as (n=) for parameters that vary from total sample.

Table 2 displays FM, FFM, and VAT, as measured by the DXA and BIA, and Table 3 displays the corresponding correlations between BIA, DXA, WHtR, and WC for FM, FFM, and VAT. FM and VAT measures were significantly correlated for the total sample. WC and BIA FFM (kg) were significantly correlated (rho 0.972, $p < 0.001$), as well as BIA FFM (kg) and WHtR (rho 0.500, $p < 0.01$). There was a strong correlation between BIA and DXA for FM (kg), (rho 0.981, $p < 0.001$) and between WC and BIA VAT (cm^3) (rho 0.944, $p < 0.001$). For each variable, BIA and DXA were more strongly correlated with WC than WHtR; in the normal weight group, there were no significant relationships between these variables (Table 3). For the overweight/obese group, all measures were significantly correlated for FM and VAT. For FFM, BIA was significantly correlated with WC and WHtR (rho 0.823, $p < 0.001$ and rho 0.470, $p < 0.05$, respectively). Again, in this group, BIA and DXA were more strongly correlated with WC than WHtR for all measures. Concordance was strong between BIA and DXA for FM and FFM (0.992 and 0.947, respectively); however, concordance was poor for VAT measured by BIA and DXA (−0.016).

Table 2. Fat mass, fat-free mass, and visceral adipose tissue volume, as measured by DXA and BIA (normal weight BMI < 25 kg/m^2 and overweight and obese BMI ≥ 25 kg/m^2).

	DXA			BIA		
	Normal Weight Group (n = 10, 6 = Female)	Overweight and Obese Group (n = 20, 10 = Female)	Whole Group (n = 30)	Normal Weight Group (n = 10, 6 = Female)	Overweight and Obese Group (n = 20, 10 = Female)	Whole Group (n = 30)
Fat mass (kg) Mean (SD)	26.60 (15.08)	31.15 (18.00)	29.63 (16.96)	27.23 (14.24)	30.36 (17.77)	29.32 (16.49)
Fat free mass (kg) Mean (SD)	57.70 (9.30)	57.62 (12.86)	57.65 (11.63)	58.92 (10.47)	58.88 (12.69)	58.90 (11.78)
Visceral adipose tissue (litres) Mean (SD)	1.25 (1.47)	1.04 (1.13)	1.11 (1.23)	0.81 (0.98)	5.24 (5.19)	3.76 (4.74)

Data presented as mean values (standard deviation). DXA: dual energy X-ray absorptiometry; BIA: bioelectrical impedance.

A one-sample t-test demonstrated that the difference between methods for VAT measurement was significantly different from zero ($t = -6.4$, $p < 0.001$) for the total sample and when the sample was split into normal weight and overweight/obese groups; therefore, it was not appropriate to construct Bland-Altman plots for this variable. Linear regression analysis showed that BIA significantly overestimated VAT compared to DXA ($t = -13.0$, $p < 0.001$). A Bland-Altman plot determined the level of agreement for FM measurements (Figure 1) and FFM measurements (Figure 2).

BIA underestimated FM by 0.32 kg (limits of agreement −3.77 kg, 4.40 kg, ±27.6%) compared with DXA. For the normal weight group, BIA underestimated FM by 0.25 kg (limits of agreement: −4.30 kg, 4.81 kg, ±34.4%) compared with DXA, and for the overweight and obese group, BIA underestimated fat mass by 0.35 kg (limits of agreement: −3.61 kg, 4.30 kg, ±25.4%) compared with DXA. There was good agreement between the methods for FM, and whilst the mean difference was smaller for the normal weight group, the limits of agreement were narrower for the overweight and obese group (Figure 1).

Table 3. Correlation matrix (Spearman's rho) between BIA, DXA, WC, and WHtR for fat-free mass, fat mass, and visceral adipose tissue (normal weight BMI < 25 kg/m^2, overweight and obese ≥ 25 kg/m^2).

	Normal Weight Group (n = 10)	Overweight and Obese Group (n = 20)	Whole Group (n = 30)
Fat free mass			
WHtR vs. BIA	0.418	0.470 *	0.500 **
WHtR vs. DXA	0.365	−0.095	0.073
WC vs. BIA	0.620	0.823 ***	0.972 ***
WC vs. DXA	0.277	0.147	0.222
BIA vs. DXA	−0.292	0.425	0.323
Fat mass			
WHtR vs. BIA	0.552	0.716 ***	0.815 ***
WHtR vs. DXA	0.588	0.747 ***	0.828 ***
WC vs. BIA	0.444	0.815 ***	0.888 ***
WC vs. DXA	0.571	0.836 ***	0.901 ***
BIA vs. DXA	0.588	0.989 ***	0.981 ***
Visceral adipose tissue			
WHtR vs. BIA	0.409	0.870 ***	0.822 ***
WHtR vs. DXA	0.091	0.653 ***	0.743 ***
WC vs. BIA	0.573	0.987 ***	0.944 ***
WC vs. DXA	0.103	0.807 ***	0.880 ***
BIA vs. DXA	0.323	0.826 ***	0.869 ***

Data presented as rho values. * $p < 0.05$; ** $p < 0.01$; *** $p < 0.001$. WHtR: waist to height ratio; WC: anatomical waist circumference.

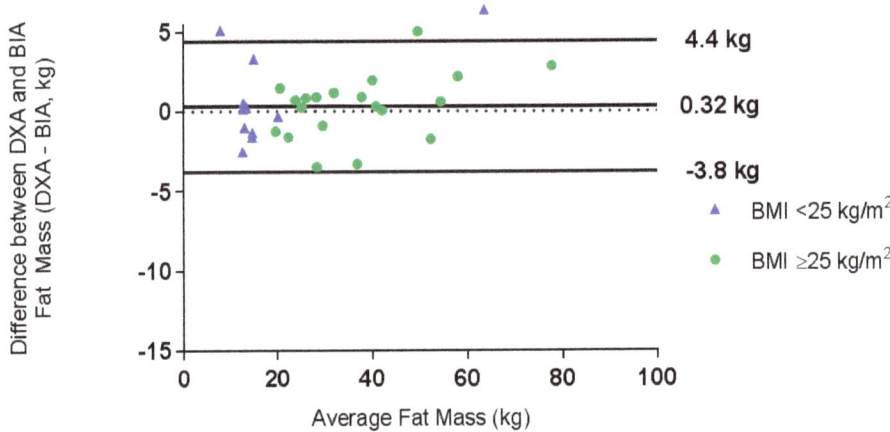

Figure 1. Bland-Altman plot of the difference between fat mass, as measured by dual energy X-ray absorptiometry (DXA) and bioelectrical impedance (BIA), against the mean fat mass (kg) for the whole group. ● BMI ≥ 25 kg/m^2, ▲ BMI < 25 kg/m^2.

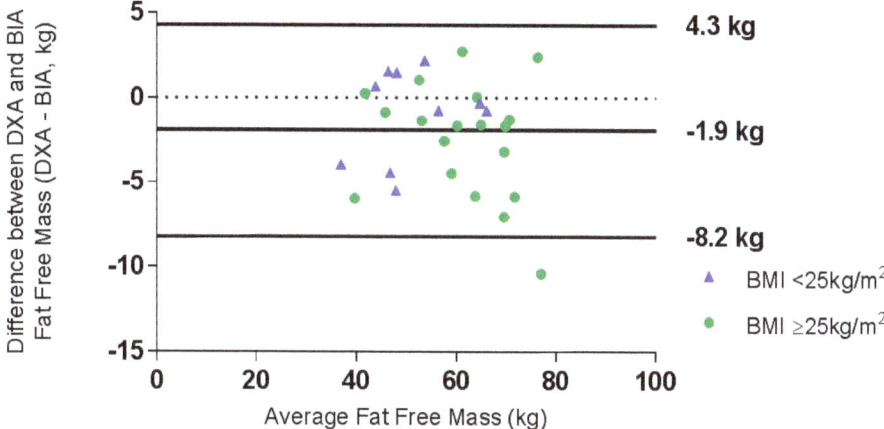

Figure 2. Bland-Altman plot of the difference between fat-free mass (kg), as measured by DXA and BIA, against the mean fat-free mass (kg) for the whole group. ● BMI ≥ 25 kg/m^2, ▲ BMI < 25 kg/m^2.

Regression analysis showed that there was no proportional bias between measures of FM or FFM for the whole group or either of the normal weight or overweight/obese groups (data not shown). BIA overestimated FFM by 0.43 kg, and whilst the limits of agreement were larger, this represented a smaller proportion of mean FFM (−8.2 kg, 4.3 kg, ±21.7%) than for FM (Figure 2). The mean difference between the methods for FFM was larger for the normal weight group, as were the limits of agreement compared to the overweight/obese group (Figure 2). Clinically acceptable equivalence (5%) was not demonstrated for both FM and FFM for the total sample, nor when split into normal weight and overweight groups. Equivalence was demonstrated at 25.8% for FM and 11% for FFM for the whole group.

4. Discussion

This study aimed to better understand the strengths and weaknesses of two relatively new instruments that purport to measure body composition, as well as VAT in adults across the spectrum of the BMI range. Both devices, the GE iDXA and seca BIA instruments, incorporate proprietary algorithms into simple-to-use instruments, but with little explanation as to their measurement derivation. A strength of the seca 515 BIA is its non-invasive nature and ease of use; however, our results indicate that the seca BIA device showed greater agreement with DXA for FM measurements, especially in individuals with larger amounts of FM. The two methods did not demonstrate clinically relevant equivalence for measures of FM or FFM; this highlights that different devices for body composition are not interchangeable.

VAT volume is an independent risk factor for a host of lifestyle-related diseases [9,10]. Quantification achievable in a clinical setting could help to prioritize patients for intervention and further characterize their risk. Finding an inexpensive and faster alternative to MRI or CT scans for the quantification of VAT volume remains a challenge. GE iDXA and seca BIA may provide practical alternatives to quantify VAT, albeit that the seca BIA systematically and significantly overestimated VAT compared to the iDXA. Pietiläinen et al. (2013) found other impedance devices have also shown poor agreement between BIA and DXA for assessment for VAT, and the specially designed BIA device, ViScan, has limited VAT prediction ability [18,37]. Previous studies have shown good agreement between DXA and MRI, or CT measures of VAT [19,38]. Concordance was also found to be low, suggesting that the two methods were not measuring the same parameter. Indeed, it is difficult to see how segmental impedance analysis, in which the trunk is measured as a whole rather than the visceral compartment per se, can specifically predict VAT. Impedance techniques with a focus on measuring the impedance of the central abdominal region would appear to hold more promise, although current devices have not shown good clinical performance to date [39,40]. Alternatively, the seca mBCA 515 Analyzer demonstrates good agreement with DXA for the quantification of total body FM, itself a helpful indicator of lifestyle disease risk, independent of VAT [41].

Waist circumference is a valuable tool in assessing central adiposity and, as such, this simple anthropometric measure should not be overlooked, as it is an informative indicator of obesity and risk of related diseases [42,43]. Although anthropometric measures were found to be significantly correlated with DXA measurements of FM and VAT (especially for the overweight and obese participants), anthropometry and BIA may not be an informative measure of body composition for individuals within the normal weight range, due to the smaller proportion of FM seen in this group. Thus, DXA may be preferred to BIA or anthropometry for body composition analysis in normal-weight individuals.

The limitations of this study were the small sample size, especially in the normal weight group, with the majority of the participants being of Caucasian descent; and not being able to draw conclusions on the generalizability of the instruments for use in body composition assessment across other ethnic groups, due to body composition variability observed between ethnicities [44]. However, the large range of BMIs explored in this study was a strength, as it allowed assessment of agreement and equivalence of measures across a wide range of body sizes. Future work should focus on validating the seca mBCA 515 Analyzer in a larger sample with a range of BMI and different ethnicities.

The limits of agreement were larger than those previously reported [25,28], with the overweight and obese group showing narrower limits of agreement than the normal weight group. These differences in mean error and limits of agreement could be attributed to a range of factors, including: (1) the use of different proprietary algorithms by each device, and; (2) the large range of BMIs explored in this study. These findings strongly suggest that for consistency, any repeated or longitudinal measures on any individual should be performed using the same device or technique.

WC and WHtR are quick, simple, and cheap methods of assessing body fatness [45]. WC is an especially good indicator of body fatness for individuals who are overweight or obese, but cannot provide information on body composition. In busy clinic settings, WC should not be overlooked as a quick and simple assessment of a patient's risk of obesity. BIA may be able to provide more detailed information on body composition than anthropometry, and has demonstrated good agreement with DXA for FM, particularly for those who are overweight or obese, as defined by BMI. However, the seca mBCA 515 Analyzer and DXA are not equivalent techniques for the range of BMIs explored in this study; thus, DXA remains more informative for body composition than the seca mBCA 515 Analyzer.

Author Contributions: Formal analysis, K.D., K.H., L.C.W. and H.T.; Investigation, K.D., A.K., A.E. and F.M.; Methodology, F.M., A.V.-G. and H.T.; Project administration, H.T.; Supervision, A.V.-G. and H.T.; Writing-original draft, K.D. and H.T.; Writing-review & editing, K.D., A.K., A.E., F.M., A.V.-G., K.H., L.C.W. and H.T.

Funding: This research received no external funding.

Acknowledgments: A.K. is in receipt of an Australian Government Research Training Program (RTP) Scholarship.

Conflicts of Interest: The authors declare no conflict of interest.

References

1. Australian Institute of Health and Welfare. *A Picture of Overweight and Obesity in Australia 2017*; Australian Institute of Health and Welfare: Canberra, Australia, 2017.
2. Bastien, M.; Poirier, P.; Lemieux, I.; Després, J.-P. Overview of Epidemiology and Contribution of Obesity to Cardiovascular Disease. *Prog. Cardiovasc. Dis.* **2014**, *56*, 369–381. [CrossRef] [PubMed]
3. Guariguata, L.; Whiting, D.R.; Hambleton, I.; Beagley, J.; Linnenkamp, U.; Shaw, J.E. Global estimates of diabetes prevalence for 2013 and projections for 2035. *Diabetes Res. Clin. Pract.* **2014**, *103*, 137–149. [CrossRef] [PubMed]
4. Britton, K.A.; Massaro, J.M.; Murabito, J.M.; Kreger, B.E.; Hoffmann, U.; Fox, C.S. Body fat distribution, incident cardiovascular disease, cancer, and all-cause mortality. *J. Am. Coll. Cardiol.* **2013**, *62*, 921–925. [CrossRef] [PubMed]

5. Lee, J.J.; Beretvas, S.N.; Freeland-Graves, J.H. Abdominal adiposity distribution in diabetic/prediabetic and nondiabetic aopulations: A meta-analysis. *J. Obes.* **2014**, *2014*, 697264. [CrossRef] [PubMed]
6. Ali, A.H.; Koutsari, C.; Mundi, M.; Stegall, M.D.; Heimbach, J.K.; Taler, S.J.; Nygren, J.; Thorell, A.; Bogachus, L.D.; Turcotte, L.P.; et al. Free fatty acid storage in human visceral and subcutaneous adipose tissue: Role of adipocyte proteins. *Diabetes* **2011**, *60*, 2300–2307. [CrossRef] [PubMed]
7. Catalán, V.; Gómez-Ambrosi, J.; Ramirez, B.; Rotellar, F.; Pastor, C.; Silva, C.; Rodríguez, A.; Gil, M.J.; Cienfuegos, J.A.; Frühbeck, G. Proinflammatory cytokines in obesity: Impact of type 2 diabetes mellitus and gastric bypass. *Obes. Surg.* **2007**, *17*, 1464–1474. [CrossRef] [PubMed]
8. Samaras, K.; Botelho, N.K.; Chisholm, D.J.; Lord, R.V. Subcutaneous and visceral adipose tissue gene expression of serum adipokines that predict type 2 diabetes. *Obesity* **2010**, *18*, 884–889. [CrossRef] [PubMed]
9. Coutinho, T.; Goel, K.; Corrêa de Sá, D.; Carter, R.E.; Hodge, D.O.; Kragelund, C.; Kanaya, A.M.; Zeller, M.; Park, J.S.; Kober, L.; et al. Combining body mass index with measures of central obesity in the assessment of mortality in subjects with coronary disease: Role of "normal weight central obesity". *J. Am. Coll. Cardiol.* **2013**, *61*, 553–560. [CrossRef] [PubMed]
10. Feliciano, E.M.C.; Kroenke, C.H.; Meyerhardt, J.A.; Prado, C.M.; Bradshaw, P.T.; Dannenberg, A.J.; Kwan, M.L.; Xiao, J.; Quesenberry, C.; Weltzien, E.K.; et al. Metabolic dysfunction, obesity, and survival among patients with early-stage colorectal cancer. *J. Clin. Oncol.* **2016**, *34*, 3664–3671. [CrossRef] [PubMed]
11. Kim, D.; Chung, G.E.; Kwak, M.-S.; Seo, H.B.; Kang, J.H.; Kim, W.; Kim, Y.J.; Yoon, J.-H.; Lee, H.-S.; Kim, C.Y. Body fat distribution and risk of incident and regressed nonalcoholic fatty liver disease. *Clin. Gastroenterol. Hepatol.* **2016**, *14*, 132–138. [CrossRef] [PubMed]
12. Dolinková, M.; Dostálová, I.; Lacinová, Z.; Michalský, D.; Haluzíková, D.; Mráz, M.; Kasalický, M.; Haluzík, M. The endocrine profile of subcutaneous and visceral adipose tissue of obese patients. *Mol. Cell. Endocrinol.* **2008**, *291*, 63–70. [CrossRef] [PubMed]
13. Kershaw, E.E.; Flier, J.S. Adipose tissue as an endocrine organ. *J. Clin. Endocrinol. Metab.* **2004**, *89*, 2548–2556. [CrossRef] [PubMed]
14. Panel, N.O. On the identification, evaluation, and treatment of overweight and obesity in adults. Clinical guidelines on the identification, evaluation, and treatment of overweight and obesity in adults—The evidence report. *Obes Res.* **1998**, *6* (Suppl. 2), 51S–209S.
15. Nambiar, S.; Truby, H.; Abbott, R.A.; Davies, P.S. Validating the waist-height ratio and developing centiles for use amongst children and adolescents. *Acta Paediatr.* **2009**, *98*, 148–152. [CrossRef] [PubMed]
16. Ashwell, M.; Gunn, P.; Gibson, S. Waist-to-height ratio is a better screening tool than waist circumference and BMI for adult cardiometabolic risk factors: Systematic review and meta-analysis. *Obes. Rev.* **2012**, *13*, 275–286. [CrossRef] [PubMed]
17. Albanese, C.V.; Diessel, E.; Genant, H.K. Clinical applications of body composition measurements using DXA. *J. Clin. Densitom.* **2003**, *6*, 75–85. [CrossRef]
18. Pietiläinen, K.H.; Kaye, S.; Karmi, A.; Suojanen, L.; Rissanen, A.; Virtanen, K.A. Agreement of bioelectrical impedance with dual-energy X-ray absorptiometry and MRI to estimate changes in body fat, skeletal muscle and visceral fat during a 12-month weight loss intervention. *Br. J. Nutr.* **2013**, *109*, 1910–1916. [CrossRef] [PubMed]
19. Kaul, S.; Rothney, M.P.; Peters, D.M.; Wacker, W.K.; Davis, C.E.; Shapiro, M.D.; Ergun, D.L. Dual-energy X-ray absorptiometry for quantification of visceral fat. *Obesity* **2012**, *20*, 1313–1318. [CrossRef] [PubMed]
20. Marinangeli, C.P.; Kassis, A.N. Use of dual X-ray absorptiometry to measure body mass during short- to medium-term trials of nutrition and exercise interventions. *Nutr. Rev.* **2013**, *71*, 332–342. [CrossRef] [PubMed]
21. Bosy-Westphal, A.; Schautz, B.; Later, W.; Kehayias, J.; Gallagher, D.; Müller, M. What makes a BIA equation unique? Validity of eight-electrode multifrequency BIA to estimate body composition in a healthy adult population. *Eur. J. Clin. Nutr.* **2013**, *67*, S14. [CrossRef] [PubMed]
22. Verney, J.; Metz, L.; Chaplais, E.; Cardenoux, C.; Pereira, B.; Thivel, D. Bioelectrical impedance is an accurate method to assess body composition in obese but not severely obese adolescents. *Nutr. Res.* **2016**, *36*, 663–670. [CrossRef] [PubMed]
23. Faria, S.L.; Faria, O.P.; Cardeal, M.D.; Ito, M.K. Validation study of multi-frequency bioelectrical impedance with dual-energy X-ray absorptiometry among obese patients. *Obes. Surg.* **2014**, *24*, 1476–1480. [CrossRef] [PubMed]

24. Shafer, K.J.; Siders, W.A.; Johnson, L.K.; Lukaski, H.C. Validity of segmental multiple-frequency bioelectrical impedance analysis to estimate body composition of adults across a range of body mass indexes. *Nutrition* **2009**, *25*, 25–32. [CrossRef] [PubMed]
25. Anderson, L.J.; Erceg, D.N.; Schroeder, E.T. Utility of multifrequency bioelectrical impedance compared with dual-energy X-ray absorptiometry for assessment of total and regional body composition varies between men and women. *Nutr. Res.* **2012**, *32*, 479–485. [CrossRef] [PubMed]
26. Leahy, S.; O'Neill, C.; Sohun, R.; Jakeman, P. A comparison of dual energy X-ray absorptiometry and bioelectrical impedance analysis to measure total and segmental body composition in healthy young adults. *Eur. J. Appl. Physiol.* **2012**, *112*, 589–595. [CrossRef] [PubMed]
27. Wang, J.-G.; Zhang, Y.; Chen, H.-E.; Li, Y.; Cheng, X.-G.; Xu, L.; Guo, Z.; Zhao, X.-S.; Sato, T.; Cao, Q.-Y.; et al. Comparison of two bioelectrical impedance analysis devices with dual energy X-ray absorptiometry and magnetic resonance imaging in the estimation of body composition. *J. Strength Cond. Res.* **2013**, *27*, 236–243. [CrossRef] [PubMed]
28. Lim, J.S.; Hwang, J.S.; Lee, J.A.; Kim, D.H.; Park, K.D.; Jeong, J.S.; Cheon, G.J. Cross-calibration of multi-frequency bioelectrical impedance analysis with eight-point tactile electrodes and dual-energy X-ray absorptiometry for assessment of body composition in healthy children aged 6–18 years. *Pediatr. Int.* **2009**, *51*, 263–268. [CrossRef] [PubMed]
29. Nambiar, S.; Truby, H.; Davies, P.S.; Baxter, K. Use of the waist–height ratio to predict metabolic syndrome in obese children and adolescents. *J. Paediatr. Child Health* **2013**, *49*, E281–E287. [CrossRef] [PubMed]
30. Bosy-Westphal, A.; Later, W.; Hitze, B.; Sato, T.; Kossel, E.; Glüer, C.-C.; Heller, M.; Müller, M.J. Accuracy of bioelectrical impedance consumer devices for measurement of body composition in comparison to whole body magnetic resonance imaging and dual X-ray absorptiometry. *Obes. Facts* **2008**, *1*, 319–324. [CrossRef] [PubMed]
31. Pateyjohns, I.R.; Brinkworth, G.D.; Buckley, J.D.; Noakes, M.; Clifton, P.M. Comparison of three bioelectrical impedance methods with DXA in overweight and obese men. *Obesity* **2006**, *14*, 2064–2070. [CrossRef] [PubMed]
32. National Health and Nutrition Examination Survey (NHANES). Anthropometry Procedures Manual. Available online: http://www.cdc.gov/nchs/data/nhanes/nhanes_09_10/BodyMeasures_09.pdf (accessed on 10th September 2018).
33. Neamat-Allah, J.; Wald, D.; Hüsing, A.; Teucher, B.; Wendt, A.; Delorme, S.; Dinkel, J.; Vigl, M.; Bergmann, M.M.; Feller, S.; et al. Validation of anthropometric indices of adiposity against whole-body magnetic resonance imaging—A atudy within the German European Prospective Investigation into Cancer and Nutrition (EPIC) Cohorts. *PLoS ONE* **2014**, *9*, e91586. [CrossRef] [PubMed]
34. Martin Bland, J.; Altman, D. Statistical methods for assessing agreement between two methods of clinical measurement. *Lancet* **1986**, *327*, 307–310. [CrossRef]
35. Schuirmann, D.J. A comparison of the two one-sided tests procedure and the power approach for assessing the equivalence of average bioavailability. *J. Pharm. Biopharm.* **1987**, *15*, 657–680. [CrossRef]
36. Lawrence, I.; Lin, K. A concordance correlation coefficient to evaluate reproducibility. *Biometrics* **1989**, 255–268.
37. Thomas, E.L.; Collins, A.L.; McCarthy, J.; Fitzpatrick, J.; Durighel, G.; Goldstone, A.P.; Bell, J.D. Estimation of abdominal fat compartments by bioelectrical impedance: The validity of the ViScan measurement system in comparison with MRI. *Eur. J. Clin. Nutr.* **2010**, *64*, 525. [CrossRef] [PubMed]
38. Neeland, I.; Grundy, S.; Li, X.; Adams-Huet, B.; Vega, G. Comparison of visceral fat mass measurement by dual-X-ray absorptiometry and magnetic resonance imaging in a multiethnic cohort: The Dallas Heart Study. *Nutr. Diabetes* **2016**, *6*, e221. [CrossRef] [PubMed]
39. Scharfetter, H.; Brunner, P.; Mayer, M.; Brandstatter, B.; Hinghofer-Szalkay, H. Fat and hydration monitoring by abdominal bioimpedance analysis: Data interpretation by hierarchical electrical modeling. *IEEE Trans. Biomed. Eng.* **2005**, *52*, 975–982. [CrossRef] [PubMed]
40. Alvero-Cruz, J.R.; García-Romero, J.C.; de Albornoz-Gil, M.C.; Jiménez, M.; Correas-Gomez, L.; Peñaloza, P.; López-Fernández, I.; Carnero, E.A. Longitudinal validity of abdominal adiposity assessment by regional bioelectrical impedance. *Eur. J. Clin. Nutr.* **2018**, *72*, 1055–1057. [CrossRef] [PubMed]
41. Festa, A.; D'Agostino, R., Jr.; Williams, K.; Karter, A.J.; Mayer-Davis, E.J.; Tracy, R.P.; Haffner, S.M. The relation of body fat mass and distribution to markers of chronic inflammation. *Int. J. Obes. Relat. Metab. Disord.* **2001**, *25*, 1407–1415. [CrossRef] [PubMed]

42. Janssen, I.; Katzmarzyk, P.T.; Ross, R. Waist circumference and not body mass index explains obesity-related health risk. *Am. J. Clin. Nutr.* **2004**, *79*, 379–384. [CrossRef] [PubMed]
43. Taylor, A.E.; Ebrahim, S.; Ben-Shlomo, Y.; Martin, R.M.; Whincup, P.H.; Yarnell, J.W.; Wannamethee, S.G.; Lawlor, D.A. Comparison of the associations of body mass index and measures of central adiposity and fat mass with coronary heart disease, diabetes, and all-cause mortality: A study using data from 4 UK cohorts. *Am. J. Clin. Nutr.* **2010**, *91*, 547–556. [CrossRef] [PubMed]
44. Deurenberg, P.; Yap, M.; Van Staveren, W.A. Body mass index and percent body fat: A meta analysis among different ethnic groups. *Int. J. Obes.* **1998**, *22*, 1164. [CrossRef]
45. Hsieh, S.D.; Yoshinaga, H.; Muto, T. Waist-to-height ratio, a simple and practical index for assessing central fat distribution and metabolic risk in Japanese men and women. *Int. J. Obes. Relat. Metab. Disord.* **2003**, *27*, 610–616. [CrossRef] [PubMed]

© 2018 by the authors. Licensee MDPI, Basel, Switzerland. This article is an open access article distributed under the terms and conditions of the Creative Commons Attribution (CC BY) license (http://creativecommons.org/licenses/by/4.0/).

Article

Reliability of Compartmental Body Composition Measures in Weight-Stable Adults Using GE iDXA: Implications for Research and Practice

Aimee L. Dordevic [1,*], Maxine Bonham [1], Ali Ghasem-Zadeh [2], Alison Evans [1], Elizabeth Barber [1], Kaitlin Day [1], Alastair Kwok [1] and Helen Truby [1]

[1] Department of Nutrition, Dietetics & Food, Monash University, Notting Hill 3168, Australia; maxine.bonham@monash.edu (M.B.); alison.evans@monash.edu (A.E.); elizabeth.barber@monash.edu (E.B.); kaitlin.day@monash.edu (K.D.); alastair.kwok@monash.edu (A.K.); helen.truby@monash.edu (H.T.)

[2] Department of Endocrinology, Department of Medicine, Austin Health, the University of Melbourne, West Heidelberg 3081, Australia; alig@unimelb.edu.au

* Correspondence: aimee.dordevic@monash.edu; Tel.: +61-3-9905-2142

Received: 7 September 2018; Accepted: 10 October 2018; Published: 12 October 2018

Abstract: The aim of this study was to explore the reliability and precision of body compartment measures, in particular visceral adipose tissue, in weight stable adults over a range of BMIs using GE-Lunar iDXA. Weight-stable participants aged 18–65 years had a total body composition scan on GE-Lunar iDXA either on three separate occasions over a three month period ($n = 51$), or on a single occasion for duplicate scans with repositioning ($n = 30$). The coefficient of variation (CV%) and least significant change (LSC) of body compartments were calculated. The CV was higher for all measures over three months (range 0.8–5.9%) compared with same-day precision-scans (all < 2%). The CV for visceral adipose tissue (VAT) was considerably higher than all other body compartments (42.2% three months, 16.2% same day scanning). To accurately measure VAT mass using the GE iDXA it is recommended that participants have a BMI ≥ 25 kg/m^2, or VAT mass > 500 g. Changes observed in VAT mass levels below 500 g should be interpreted with caution due to lack of precision and reliability. All other compartmental measures demonstrated good reliability, with less than 6% variation over three months.

Keywords: adiposity; body composition; dual X-ray absorptiometry; visceral adipose tissue

1. Introduction

Dual energy X-ray absorptiometry (DXA) is one of the most accessible, simple, quick, relatively non-invasive measures of body composition [1,2]. It is now widely used in human studies where changes in body compartment composition attains importance [3–7], providing a measure of physiological responses to obesity interventions. DXA is superior to simple anthropometrics such as body mass index (BMI) as an outcome measure in weight management studies, in particular to detect changes in fat and lean body mass. The presence of visceral adipose tissue (VAT), as a component of total fat mass, has become more pertinent in recent years with further understanding of the differential roles of subcutaneous adipose tissue (SAT) and VAT, especially in terms of metabolic activity. Therefore, being able to compartmentalize body fat into both SAT and VAT has become more relevant. This has been recently reviewed by Marinangeli and Kassis [8] in relation to weight management studies. To further understand metabolic risks associated with different body compositions it has been recommended to include a fast and valid measure of body compartment changes, such as VAT, in obesity treatment [9].

Deposition of VAT in the android region is strongly associated with an increase in chronic disease risk [10,11]. A metabolically abnormal phenotype has been linked with increased body fat levels in people with healthy weight status [12–14], and is suggested to be a result of increased VAT in those individuals [14]. As such, it is important to be able to reliably measure the impact of interventions on VAT levels in a range of body composition types. However, VAT cannot be clearly differentiated from SAT by anthropometric measures alone or other non-invasive measures of body composition [15–17]. Until recently, quantifying VAT has relied on more complex and specialist techniques such as CT and MRI scans, both of which have strengths and limitations including higher X-ray dose by CT, higher cost, and they require specialist expertise to interpret findings.

The Lunar iDXA scanner (GE Medical Systems Lunar, Madison, WI, USA), with its CoreScan software that calculates both VAT mass (g) and VAT volume (cm^3), was the first DXA instrument that reported the ability to quantify VAT. Its testing against the reference method of CT scan was reported by Kaul et al. in 2012 [18]. The calculation of VAT from a non-invasive, low radiation technique therefore provides the opportunity to measure changes in fat components. As such, the GE iDXA is a potentially pivotal tool for monitoring the biological impact and the associated health benefits of lifestyle interventions.

However, to accurately report true biological changes from DXA imaging, a measure of precision (reproducibility) of the scanner is used, commonly reported as a percentage of the coefficient of variation (CV) [7,19,20]. The CV for body composition measurements has been reported to have high variance, ranging between 1% and 17% [21,22], and appears to be dependent on the region of interest being analyzed. A recent study reported on precision of VAT measurements from two consecutive total body scans [21]; the CV range was 5.4–17%, and was BMI-dependent, with increased variability observed in the lower BMI ranges.

Previous reports on the precision error of DXA scans have not investigated the reliability of measurements longitudinally: the current recommended procedure is consecutive repeat scans on the same day with re-positioning [21,23,24]. Short term precision error studies are likely to find low variation in measurements, as extraneous variables such as changes in machine calibration, instrument-functioning drift, scan analysis, and inter- or intra-operator errors [25] may be minimized or not encountered. However, long term stability is vital for correct interpretation of lifestyle intervention studies that aim to measure true body composition changes induced by the intervention, rather than normal biological fluctuations or instrument variation.

In obesity interventions, assessment and monitoring of body composition changes occur over long periods of time. Therefore, temporal reliability analyses may be more reflective of study procedures, allowing better interpretation of results for body composition over usual intervention periods [26]. Since there is no body composition phantom available for visceral fat variability measurement, the longitudinal stability of the GE iDXA instrument for body composition measurements, in particular VAT mass, is crucial for correct interpretation of findings.

This study aimed to assess the variability of body composition measures of weight-stable adults, taken on the GE iDXA. It did this through the assessment of the CV (%) and least significant change (LSC) of measurements for three repeated total body scans over three months, which is the minimum period typically required to measure clinically significant changes in body composition in response to nutrition and lifestyle interventions. Additionally, the precision of the same instrument using the standard protocol of two repeated scans on the same day with subject re-positioning was also performed. We hypothesized that the variability between measurements over three months for each body segment including total body, android, gynoid and VAT would be higher than those observed for the same-day precision measures.

2. Materials and Methods

2.1. Participants

Reliability, three-month study: Sixty-five weight stable adults aged 18 to 65 years were recruited by advertisement posted within Monash University and the local community. Weight stability was self-reported as weight change no more than ±2 kg for at least three months prior to participation. Participants attended the Be Active, Sleep, Eat (BASE) Facility at Monash University, Melbourne, on three separate occasions over a three-month period.

Same-day precision: Thirty adults aged 18 to 65 years were recruited by advertisement posted within Monash University and the local community. Participants attended the Be Active, Sleep, Eat (BASE) Facility at Monash University, Melbourne on a single occasion for duplicate scans.

No incentive was offered for completion of either study but all participants were given a copy of their body composition scan at their final visit. All experimental procedures were conducted in accordance with the Declaration of Helsinki and were formally approved by the Monash University Human Research Ethics Committee (CF13/1432-2013000751; CF15/2790-2015001139) and participants provided full informed consent.

2.2. Sample Size

The sample size was estimated based on previously reported data that investigated the reproducibility of DXA scans [27]. It has also previously been estimated that precision studies recruit at least 30 participants to be scanned twice or at least 15 participants scanned three times [28].

2.3. Procedures

Reliability, three-month study: Participants attended the laboratory after an overnight fast between 8 am and 10 am. Each participant was required to attend at the same time of day for each visit. Prior to the DXA scan, participants were required to change in to a gown and remove all radio-opaque objects. Height (Holtain stadiometer to 0.1 cm, Holtain Ltd., Crosswell, Pembrokeshire, UK) and weight (Seca Scale 720 to 0.01 kg, Seca Group, Hamburg, Germany) were measured by standard anthropometric techniques to ensure weight stability throughout the assessment period and for the correct scanning mode to be calculated by the GE LUNAR iDXA Narrow-Angle Dual Energy X-ray Densitometer with SmartFAN™ (GE Medical, Software Lunar DPX enCORE 2012 version 14.0, Madison, WI, USA). Participants were then positioned and scanned according to manufacturer's guidelines for a total body composition scan. BMI was calculated as weight (kg)/height (m^2).

Same-day precision: The protocol for the precision study was the same as the reliability study, except that participants were asked to stand-up after the first scan, then lie down again for repositioning for the second scan.

Positioning: Participants were positioned for a total body scan on the scanner using standardized procedures. Briefly, participants were placed in supine position with the longitudinal center of the table bisecting the trunk. All parts of the body were in the scan field, except where the participant did not fit within the scan boundary, where arms were placed outside scan regions to obtain VAT data. The top of the participant's head was located 3 cm below the top scan line. Participants were asked to slightly extend their chin with hands placed in a neutral position, but with space allowed between arms and trunk. Velcro straps were secured at ankle level to minimize movement for the duration of the scan.

2.4. Scan Analysis Procedures

All DXA scans and analyses were performed by the same radiographer (AE) who ensured that calibration and phantom scans were performed and passed each day prior to scanning. The manufacturer's guidelines were followed to ensure the quality of scanning and analyses. Scans were analyzed according to the manufacturer's instructions. Total body composition was calculated from the whole scan, whereas android and gynoid regions were manually identified by the radiographer (AE) using standard procedures. The android region of interest (ROI) is the area between ribs and iliac crests, the lateral boundaries occur between the trunk and arms, the lower boundary is the top of the iliac crest, and the upper boundary is determined as 20% of the distance between the pelvis and neck cuts. The gynoid ROI is the hip area and includes the area around the proximal femur. The outer leg cuts are the lateral boundaries, the upper boundary is below the pelvis cut by 1.5× android ROI height. The height of the gynoid ROI is determined as 2× android ROI height. Figure 1 shows an example scan including regions of interest. VAT is calculated by the Lunar DPX enCORE software from the android region, determined at L3–L5 level.

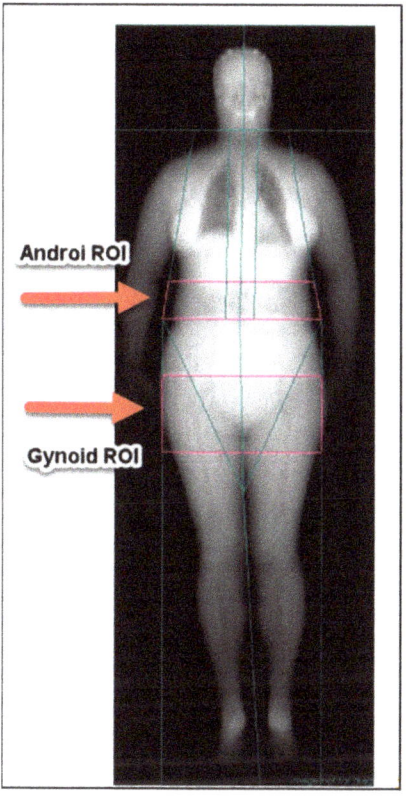

Figure 1. Example scan image with android (top arrow) and gynoid regions (bottom arrow) identified from the GE LUNAR iDXA Narrow-Angle Dual Energy X-ray Densitometer with SmartFAN™ (GE Medical, Software Lunar DPX enCORE 2012 version 14.0, Madison, WI, USA).

2.5. Statistical Analysis

Continuous variables are reported as mean and standard deviation (SD) unless reported otherwise. In order to minimize variations that were due to actual changes in body weight and composition, participants who did not meet the criterion for weight stability (±2 kg) for the duration of the reliability study were not included in the analyses. The measurement errors were calculated as CV (%) and the square root of the mean of the sum of the squares of differences (RMSSD) between scans, from which the LSC (at 95% confidence interval) was calculated as recommended by the International Society for Clinical Densitometry [29]. Data were tested for normality using the Shapiro-Wilk test. Differences between groups were assessed by the t-test for parametric data and the Mann-Whitney U test for non-parametric data as reported. For the reliability data, Spearman rank correlation coefficients were calculated for BMI versus VAT mass, and for VAT CV with BMI and fat mass variables. To explore participant characteristics for reliability of VAT measures, a chi-squared test of independence was applied to categories to test whether the variability of measures differed between groups. The categories were determined by applying cut-off levels to the variables in the correlation scatterplots. The cut-off for CV was applied at 10% as the maximum level of acceptable variability, BMI at 25 kg/m^2, and VAT mass 500 g as the point at which most participants did not exceed 10% variability in repeated measures. To explore the impact of sex, and BMI categories (healthy weight < 25 kg/m^2, and overweight + obese ≥ 25 kg/m^2) on the outcome measures, a two-way analysis between groups analysis of variance (ANOVA) was performed. All analyses were performed using IBM SPSS Statistics (Version 22, Armonk, NY, USA).

3. Results

3.1. Three-Month Reliability Study

3.1.1. Participants' Baseline Characteristics

Of the 65 participants, four did not complete the study due to other commitments, and 11 participants did not remain weight stable (±2 kg) over the three-month period and were excluded from the analyses. The height, weight and BMI of the remaining 51 weight stable participants (88% female) are presented in Table 1. The mean age was 35.1 (SD 14.5) years and the median (range) 29.8 (18.7–64.3) years. The CV for body weight was 0.8% over three months.

Table 1. Participant characteristics and body composition and coefficient of variation by region of interest over three months.

Number of Participants (Male n, (%))								
	Visit 1			Visit 2			Visit 3	
Total								
Height (cm)	165.0 (149.1–178.5)			165.3 (148.8–178.7)			164.9 (148.3–178.3)	
Weight (kg)	59.8 (49.5–83.7)			60.2 (49.2–83.6)			59.7 (47.6–84.0)	
BMI (kg/m²)	22.2 (18.6–31.5)			22.3 (18.3–31.7)			22.4 (18.2–31.7)	
Male								
Height (cm)	172.0 (167.5–178.5)			171.6 (168.1–178.7)			171.9 (167.8–178.4)	
Weight (kg)	77.6 (69.9–82.5)			75.5 (69.0–81.6)			77.5 (69.4–81.9)	
BMI (kg/m²)	25.5 (23.8–28.2)			25.1 (23.3–27.9)			25.5 (23.4–27.9)	
Female								
Height (cm)	164.5 (149.1–176.4)			164.3 (148.8–176.4)			164.2 (148.3–176.4)	
Weight (kg)	58.7 (49.5–83.7)			57.9 (49.2–83.6)			58.4 (47.6–84.0)	
BMI (kg/m²)	21.8 (18.6–31.5)			21.9 (18.3–31.7)			22.0 (18.2–31.7)	

Measure (Region of Interest)	Visit 1		Visit 2		Visit 3		CV%	RMSSD (LSC 95% CI)		
	Mean (SD)	Range	Mean (SD)	Range	Mean (SD)	Range		V1–V2	V2–V3	V1–V3
A-FM (kg)	1.33 (0.97)	0.27–4.81	1.33 (0.98)	0.30–5.01	1.32 (0.96)	0.25–4.89	5.9	0.10 (0.27)	0.11 (0.31)	0.12 (0.34)
G-FM (kg)	3.53 (1.37)	1.28–7.76	3.54 (1.35)	1.20–7.62	3.55 (1.40)	1.25–8.07	2.8	0.15 (0.43)	0.15 (0.40)	0.19 (0.53)
TB-FM (kg)	18.8 (7.82)	7.62–47.3	18.9 (7.93)	8.10–47.7	18.8 (7.94)	7.81–47.7	2.5	0.73 (2.03)	0.60 (1.67)	1.00 (2.76)
A-LM (kg)	3.01 (0.54)	2.18–4.69	2.98 (0.56)	2.16–4.61	2.99 (0.58)	1.91–4.80	3.1	0.14 (0.39)	0.16 (0.46)	0.14 (0.39)
G-LM (kg)	6.60 (1.29)	4.67–10.2	6.58 (1.30)	4.50–10.2	6.60 (1.31)	4.45–10.1	1.6	0.15 (0.42)	0.17 (0.46)	0.16 (0.43)
TB-LM (kg)	41.0 (7.55)	30.6–61.3	41.1 (7.61)	30.4–61.4	41.1 (7.68)	29.1–62.0	1.2	0.77 (2.14)	0.80 (2.21)	0.86 (2.37)
A-TM (kg)	4.38 (1.23)	2.71–8.51	4.36 (1.22)	2.68–8.42	4.36 (1.27)	2.52–8.45	2.3	0.15 (0.43)	0.14 (0.40)	0.16 (0.43)
G-TM (kg)	10.4 (1.92)	6.81–15.8	10.4 (1.87)	6.86–15.4	10.4 (1.95)	6.65–15.7	1.3	0.22 (0.62)	0.22 (0.60)	0.20 (0.55)
TB-TM (kg)	62.2 (11.9)	43.1–98.2	62.3 (11.9)	43.9–98.9	62.3 (12.1)	42.7–98.7	0.8	0.79 (2.20)	0.67 (1.85)	0.92 (2.56)
A-%Fat	28 (12)	9–58	28 (12)	9–60	28 (11)	10–58	5.5	2.0 (5.5)	2.3 (6.3)	2.7 (7.5)
G-%Fat	34 (9)	16–52	34 (9)	15–51	34 (9)	15–53	2.2	1.2 (3.3)	1.1 (3.1)	1.4 (3.8)
TB-%Fat	30 (8)	17–50	30 (8)	16–51	30 (8)	16–50	2.5	1.1 (3.1)	1.1 (3.1)	1.6 (4.4)
VAT Mass (g)	303.7 (504.9)	0–2540.0	301.4 (516.6)	0–2621.7	280.9 (464.1)	0–2273.1	42.2	50.8 (140.7)	82.7 (229.0)	74.5 (206.3)
VAT Vol (cm³)	322.0 (535.2)	0–2692.4	319.5 (547.6)	0–2779.0	297.7 (491.9)	0–2409.5	42.2	66.4 (184.0)	70.2 (194.5)	65.4 (181.2)
VAT Mass (g) ^	350.8 (529.1)	0.49–2540.0	348.3 (542.1)	0.46–2621.7	324.9 (485.8)	2.18–2273.1	29.3	54.6 (151.3)	88.7 (245.8)	79.6 (220.5)
VAT Vol (cm³) ^	371.8 (560.8)	0.51–2692.4	369.2 (574.6)	0.48–2779.0	344.4 (514.9)	2.32–2409.5	29.3	57.9 (160.4)	94.0 (260.5)	84.4 (233.7)

Participant characteristics are reported median (5th and 95th percentile A = Android). BMI = body mass index; FM = Fat mass; G = Gynoid; LM = Lean mass; CV = coefficient of variation; LSC = Least significant change; RMSSD = Root mean square of the standard deviation; TB = Total body; TM = Total mass; V1 = visit 1, V2 = visit 2, V3 = visit 3; VAT = Visceral adipose tissue; ^ = Included only participants with VAT > 0 g for all three visits (n = 44). Italics: Datas are different to above rows.

3.1.2. Body Composition Variability Over Three Months

The android region (from which VAT is calculated) demonstrated the highest variability in all measures of body composition compared with the total body and gynoid region over the three visits (Table 1). The variability of measures in the android region ranged from 2.3% to 5.9%. Whereas the variability between repeated body composition measures that were calculated for the total body, and gynoid region, ranged from 0.8% to 2.8% (Table 1).

Men and women differed in body composition measures: men were taller ($p = 0.004$), weighed more ($p = 0.013$), had decreased gynoid ($p < 0.001$) and total ($p = 0.009$) fat mass, and increased lean mass in all regions ($p < 0.001$). VAT mass was not different between men and women ($p = 0.321$) (Supplementary Table S1). While CV values for women tended to be higher, the levels of variation were not statistically different from men (Supplementary Table S1).

Participants with BMI < 25 kg/m^2 had significantly lower fat mass and total mass for all compartments (all $p < 0.01$), including VAT mass ($p = 0.019$) when compared with participants with BMI ≥ 25 kg/m^2. However, analysis by ANOVA did not reveal any significant differences in variability between these groups (Supplementary Table S1).

The CVs for VAT mass and volume were both 42.2%. The measure for VAT mass was detected as 0 g on at least one occasion for seven participants. As such, CVs for VAT mass and volume have also been reported for $n = 44$ (VAT mass > 0 g at all three visits), and remained considerably higher than all other scan measures, both 29.3%. The highest LSC across the three visits for VAT mass and VAT volume was 245.8 g and 260.5 cm^3, respectively (Table 2). The participants for which VAT was measured as 0 g on at least one occasion had lower BMI ($p = 0.036$), android fat mass ($p = 0.037$), android total mass ($p = 0.048$), as well as VAT mass and volume (both $p < 0.001$) (Supplementary Table S2).

BMI was positively correlated with VAT mass (Spearman's correlation coefficient, $r_s = 0.598$, $p < 0.001$). The CVs of VAT mass were negatively correlated with weight ($r_s = -0.334$, $p = 0.02$), BMI ($r_s = -0.537$, $p < 0.001$) (Figure 2B), total fat mass ($r_s = -0.489$, $p < 0.001$), android fat mass ($r_s = -0.694$, $p < 0.001$) and VAT mass ($r_s = -0.795$, $p < 0.001$, Figure 2A). All correlations indicated that those with higher fat mass demonstrated lower CV for VAT measures over three months. Only 4 out of 12 (33%) participants with a BMI > 25 kg/m^2 demonstrated CV greater than 10% for VAT, whereas 22 of 35 (63%) participants with a BMI less than 25 kg/m^2 showed VAT variability greater than 10%. Similarly, participants with VAT mass > 500 g (1 out of 10, 10%) were less likely to have increased variability $>10\%$ than people with VAT mass < 500 g (32 out of 38, 84%). People were less likely to have increased variability ($>10\%$) if their BMI was above 25 kg/m^2 ($p = 0.001$) and VAT mass was over 500 g ($p < 0.001$).

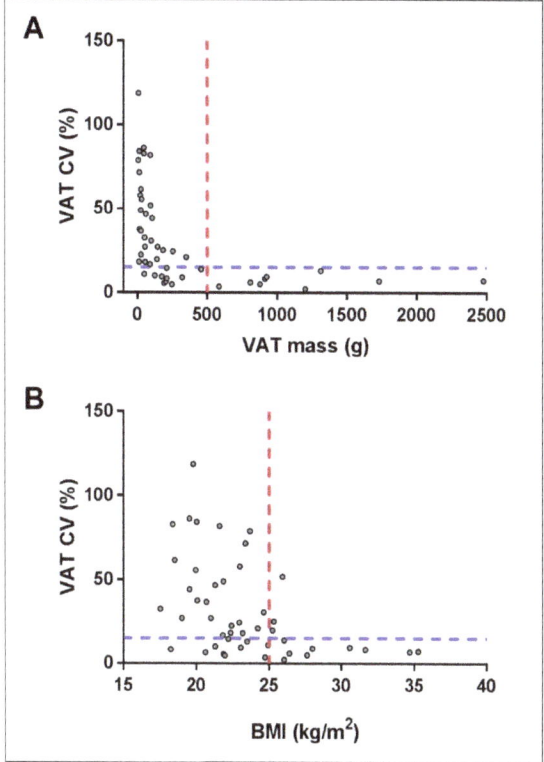

Figure 2. Correlation scatterplot between visceral adipose tissue (VAT) mass coefficient of variation (CV%) and (**A**) VAT mass (g) $r_s = -0.795$, $p < 0.001$; and (**B**) body mass index (BMI) (kg/m^2) $r_s = -0.537$, $p < 0.001$. The dashed lines represent the cut off lines for VAT (500 g) and BMI (25 kg/m^2) to increase the probability of more reliable CV% for VAT assessments.

3.2. Same-Day Repeated-Scan Precision

Thirty participants, of mean age (SD) 30.9 (10.5) years, median (range) 27.5 (18–49) years, completed the precision study. Height, weight, BMI, and scan data are presented in Table 2. The CVs for all the body compartments for fat mass, lean mass and total mass were less than 2%, whereas the CVs for VAT mass and volume were both 16.2% (Table 2). VAT mass was detected as 0 g on one occasion for one participant, therefore CV is also reported for $n = 29$ for these variables, both 11.8% (Table 2). The characteristics of the participant for which VAT was measured as 0 g were weight 60.7 kg, BMI 22 kg/m^2, similar to the participants in the three-month study who had measured 0 g VAT.

Table 2. Participant characteristics and scan results with coefficient of variation for body composition measurements for participants in the same-day repeated-scan precision study.

Characteristics			
		Men	Women
Number of participants (Male n, (%))	30 (14 (47%))		
Height (cm) Median (5th–95th percentile)	171.4 (161.9–184.6)	176.6 (169.7–192.3)	165.3 (161.9–184.2)
Weight (kg) Median (5th–95th percentile)	77.8 (51.7–131.9)	102.8 (55.8–145.1)	69.9 (51.7–126.9)
BMI (kg/m^2) Median (5th–95th percentile)	26.5 (18.9–39.2)	34.2 (18.9–42.53)	24.4 (19.0–37.4)

Measure	Scan 1 Mean (SD)	Range	Scan 2 Mean (SD)	Range	CV%	RMSSD (LSC 95% CI)
A-FM (kg)	2.32 (1.77)	0.36–6.56	2.34 (1.81)	0.36–6.60	1.87	0.06 (0.18)
G-FM (kg)	4.75 (2.64)	1.77–11.96	4.79 (2.74)	1.77–12.43	1.28	0.15 (0.43)
TB-FM (kg)	26.80 (15.01)	10.51–60.09	26.86 (15.14)	10.78–60.10	0.74	0.31 (0.85)
A-LM (kg)	3.82 (0.87)	2.32–5.93	3.82 (0.87)	2.29–6.01	1.11	0.08 (0.23)
G-LM (kg)	8.74 (2.21)	5.12–13.46	8.75 (2.23)	5.01–13.59	0.60	0.15 (0.43)
TB-LM (kg)	53.67 (12.54)	32.79–79.23	53.69 (12.46)	32.77–79.93	0.48	0.48 (1.34)
A-TM (kg)	6.19 (2.44)	3.33–11.02	6.21 (2.48)	3.25–11.22	0.63	0.08 (0.21)
G-TM (kg)	13.81 (4.36)	8.60–23.64	13.86 (4.46)	8.57–24.33	0.58	0.18 (0.50)
TB-TM (kg)	83.41 (25.29)	51.58–136.13	83.50 (25.42)	51.60–136.22	0.20	0.40 (1.10)
A-%Fat	33 (15)	8–61	33 (15)	8–61	1.75	0.9 (2.5)
G-%Fat	33 (9)	16–52	33 (10)	16–53	1.02	0.6 (1.7)
TB-%Fat	30 (9)	17–48	30 (9)	17–48	0.80	0.4 (1.1)
VAT Mass (g)	776.9 (808.8)	28.0–2978.2	766.7 (807.5)	0.0–2999.2	16.2	65.5 (181.4)
VAT Vol (cm^3)	823.5 (857.4)	29.7–3156.9	812.7 (856.0)	0.0–3179.1	16.2	82.2 (227.8)
VAT Mass (g) ^	802.4 (810.8)	28.0–2978.2	793.2 (808.5)	23.4–2999.2	11.8	66.4 (184.0)
VAT Vol (cm^3) ^	850.5 (859.4)	29.7–3156.9	840.7 (857.0)	24.8–3179.1	11.8	82.5 (228.6)

A = Android; FM = Fat mass; G = Gynoid; LM = Lean mass; LSC = Least significant change; STM = Soft tissue mass; V1 = Visit 1; V2 = Visit 2; V3 = Visit 3; TB = Total body; TM = Total mass; VAT = Visceral adipose tissue; ^ = Included only participants with VAT > 0 g for all three visits (n = 29).

Men and women differed slightly in body composition measures compared to the three-month cohort; men were taller (p = 0.003), had higher levels of android fat (p = 0.035), and android (p = 0.004), gynoid (p = 0.006), and total body (p = 0.003) lean mass. VAT mass was higher in men compared with women (p = 0.003) (Supplementary Table S1). CV values were not different between men (Supplementary Table S1).

Participants with BMI < 25 kg/m^2 had significantly lower fat mass, lean mass, and total mass for all compartments (all p < 0.01), including VAT mass (p < 0.001) when compared with participants with BMI $\geq$ 25 kg/m^2. However, analysis by ANOVA did not reveal any significant differences in variability between these groups (Supplementary Table S1).

4. Discussion

As little as 5% loss of total body weight can result in clinically meaningful risk reduction in obesity-associated morbidities [30,31]. Body composition, not just weight-status, is an important indicator of disease risk [32] and in particular, increased VAT in the android region [33], even in healthy-weight individuals [12–14]. As such, intervention studies may aim to target reductions in VAT mass and consequent metabolic disease risk. Therefore, it is important to be able to reliably measure small compartmental changes over time. The iDXA is generally recognized as a reliable measure of body composition, however as with any laboratory and imaging instrument, outputs can vary over time due to factors such as changes in instrument calibration, fluctuation of component function, and others [34]. Despite stability in total body weight (0.8%), the CVs of android, gynoid and total body fat and lean mass were increased over three months compared with both our own same-day precision data and previously published results [24,35,36]. However, these percentages of variation were still considered within acceptable scientific limits (< 6%) [36,37]. A key strength of this study was that a single radiographer was used to reduce variability associated with different operations and this was confirmed by very low variability in the bone mineral density measures over three months (<2.0% data not shown), and as such the variability in body composition measures reported here were likely due to the long-term variability of the scanner rather than possibly attributed to operator errors or inconsistencies in positioning of participants.

High levels of variability were demonstrated in VAT mass and volume, 11.8% with same day scanning, and greater than 30% over three months. The highest variability over the three month period was observed in participants with a lower volume of VAT. Previously reported same-day precision of VAT on the iDXA, was also increased for participants with a weight in the healthy (BMI 18–25 kg/m^2) range (17%) compared with participants with overweight and obesity (approximately 5%) [21]. The VAT measures are calculated from the compartmentalization of the android region of the total body scan. All composition measures showed higher variability in this region than the gynoid and total body regions. This is supported by previously published results that demonstrated poor DXA scan reproducibility in the upper body segments compared with the lower regions of the body [36]. As the android region is where the gastrointestinal tract is located, factors that may influence the increased variability include hydration status and whether the participant has consumed food. It is therefore speculated that to increase reliability of scans of this compartment, any variables that may influence its composition be minimized, and as such participants should present to study measurements days fasted and at the same time of day.

A LSC of 260 g for VAT mass was measured, indicating that any changes below this level will not be accurately detectable by iDXA in this cohort. This LSC value must be interpreted with consideration that one of the limitations of the present study of was a higher number of participants within the 'healthy BMI range' who demonstrated significantly increased variation in repeated VAT measures compared with participants with BMI $\geq$ 25kg/m^2. In future studies that aim to investigate VAT changes in adults with overweight and obesity as defined by a BMI $\geq$ 25 kg/m^2 and $\geq$ 30 kg/m^2, respectively, the LSC may be lower. Nonetheless, based on the present study, a change >260 g or more is recommended to be confident of a significant change in VAT mass.

Of particular concern was that VAT was detected as 0 g on at least one occasion for seven people in the three-month study, and one person in the precision study. The participants weighed significantly less, and had less fat mass in the android region than participants where VAT was detected on all three occasions. The average BMI was 20 kg/m^2, and VAT mass, when detectable, was measured to be generally less than 20 g. For the whole sample, measurement of VAT mass was less reliable in participants with a BMI below 25 kg/m^2. However, as only eleven participants in this study had a BMI over 25 kg/m^2, it may limit the generalizability of these findings. Regardless, our results indicate that for reliable measurements of changes in VAT using the iDXA, participants need to have a BMI above 25 kg/m^2. More specifically, the results obtained from the 51 participants who completed the three-month reliability study indicate that reliable measures of VAT mass can only be obtained in people with more than 2 kg android fat mass or 500 g VAT mass. As BMI was positively correlated with VAT mass and negatively associated with variability in VAT, it may serve as a useful indicator when planning nutrition and lifestyle studies aimed at reducing VAT. BMI has previously been shown to predict VAT in young adults; waist circumference may also be a reliable marker [38].

Men and women differ in body composition [39], and the variability of measures over time may be impacted by sex. Adiposity levels in women are associated with menstrual cycle sex hormone patterns [40]; some studies also suggest that body composition is altered during the menstrual cycle [41,42] whereas others have reported no significant impact of cycle phase on body composition measures [43]. The present study did not control for the menstrual cycle of participants; if fluctuations in adiposity were occurring, they may have contributed to the increased level of variability observed between visits.

The iDXA has previously been validated for the measurement of VAT and demonstrated good agreement between VAT measures with computed tomography (CT) scans in men and women across a range of BMI values [18] and good correlation with MRI [44]. Furthermore, earlier studies have demonstrated that major shifts in VAT can occur in adults with none to modest observed change in body weight [45–47]. Therefore, the variability observed in the current study may have been representative of true, normal fluctuation of VAT in weight-stable participants over three months, rather than scan variation. Further studies that compare measures of VAT from the iDXA with scans from CT or magnetic resonance imaging (MRI) to determine accuracy over time are required.

5. Conclusions

Despite the CV for total body mass remaining below 1% for both study arms, the variability of measures collected over three months for all body segments was increased compared with repeated same-day scanning. In the case of the variability in VAT, this will make it difficult to assess true loss or gain of VAT during weight loss interventions, particularly in individuals with VAT mass <500 g.

For future studies that aim to assess changes in VAT mass using the GE iDXA it is recommended that to increase likelihood of accurate interpretation, participants should have a BMI at least 25 kg/m^2, or VAT greater than 500 g. Data obtained from participants with VAT mass levels below 500 g should be interpreted with caution. Furthermore, we suggest that VAT changes in people with BMI lower than 25 kg/m^2 would be better to be reported as absolute value rather than percentage changes.

Supplementary Materials: The following are available online at http://www.mdpi.com/2072-6643/10/10/1484/s1, Table S1 (attachment): Comparisons of body composition and variability for sex and BMI; Table S2 (attachment): Participant characteristics and body composition: Participants with VAT detected as 0 g.

Author Contributions: Conceptualization, M.B. and H.T.; data curation, A.L.D., A.E., E.B., K.D. and A.K.; formal analysis, A.L.D., A.G.-Z. and A.E.; methodology, A.L.D., M.B. and H.T.; project administration, A.L.D. and E.B.; writing: original draft, A.L.D.; writing: review & editing, M.B., A.G.-Z., A.E., E.B., K.D., A.K. and H.T.

Funding: This research received no external funding.

Acknowledgments: The authors would like to acknowledge the participants in this study for their contribution of time. A.K. is in receipt of an Australian Government Research Training Program (RTP) Scholarship.

Conflicts of Interest: The authors declare no conflict of interest.

References

1. Newton, R.L.; Alfonso, A.; White, M.A.; York-Crowe, E.; Walden, H.; Ryan, D.; Bray, G.A.; Williamson, D. Percent body fat measured by BIA and DEXA in obese, African-American adolescent girls. *Int. J. Obes.* **2005**, *29*, 594–602. [CrossRef] [PubMed]
2. Watts, K.; Naylor, L.H.; Davis, E.A.; Jones, T.W.; Beeson, B.; Bettenay, F.; Siafarikas, A.; Lana, B.; Ackland, T.; Green, D.J. Do skinfolds accurately assess changes in body fat in obese children and adolescents? *Med. Sci. Sports Exerc.* **2006**, *38*, 439–444. [CrossRef] [PubMed]
3. Kelly, T.L.; Wilson, K.E.; Heymsfield, S.B. Dual energy X-Ray absorptiometry body composition reference values from NHANES. *PLoS ONE* **2009**, *4*, e7038. [CrossRef] [PubMed]
4. Steinsbekk, S.; Wichstrom, L.; Odegard, R.; Mehus, I. Change in body fat during a family-based treatment of obesity in children: The relative importance of energy intake and physical activity. *Obes. Facts* **2013**, *5*, 515–526. [CrossRef] [PubMed]
5. Manios, Y.; Moschonis, G.; Koutsikas, K.; Papoutsou, S.; Petraki, I.; Bellou, E.; Naoumi, A.; Kostea, S.; Tanagra, S. Changes in body composition following a dietary and lifestyle intervention trial: The postmenopausal health study. *Maturitas.* **2009**, *62*, 58–65. [CrossRef] [PubMed]
6. Cohen, A.; Dempster, D.W.; Recker, R.R.; Lappe, J.M.; Zhou, H.; Zwahlen, A.; Müller, R.; Zhao, B.; Guo, X.; Lang, T. Abdominal fat is associated with lower bone formation and inferior bone quality in healthy premenopausal women: A transiliac bone biopsy study. *J. Clin. Endocrinol. Metab.* **2013**, *98*, 2562–2572. [CrossRef] [PubMed]
7. Freedman, D.S.; Thornton, J.C.; Mei, Z.; Wang, J.; Dietz, W.H.; Pierson, R.N., Jr.; Horlick, M. Height and adiposity among children. *Obes. Res.* **2004**, *12*, 846–853. [CrossRef]
8. Marinangeli, C.P.; Kassis, A.N. Use of dual X-ray absorptiometry to measure body mass during short- to medium-term trials of nutrition and exercise interventions. *Nutr. Rev.* **2013**, *71*, 332–342. [CrossRef]
9. Millstein, R.A. Measuring outcomes in adult weight loss studies that include diet and physical activity: A systematic review. *J. Nutr. Metab.* **2014**. [CrossRef] [PubMed]

10. Wensveen, F.M.; Valentic, S.; Sestan, M.; Wensveen, T.T.; Polic, B. The "Big Bang" in obese fat: Events initiating obesity-induced adipose tissue inflammation. *Eur. J. Immunol.* **2015**, *45*, 2446–2456. [CrossRef] [PubMed]
11. Zhang, M.; Hu, T.; Zhang, S.; Zhou, L. Associations of different adipose tissue depots with insulin resistance: A systematic review and meta-analysis of observational studies. *Sci. Rep.* **2015**, *5*, 18495. [CrossRef] [PubMed]
12. Batsis, J.A.; Sahakyan, K.R.; Rodriguez-Escudero, J.P.; Bartels, S.J.; Somers, V.K.; Lopez-Jimenez, F. Normal weight obesity and mortality in United States subjects >/=60 years of age (from the Third National Health and Nutrition Examination Survey). *Am. J. Cardiol.* **2013**, *112*, 1592–1598. [CrossRef] [PubMed]
13. Shea, J.L.; King, M.T.; Yi, Y.; Gulliver, W.; Sun, G. Body fat percentage is associated with cardiometabolic dysregulation in BMI-defined normal weight subjects. *Nutr. Metab. Cardiovasc. Dis.* **2012**, *22*, 741–747. [CrossRef] [PubMed]
14. De Lorenzo, A.; Bianchi, A.; Maroni, P.; Iannarelli, A.; Daniele, N.D.; Iacopino, L.; Renzo, L.D. Adiposity rather than BMI determines metabolic risk. *Int. J. Cardiol.* **2013**, *166*, 111–117. [CrossRef] [PubMed]
15. von Hurst, P.R.; Walsh, D.C.I.; Conlon, C.A.; Ingram, M.; Kruger, R.; Stonehouse, W. Validity and reliability of bioelectrical impedance analysis to estimate body fat percentage against air displacement plethysmography and dual-energy X-ray absorptiometry. *Nutr. Diet.* **2016**, *73*, 197–204. [CrossRef]
16. Kuk, J.L.; Lee, S.; Heymsfield, S.B.; Ross, R. Waist circumference and abdominal adipose tissue distribution: Influence of age and sex. *Am. J. Clin. Nutr.* **2005**, *81*, 1330–1334. [CrossRef] [PubMed]
17. Camhi, S.M.; Bray, G.A.; Bouchard, C.; Greenway, F.L.; Johnson, W.D.; Newton, R.L.; Ravussin, E.; Ryan, D.H.; Smith, S.R.; Katzmarzyk, P.T. The relationship of waist circumference and BMI to visceral, subcutaneous, and total body fat: Sex and race differences. *Obesity (Silver Spring)* **2011**, *19*, 402–408. [CrossRef] [PubMed]
18. Kaul, S.; Rothney, M.P.; Peters, D.M.; Wacker, W.K.; Davis, C.E.; Shapiro, M.D.; Ergun, D.L. Dual-energy X-ray absorptiometry for quantification of visceral fat. *Obesity (Silver Spring)* **2012**, *20*, 1313–1318. [CrossRef] [PubMed]
19. Leonard, C.M.; Roza, M.A.; Barr, R.D.; Webber, C.E. Reproducibility of DXA measurements of bone mineral density and body composition in children. *Pediatr. Radiol.* **2009**, *39*, 148–154. [CrossRef] [PubMed]
20. Alwis, G.; Rosengren, B.; Stenevi-Lundgren, S.; Duppe, H.; Sernbo, I.; Karlsson, M.K. Normative dual energy X-ray absorptiometry data in Swedish children and adolescents. *Acta. Paediatr.* **2013**, *99*, 1091–1099. [CrossRef] [PubMed]
21. Mellis, M.G.; Oldroyd, B.; Hind, K. In vivo precision of the GE Lunar iDXA for the measurement of visceral adipose tissue in adults: The influence of body mass index. *Eur. J. Clin. Nutr.* **2014**, *68*, 1365–1367. [CrossRef] [PubMed]
22. Carver, T.E.; Christou, N.V.; Court, O.; Lemke, H.; Andersen, R.E. In vivo precision of the GE lunar iDXA for the assessment of lumbar spine, total hip, femoral neck, and total body bone mineral density in severely obese patients. *J. Clin. Densitom.* **2014**, *17*, 109–115. [CrossRef] [PubMed]
23. Lohman, M.; Tallroth, K.; Kettunen, J.A.; Marttinen, M.T. Reproducibility of dual-energy X-ray absorptiometry total and regional body composition measurements using different scanning positions and definitions of regions. *Metabolism* **2009**, *58*, 1663–1668. [CrossRef] [PubMed]
24. Kaminsky, L.A.; Ozemek, C.; Williams, K.L.; Byun, W. Precision of total and regional body fat estimates from dual-energy X-ray absorptiometer measurements. *J. Nutr. Health Aging* **2014**, *18*, 591–594. [CrossRef] [PubMed]
25. Baim, S.; Wilson, C.R.; Lewiecki, E.M.; Luckey, M.M.; Downs, R.W., Jr.; Lentle, B.C. Precision assessment and radiation safety for dual-energy X-ray absorptiometry: Position paper of the International Society for Clinical Densitometry. *J. Clin. Densitom.* **2005**, *8*, 371–378. [CrossRef]
26. Kyle, U.G.; Bosaeus, I.; De Lorenzo, A.D.; Deurenberg, P.; Elia, M.; Gomez, J.M.; Heitmann, B.L.; Kent-Smith, L.; Melchior, J.C.; Pirlich, M.; et al. Bioelectrical impedance analysis—Part I: Review of principles and methods. *Clin. Nutr.* **2004**, *23*, 1226–1243. [CrossRef] [PubMed]
27. Hind, K.; Oldroyd, B. In-vivo precision of the GE Lunar iDXA densitometer for the measurement of appendicular and trunk lean and fat mass. *Eur. J. Clin. Nutr.* **2013**, *67*, 1331–1333. [CrossRef] [PubMed]
28. Khan, A.A.; Bachrach, L.; Brown, J.P.; Hanley, D.A.; Josse, R.G.; Kendler, D.L.; Leib, E.S.; Lentle, B.C.; Leslie, W.D.; Lewiecki, E.M.; et al. Standards and guidelines for performing central dual-energy X-ray absorptiometry in premenopausal women, men, and children. *J. Clin. Densitom.* **2004**, *7*, 51–64. [CrossRef]

29. International Society for Clinical Densiotometry (ISCD). Bone Densitometry Precision Calculating Tool. Available online: http://www.iscd.org/resources/calculators/precision-calculator/faq/ (accessed on 13 March 2017).
30. Wing, R.R.; Lang, W.; Wadden, T.A.; Safford, M.; Knowler, W.C.; Bertoni, A.G.; Hill, G.O.; Brancati, F.L.; Peters, A.; Wagenknecht, L.; et al. Benefits of modest weight loss in improving cardiovascular risk factors in overweight and obese individuals with type 2 diabetes. *Diabetes Care.* **2011**, *34*, 1481–1486. [CrossRef] [PubMed]
31. Blackburn, G. Effect of degree of weight loss on health benefits. *Obes. Res.* **1995**, *3* (Suppl. S2), 211s–216s. [CrossRef] [PubMed]
32. Dulloo, A.G.; Jacquet, J.; Solinas, G.; Montani, J.P.; Schutz, Y. Body composition phenotypes in pathways to obesity and the metabolic syndrome. *Int. J. Obes.* **2010**, *34* (Suppl. 2), S4–S17. [CrossRef]
33. Smith, J.D.; Borel, A.L.; Nazare, J.A.; Haffner, S.M.; Balkau, B.; Ross, R.; Massien, C.; Alméras, N.; Després, J.-P. Visceral adipose tissue indicates the severity of cardiometabolic risk in patients with and without type 2 diabetes: Results from the INSPIRE ME IAA study. *J. Clin. Endocrinol. Metab.* **2012**, *97*, 1517–1525. [CrossRef] [PubMed]
34. Lewiecki, E.M.; Binkley, N.; Morgan, S.L.; Shuhart, C.R.; Camargos, B.M.; Carey, J.J.; Gordon, C.M.; Jankowski, L.G.; Lee, J.-K.; Leslie, W.D.; et al. Best Practices for Dual-Energy X-ray Absorptiometry Measurement and Reporting: International Society for Clinical Densitometry Guidance. *J. Clin. Densitom.* **2016**, *19*, 127–140. [CrossRef] [PubMed]
35. Carver, T.E.; Christou, N.V.; Andersen, R.E. In vivo precision of the GE iDXA for the assessment of total body composition and fat distribution in severely obese patients. *Obesity (Silver Spring)* **2013**, *21*, 1367–1369. [CrossRef] [PubMed]
36. Hind, K.; Oldroyd, B.; Truscott, J.G. In vivo precision of the GE Lunar iDXA densitometer for the measurement of total body composition and fat distribution in adults. *Eur. J. Clin. Nutr.* **2011**, *65*, 140–142. [CrossRef] [PubMed]
37. Guo, Y.; Franks, P.W.; Brookshire, T.; Tataranni, P.A. The intra- and inter-instrument reliability of DXA based on ex vivo soft tissue measurements. *Obes. Res.* **2004**, *12*, 1925–1929. [CrossRef] [PubMed]
38. Borruel, S.; Molto, J.F.; Alpanes, M.; Fernandez-Duran, E.; Alvarez-Blasco, F.; Luque-Ramirez, M.; Escobar-Morreale, H.F. Surrogate markers of visceral adiposity in young adults: Waist circumference and body mass index are more accurate than waist hip ratio, model of adipose distribution and visceral adiposity index. *PLoS ONE* **2014**, *9*, e114112. [CrossRef] [PubMed]
39. Larsson, I.; Lissner, L.; Samuelson, G.; Fors, H.; Lantz, H.; Naslund, I.; Carlsson, L.M.S.; Sjöström, L.; Bosaeus, I. Body composition through adult life: Swedish reference data on body composition. *Eur. J. Clin. Nutr.* **2015**, *69*, 837–842. [CrossRef] [PubMed]
40. Yeung, E.H.; Zhang, C.; Albert, P.S.; Mumford, S.L.; Ye, A.; Perkins, N.J.; Wactawski-Wende, J.; Schisterman, E.F. Adiposity and sex hormones across the menstrual cycle: The BioCycle Study. *Int. J. Obes. (Lond.)* **2013**, *37*, 237–243. [CrossRef] [PubMed]
41. Gleichauf, C.N.; Roe, D.A. The menstrual cycle's effect on the reliability of bioimpedance measurements for assessing body composition. *Am. J. Clin. Nutr.* **1989**, *50*, 903–907. [CrossRef] [PubMed]
42. Kirchengast, S.; Gartner, M. Changes in fat distribution (WHR) and body weight across the menstrual cycle. *Coll. Antropol.* **2002**, *26*, 47–57. [PubMed]
43. Haddad, L.; Milke, P.; Zapata, L.; de la Fuente, J.R.; Vargas-Vorackova, F.; Lorenzana-Jimenez, M.; Corte, G.; Tamayo, J.; Kaplan, M.; Márquez, M.; et al. Effect of the menstrual cycle in ethanol pharmacokinetics. *J. Appl. Toxicol.* **1998**, *18*, 15–18. [CrossRef]
44. Cheung, A.S.; de Rooy, C.; Hoermann, R.; Gianatti, E.J.; Hamilton, E.J.; Roff, G.; Zajac, J.D.; Grossmann, M. Correlation of visceral adipose tissue measured by Lunar Prodigy dual X-ray absorptiometry with MRI and CT in older men. *Int. J. Obes. (Lond.)* **2016**, *40*, 1325–1328. [CrossRef] [PubMed]
45. Mourier, A.; Gautier, J.F.; De Kerviler, E.; Bigard, A.X.; Villette, J.M.; Garnier, J.P.; Duvallet, A.; Guezennec, C.Y.; Cathelineau, G. Mobilization of visceral adipose tissue related to the improvement in insulin sensitivity in response to physical training in NIDDM. Effects of branched-chain amino acid supplements. *Diabetes Care* **1997**, *20*, 385–391. [CrossRef] [PubMed]

46. Toro-Ramos, T.; Goodpaster, B.H.; Janumala, I.; Lin, S.; Strain, G.W.; Thornton, J.C.; Kang, P.; Courcoulas, A.P.; Pomp, A.; Gallagher, D. Continued loss in visceral and intermuscular adipose tissue in weight-stable women following bariatric surgery. *Obesity (Silver Spring)* **2015**, *23*, 62–69. [CrossRef] [PubMed]
47. Chaston, T.B.; Dixon, J.B. Factors associated with percent change in visceral versus subcutaneous abdominal fat during weight loss: Findings from a systematic review. *Int. J. Obes. (Lond.)* **2008**, *32*, 619–628. [CrossRef] [PubMed]

© 2018 by the authors. Licensee MDPI, Basel, Switzerland. This article is an open access article distributed under the terms and conditions of the Creative Commons Attribution (CC BY) license (http://creativecommons.org/licenses/by/4.0/).

Article

Association between Physical Condition and Body Composition, Nutrient Intake, Sociodemographic Characteristics, and Lifestyle Habits in Older Spanish Adults

Maria del Mar Bibiloni [1,2], Joanne Karam [1,3], Cristina Bouzas [1], Raquel Aparicio-Ugarriza [4], Raquel Pedrero-Chamizo [4], Antoni Sureda [1,2], Marcela González-Gross [2,4] and Josep A. Tur [1,2,*]

1. Research Group on Community Nutrition and Oxidative Stress, University of the Balearic Islands, E-07122 Palma de Mallorca, Spain; mar.bibiloni@uib.es (M.d.M.B.); joannem.karam@gmail.com (J.K.); cristinabouvel@gmail.com (C.B.); tosugo@hotmail.com (A.S.)
2. CIBEROBN (Physiopathology of Obesity and Nutrition CB12/03/30038), 28029 Madrid, Spain; marcela.gonzalez.gross@upm.es
3. Faculty of Health Sciences, University of Balamand, Balamand Al Kurah, P.O. Box 166378, Achrafieh, Beirut 1100-2807, Lebanon
4. ImFINE Research Group, Department of Health and Human Performance, Faculty of Physical Activity and Sport Sciences (INEF), Technical University of Madrid, 28040 Madrid, Spain; apariciougarriza.raquel@gmail.com (R.A.-U.); Raquel.pedrero@gmail.com (R.P.-C.)
* Correspondence: pep.tur@uib.es; Tel.: +34-971-1731; Fax: +34-971-173184

Received: 23 July 2018; Accepted: 23 October 2018; Published: 1 November 2018

Abstract: In this study, we assessed physical condition and its association with body composition, nutrient intake, sociodemographic characteristics, and lifestyle habits in older Spanish adults. In this cross-sectional study, we investigated 380 individuals (54% women; men aged 55–80 years and women aged 60–80 years) with no previously documented cardiovascular disease. A general questionnaire was used, and body weight, height, fat, appendicular skeletal muscle mass, and waist circumference were assessed. Physical condition measurements included handgrip strength (HGS) and agility/dynamic balance by eight-foot time up-and-go (8-f TUG) test. The lowest maximum HGS score (kg) was found in older participants, inactive men, and men with abdominal obesity. The highest maximum 8-f TUG score (s) was found in older and inactive, low education, low income, and abdominal obesity and overfat participants; 24.5% of participants had low maximum HGS and 36.8% had a high 8-f TUG score. Sex- and/or age-adjusted odds ratio (OR) for low maximum HGS in women, older participants, overweight and overfat participants were 4.6, 2.9, 0.6 and 0.6 respectively. Sex and/or age adjusted OR for high maximum 8-f TUG in women, overweight, overfat, and abdominally obese participants were 2.4, 1.6, 1.7, and 3.4, respectively; in participants with higher education, those who earned €900 or more per month, and slightly active and active participants had OR values of 0.4, 0.4, and 0.3, respectively. Sarcopenia incidence was 0.3%; however, 4.5% of men and 19.1% of women registered low physical condition (high and low scores in 8-f TUG and HGS tests, respectively). Overall, 36.8%, 24.5%, and 0.3% of participants had high maximum 8-f TUG score, low maximum HGS, and sarcopenia, respectively. Prevalence of these low values varies according to sociodemographic and body composition variables.

Keywords: physical condition; handgrip muscle strength; 8-foot time up-and-go; body composition; sarcopenia

1. Introduction

The current prevalence of and the expected increase in the elderly population is an important health challenge in our society. In 2050, almost 30% of the European population will be over 65 years old [1], and in Spain, it is estimated that 37% of the population will be over 64 years old by 2052 [2]. With an aging population, an increase in age-related diseases, including frailty, is expected.

Adverse health outcomes of aging, including falls, hospitalisation, institutionalization, and mortality, are the effect of impaired homeostatic reserve and reduced capacity of the organism to withstand stress, characterised by physical weakness, reduced physical activity, and performance that usually accompany frailty [3,4]. A key component of frailty is sarcopenia—a progressive loss of skeletal muscle mass and low muscle strength or performance that occurs with advancing age [4,5]. Sarcopenia is defined as a low muscle mass accompanied by either low muscle strength or low physical performance [4]. Low handgrip strength (HGS) and high eight-foot time up-and-go (8-f TUG) are used in the diagnosis of sarcopenia [4]; however, the prevalence of sarcopenia varies depending on the criteria used for diagnosis [6,7]. The European Working Group on Sarcopenia in Older People (EWGSOP) differentiated between presarcopenia (low muscle mass), sarcopenia (low muscle mass plus low muscle strength or physical condition), and severe sarcopenia (low muscle mass plus low muscle strength plus physical condition) [8].

Muscle strength has been described as a strong predictor of mortality and hospitalization in people aged 80 years and older [9]. Muscle homeostasis, under normal circumstances, is influenced by nutritional factors and level of physical activity [5], and also by chronic diseases and certain drug treatments [4]. Accordingly, moderate-to-vigorous physical activity may reduce the risk of severe sarcopenia and sarcopenic obesity among older men. Reducing sedentary time and increasing light physical activity and sedentary breaks may also protect against sarcopenic obesity [10]. Body composition and body measurements were shown to be associated with physical function; the Health, Aging, and Body Composition (Health ABC) study cohort reported poorer physical function in women due to their higher proportion of body fat compared to men [11]. In addition, increased body mass index (BMI) and waist circumference are associated with decreased cardiorespiratory fitness [12]; hence, a direct relation exists between BMI, waist circumference, body fat, and physical condition.

Early declines in physical condition can be detected through observation of a decline in the ability to perform mobility tasks activities of daily living, instrumental activities of daily living, or increased time to complete them. These symptoms need to reach a threshold before being recognized as a problem [13]. Early identification of a decline in the physical condition and appropriate interventions could help prevent functional impairments, such as impairments in walking and stairs climbing that often result in falls and physical frailty [14]. Therefore, the aim of this work was to assess physical condition, using HGS and 8-f TUG, and its association with nutrient intake, body composition, sociodemographic characteristics, and lifestyle habits in older Spanish adults.

2. Methods

2.1. Study Design, Population, and Ethics

The sample consisted of 380 participants (54% women) in a cross-sectional study conducted from 2013 to 2014 into two different areas (Balearic Islands, $n = 211$, and Madrid, $n = 169$) assessing the effect of lifestyle factors on health of older adults living in Spain [15]. Men aged between 55 and 80 and women aged between 60 and 80 [16] were recruited in social and municipal clubs, health centers, and sport clubs. Exclusion criteria included previously documented cardiovascular disease, being institutionalized, suffering from a physical or mental illness that would have limited participation in physical fitness or ability to respond for themselves to our questionnaires, chronic alcoholism or drug addiction, and intake of drugs for clinical research over the past year. The study was conducted according to the Declaration of Helsinki guidelines, and all procedures were approved by the Ethical

Committee of the Technical University of Madrid. Written informed consent was obtained from all participants.

2.2. Body Composition

Anthropometric measurements (height, waist circumference (WC), appendicular skeletal muscle mass (ASM), body weight, and body fat) were recorded by licensed observers. Height and WC measurements were performed according to the International Standards for Anthropometric Assessment of the International Society for the Advancement of Kinanthropometry (ISAK) [17]. Height was determined using a mobile anthropometer (Seca 213, SECA Deutschland, Hamburg, Germany) to the nearest millimeter, with the subject's head in the Frankfurt plane. WC was measured as the smallest horizontal girth between the costal margins and the iliac crests at minimal respiration using a flexible, non-extensible plastic tape with 0.1 cm precision (Kawe 43972, Kirchner & Wilhelm GmbH + Co., KG, Asperg, Germany). Body weight, body fat, and ASM were determined using a Segmental Body Composition Analyzer (Tanita BC-418, Tanita, Tokyo, Japan). One measurement was taken without excessive exercise 12 h before the measurement and/or no excessive eating and drinking the day before measurement. The participants were weighed in bare feet and light clothes, and subtracting 0.6 kg for their clothes. Weight and height measures were used to calculate body mass index (kg/m^2). Further information may be found in the technical leaflets of this analyser [18]. According to the anthropometric reference parameters for the Spanish elderly [19,20], the prevalence of overweight and obesity was defined as BMI ≥ 27.0 kg/m^2. Overfat (excessive body fat) was defined according to body fat ranges for Standard Adults reported by Gallagher et al. [21]. WC and height measures were used to calculate waist-to-height ratio (WHtR). Abdominal obesity was defined as a WHtR ≥ 0.5 [22]. ASM and height measures were used to calculate appendicular skeletal muscle mass index (ASMI, kg/m^2) and low ASMI was defined as <7.26 kg/m^2 in men and <5.5 kg/m^2 in women [23].

2.3. Socioeconomic and Lifestyle Determinants

A specific questionnaire developed by the EXERNET network [24] that included the following questions was used: age, marital status, educational level, income, and smoking habits. The respondents were grouped in binary categories as follow: (a) age: <65 (men) and <67 (women) years old, and $\geq$65 (men) and $\geq$67 (women) years old; (b) marital status: single (single, unmarried, divorced, or widowed), and in a relationship (i.e., including married and unmarried, divorced or widowed living with a partner); (c) educational level: illiterate or primary ($\leq$6 years), and secondary or college-level education (>6 years); (d) participants' income: <€900 /month, and $\geq$€900/month; and (e) smoking habits: smoker ($\geq$1 cigarette/day) and non-smoker.

Physical activity data were analyzed using the validated Spanish version of the Minnesota Leisure Time Physical Activity Questionnaire [25,26], and the participants were classified according to their leisure-time physical activity (LTPA) in the past 5 years. Individuals with $\leq$1.5 h/week of physical activity were categorised as "inactive". Individuals who completed $\geq$4 h/week of physical activity were categorised as "active". People who could not be included into the "inactive" and "active" groups were categorised as "slightly active".

2.4. Physical Condition and Sarcopenia Definition

The physical condition assessment included muscle strength based on HGS and agility/dynamic balance based on the 8-f TUG test.

2.4.1. Handgrip Strength Test (HGS)

Grip muscular strength was measured using a digital handheld dynamometer (TKK 5401 Grip-D; Takey, Tokyo, Japan). Participants were instructed to stand upright with the dynamometer beside, but not against, their body. Measurements were performed two times for each hand. The best of all attempts was used to perform the analysis [27]. According to Cruz-Jentoft et al. [4], low handgrip strength was defined as <20 kg in women and <30 kg in men.

2.4.2. Agility/Dynamic Balance Test (8-f TUG)

Participants were instructed to rise from a chair without the use of arms, walk around the cone placed 2.45 m from the chair, and return to the original sitting position. Further instructions were to complete the test as quickly as possible but without running. Measurements were performed two times and the best of all attempts was used to perform the analysis [28]. Low execution time in the 8-f TUG test was defined using the cut-off points for age and sex presented in the study by Rikli and Jones. Since there is no cut-off for men aged 55–60 years we used the same cut-offs of men aged 60–64 years [29].

The algorithm provided by EWGSOP was adopted to determine whether the study individuals were sarcopenic [4]. Presarcopenia was defined as a low ASMI. Sarcopenia was defined as a low ASMI and either high 8-f TUG score or low HGS. Finally, severe sarcopenia was defined as a low ASMI combined with a high 8-f TUG score and low HGS [23].

2.5. Dietary Intake Assessment

Dietary intake was assessed by two non-consecutive 24 h recalls. Volumes and portion sizes were reported in natural units, household measures, or with the aid of a book of photographs [30]. Conversion of food into energy intakes and macronutrient content (carbohydrate, protein, total fat, polyunsaturated fatty acids (PUFA), monounsaturated fatty acids (MUFA), saturated fatty acids (SFA), cholesterol, and fiber) was completed using a self-made computerized program based on Spanish food composition table [31]. Energy intakes ranged between 1021 and 3515 kcal/day for men and 652 and 2996 kcal/day for women. Under-reporters (energy intake/basal metabolic rate <0.96) were 23.9% (50 men and 41 women) [32]; however, when macronutrient intake was compared between under-reporters and non-under-reporters, statistically significant differences were found only for protein in both sexes, and SFA and fiber in women. As such, under-reporters were not excluded from the present analysis.

2.6. Statistics

Analyses were performed with the SPSS statistical software package version 24.0 (SPSS Inc., Chicago, IL, USA). Maximum HGS and the maximum 8-f TUG test were calculated for men and women according to different sociodemographic, body composition, and lifestyle variables. The normality of the data was assessed using the Kolmogorov-Smirnov test. We found that dependent variables (maximum HGS and maximum 8-f TUG) were not normally distributed for sex and many sociodemographic, body composition, and lifestyle variables. Results are expressed as the median (interquartile range, IQR). The Mann-Whitney U test was used to compare the median of two independent groups, and the Kruskal-Wallis test was used to compare the median of three independent groups (i.e., LTPA physical variable). The differences in prevalence across normal and low maximum HGS, and normal and high maximum 8-f TUG score participants, according to sociodemographic, body composition, and lifestyle variables, were examined by using the Chi-square test. Logistic regression analyses, with the calculation of corresponding odds ratio (OR) and the 95% confidence interval (95% CI), were used to compare participants with low maximum HGS or high maximum 8-f TUG and the other participants as reference value (dependent variable) in selected sociodemographic, body composition, and lifestyle variables. Univariate analysis was first carried out for all the sociodemographic, body composition, and lifestyle variables (crude OR). Secondly, results were adjusted for sex and age to control for confounders. Results were considered statistically significant if $p < 0.05$ (two-tailed). Scatter plots were used to illustrate the correlations between the outcome measures used for sarcopenia diagnosis (HGS and 8-f TUG test). Analyses were stratified by sex.

3. Results

The maximum HGS and 8-f TUG score among Spanish older adults are shown in Table 1. Median maximum HGS was 37.2 kg (IQR: 11.1) in men and 21.8 kg (IQR: 6.0) in women. Median maximum HGS was lowest in men and women aged 65 and 67 or older, respectively. There were no significant differences in other sociodemographic variables. Men with abdominal obesity ($p = 0.017$) had lower maximum HGS. In men, significant differences in maximum HGS were also found by LTPA groups, with the lowest median maximum HGS in inactive men (35.6 kg, IQR: 6.2).

Table 1. Maximum handgrip strength (HGS) and maximum eight-foot time up-and-go (8-f TUG) score among older adults according to sociodemographic, body composition and lifestyle variables stratified by sex.

Variable	N	Maximum HGS (kg)		Maximum 8-f TUG (s)	
	Men/Women	Men	Women	Men	Women
Sociodemographics					
All	176/204	37.2 (11.1)	21.8 (6.0)	4.6 (1.1)	5.2 (1.0)
Age (years)					
<65 (men)/67 (women)	83/96	40.9 (9.7)	22.7 (5.4)	4.4 (1.0)	5.0 (1.2)
≥65 (men)/67 (women)	93/108	36.3 (9.0)	20.3 (6.6)	4.9 (1.1)	5.3 (1.0)
p		<0.001	0.007	<0.001	0.003
Marital status					
Married/Coupled	153/130	37.2 (11.3)	22.0 (5.9)	4.7 (1.1)	5.3 (1.1)
Single	23/74	36.7 (7.8)	21.5 (6.5)	4.6 (1.3)	5.2 (1.0)
p		0.448	0.629	0.242	0.794
Educational level					
Primary	61/100	36.5 (9.7)	21.4 (6.3)	4.9 (1.1)	5.5 (1.1)
Secondary or college	115/104	38.1 (11.0)	22.2 (5.4)	4.6 (1.1)	5.0 (0.9)
p		0.124	0.398	0.011	<0.001
Income					
<900 €	27/106	36.3 (13.4)	21.9 (6.2)	4.9 (1.3)	5.4 (1.2)
≥900 €	149/98	37.4 (10.9)	21.8 (5.9)	4.6 (1.0)	5.0 (0.9)
p		0.253	0.662	0.040	<0.001
Body composition					
BMI (kg/m^2)					
<27.0	74/113	36.8 (13.0)	21.4 (6.0)	4.4 (1.1)	5.1 (1.0)
≥27.0	102/91	37.5 (9.6)	22.5 (5.8)	4.8 (0.9)	5.4 (1.2)
p		0.989	0.202	0.128	0.007
Overfat					
No	59/83	41.1 (12.2)	20.4 (6.4)	4.3 (1.0)	5.1 (0.8)
Yes	117/121	36.7 (8.1)	22.5 (5.6)	4.8 (0.9)	5.3 (1.2)
p		0.063	0.143	<0.001	0.010
Abdominal obesity					
No	23/62	43.3 (10.2)	20.2 (6.3)	4.2 (0.9)	5.0 (0.7)
Yes	153/142	36.9 (10.5)	22.4 (5.9)	4.7 (1.0)	5.3 (1.0)
p		0.017	0.140	<0.001	0.002
Lifestyle variables					
Smoking habit					
Non-smoker	161/191	37.2 (11.3)	21.7 (5.5)	4.6 (1.1)	5.2 (1.0)
Smoker	15/13	37.4 (9.6)	22.9 (6.4)	4.7 (1.3)	5.2 (1.7)
p		0.836	0.216	0.717	0.652

Table 1. Cont.

Variable	N	Maximum HGS (kg)		Maximum 8-f TUG (s)	
	Men/Women	Men	Women	Men	Women
LTPA					
Inactive	66/92	35.6 (6.2) [a,b]	20.9 (6.2)	5.0 (1.0) [a,b]	5.5 (1.1) [a,b]
Slightly active	43/59	38.7 (10.7)	22.1 (6.3)	4.4 (1.0)	5.2 (0.9)
Active	67/53	40.9 (10.2)	22.4 (5.5)	4.4 (1.0)	4.8 (1.1)
p		0.001	0.310	<0.001	<0.001

Abbreviations: BMI, body mass index; LTPA, leisure-time physical activity. Values are expressed as median (interquartile range, IQR). Significant differences in maximum HGS and 8-f TUG medians between sociodemographic, body composition and lifestyle variables groups in men and women were tested by Mann-Whitney U test or Kruskal-Wallis test. Significant differences between ($p < 0.05$) [a] Inactive vs. Slightly active, and [b] Inactive vs. Active were obtained.

Median maximum 8-f TUG was 4.6 s (IQR: 1.1) for men and 5.2 s (IQR: 1.0) for women. Men older than 65 and women older than 67 had higher median maximum 8-f TUG score than younger participants. Whereas no significant differences in maximum 8-f TUG score were found in marital status, educational and income levels had an impact on 8-f TUG. Men and women with a primary education had higher maximum 8-f TUG score than high-education participants. Lower income was also associated with higher maximum 8-f TUG score for men and women. Participants with overweight, overfat, and abdominal obesity had higher median maximum 8-f TUG score than their leaner counterparts (results were significant except for BMI in men). Significant association with LTPA groups was found, with inactive men and women showing the highest median maximum 8-f TUG score.

Prevalence of normal and low maximum HGS and 8-f TUG score among Spanish older adults according to sociodemographic, body composition, and lifestyle variables is shown in Table 2. Overall, 24.5% of the participants had low maximum HGS. More women (36.8%) than men (10.2%) were below the cut-off values established for the HGS ($p < 0.001$). More men and women older than 65 and 67, respectively, showed low maximum HGS than younger counterparts ($p < 0.001$). Prevalence of low maximum HGS was higher in participants who were single (35.1%) and those with an income lower than €900 (33.1%) compared to married or coupled participants (20.8%) and those with an income of €900 or higher (19.8%) ($p < 0.010$). No significant differences in prevalence of low HGS and educational level were found. Overweight, overfat, and abdominally obese participants had lower prevalence of low maximum HGS than leaner counterparts. Despite the lack of statistical significance, participants who were slightly active and active showed lower prevalence of low maximum HGS than inactive participants (21.2% and 29.1%, respectively, $p = 0.076$).

Sex, age, marital status, income, overweight, overfat, and abdominal obesity status were significantly associated with low maximum HGS in univariate logistic regressions. Results in sex- and/or age-adjusted analysis illustrate that the odds of low maximum HGS were 4.6 (95% CI: 2.6–8.2) and 2.9 (95% CI: 1.7–4.8) times higher for women and older participants, respectively, compared with men and younger participants. In both overweight and overfat participants, the odds of low maximum HGS were 0.6 times lower for overweight (95% CI: 0.4–1.0) and overfat (95% CI: 0.3–1.0) participants compared with their leaner counterparts. However, the OR for low maximum HGS lost its statistical significant association with the income variable after adjusting for sex and age.

Table 2. Prevalence of low/normal maximum HGS and high/normal 8-f TUG score according to sociodemographic, body composition, and lifestyle variables.

Variables	n	Maximum HGS					Maximum 8-f TUG				
		Normal	Low	p	Crude OR (95% CI) [†]	Sex- and/or Age-Adjusted OR (95% CI) [‡]	Normal	High	p	Crude OR (95% CI) [†]	Sex- and/or Age-Adjusted OR (95% CI) [‡]
Sociodemographics											
All	380	287 (75.5)	93 (24.5)				240 (63.2)	140 (36.8)			
Sex				<0.001					<0.001		
Men	176	158 (89.8)	18 (10.2)		1.00 (ref.)	1.00 (ref.)	128 (72.7)	48 (27.3)		1.00 (ref.)	1.00 (ref.)
Women	204	129 (63.2)	75 (36.8)		5.10 (2.90–8.98)	4.59 (2.56–8.23)	112 (54.9)	92 (45.1)		2.19 (1.42–3.37)	2.38 (1.52–3.72)
Age (years)				<0.001					0.133		
<65/67	179	151 (84.4)	28 (15.6)		1.00 (ref.)	1.00 (ref.)	106 (59.2)	73 (40.8)		1.00 (ref.)	1.00 (ref.)
≥65/67	201	136 (67.7)	65 (32.3)		2.58 (1.56–4.25)	2.85 (1.68–4.82)	134 (66.7)	67 (33.3)		0.73 (0.48–1.10)	0.72 (0.47–1.10)
Marital status				0.005					0.758		
Married/Coupled	283	224 (79.2)	59 (20.8)		1.00 (ref.)	1.00 (ref.)	180 (63.6)	103 (36.4)		1.00 (ref.)	1.00 (ref.)
Single	97	63 (64.9)	34 (35.1)		2.05 (1.24–3.40)	1.08 (0.61–1.91)	60 (61.9)	37 (38.1)		1.08 (0.67–1.73)	0.90 (0.54–1.49)
Educational level				0.531					<0.001		
Primary	161	119 (73.9)	42 (26.1)		1.00 (ref.)	1.00 (ref.)	83 (51.6)	78 (48.4)		1.00 (ref.)	1.00 (ref.)
Secondary or college	219	168 (76.7)	51 (23.3)		0.86 (0.54–1.38)	1.22 (0.73–2.05)	157 (71.7)	62 (28.3)		0.42 (0.27–0.64)	0.43 (0.27–0.66)
Income				0.004					<0.001		
<900 €	133	89 (66.9)	44 (33.1)		1.00 (ref.)	1.00 (ref.)	65 (48.9)	68 (51.1)		1.00 (ref.)	1.00 (ref.)
≥900 €	247	198 (80.2)	49 (19.8)		0.50 (0.31–0.81)	1.00 (0.58–1.71)	175 (70.9)	72 (29.1)		0.39 (0.25–0.61)	0.44 (0.27–0.71)
Body composition											
BMI (kg/m²)				0.005					0.128		
<27.0	185	128 (69.2)	57 (30.8)		1.00 (ref.)	1.00 (ref.)	124 (67.0)	61 (33.0)		1.00 (ref.)	1.00 (ref.)
≥27.0	195	159 (81.5)	36 (18.5)		0.51 (0.32–0.82)	0.59 (0.35–1.00)	116 (59.5)	79 (40.5)		1.38 (0.91–2.11)	1.61 (1.04–2.49)
Overfat				0.023					0.041		
No	142	98 (69.0)	44 (31.0)		1.00 (ref.)	1.00 (ref.)	99 (69.7)	43 (30.3)		1.00 (ref.)	1.00 (ref.)
Yes	238	189 (79.4)	49 (20.6)		0.58 (0.36–0.93)	0.58 (0.34–0.98)	141 (59.2)	97 (40.8)		1.58 (1.02–2.46)	1.72 (1.10–2.72)
Abdominal obesity				0.008					0.002		
No	85	55 (64.7)	30 (35.3)		1.00 (ref.)	1.00 (ref.)	66 (77.6)	19 (22.4)		1.00 (ref.)	1.00 (ref.)
Yes	295	232 (78.6)	63 (21.4)		0.50 (0.30–0.84)	0.57 (0.31–1.03)	174 (59.0)	121 (41.0)		2.42 (1.38–4.23)	3.38 (1.87–6.09)
Lifestyle variables											
Smoking habit				0.193					0.898		
Non-smoker	352	263 (74.7)	89 (25.3)		1.00 (ref.)	1.00 (ref.)	222 (63.1)	130 (36.9)		1.00 (ref.)	1.00 (ref.)
Smoker	28	24 (85.7)	4 (14.3)		0.49 (0.17–1.46)	0.61 (0.19–1.95)	18 (64.3)	10 (35.7)		0.95 (0.43–2.12)	0.97 (0.43–2.19)
LTPA				0.076					<0.001		
Inactive	158	112 (70.9)	46 (29.1)		1.00 (ref)	1.00 (ref.)	77 (48.7)	81 (51.3)		1.00 (ref)	1.00 (ref.)
Slightly active/Active	222	175 (78.8)	47 (21.2)		0.65 (0.41–1.05)	0.79 (0.47–1.32)	163 (73.4)	59 (26.6)		0.34 (0.22–0.53)	0.33 (0.21–0.52)

Abbreviations: BMI, body mass index; HGS, handgrip strength; 8-f TUG, 8-foot time up-and-go; LTPA, leisure-time physical activity; OR, odds ratio; CI, confidence interval. [†] Logistic regression analysis considering the effect of one explanatory variable. [‡] Logistic regression analysis considering the effect of one explanatory variable and adjusted for sex and age.

Conversely, 36.8% of participants had a high 8-f TUG score. More women (45.1%) than men (27.3%) were above the cut-off values established for the 8-f TUG test ($p < 0.001$). Prevalence of high 8-f TUG was higher in participants with primary education (48.4%) and an income lower than €900 (51.1%) than more educated participants (28.3%) and those with higher income (29.1%) ($p < 0.001$). More overfat (40.8%) and abdominal obese (41.0%) participants had a higher 8-f TUG score than leaner participants (30.3% and 22.4%, respectively, $p < 0.050$). Inactive participants also had a higher prevalence of high 8-f TUG than slightly active and active ones ($p < 0.001$). Age group, marital status, BMI status, and smoking habits were not significantly associated with 8-f TUG prevalence.

Sex, educational level, income, overfat, abdominal obesity, and LTPA were significantly associated with high maximum 8-f TUG in univariate logistic regressions. Results in sex- and/or age-adjusted analysis illustrated that the odds of a high maximum 8-t TUG were, respectively, 2.4 (95% CI: 1.5–3.7), 1.6 (95% CI: 1.0–2.5), 1.7 (95% CI: 1.1–2.7) and 3.4 (95% CI: 1.9–6.1) times higher for women, overweight, overfat, and abdominal obesity participants compared with the reference groups. In more educated participants, participants with an income of 900 euros or higher per month, and slightly active and active, the odds of a high maximum 8-f TUG were 0.4 (95% CI: 0.3–0.7), 0.4 (95% CI: 0.3–0.7), and 0.3 (95% CI: 0.2–0.5) times lower compared with the reference groups, respectively. Furthermore, educational and income levels maintained statistical significant association with high maximum 8-f TUG in multivariable analysis adjusted by sex and age (secondary or college: OR: 0.50, 95% CI: 0.32–0.80; income $\geq$ €900/month: 0.56, 95% CI: 0.34–0.94).

Figure 1 illustrates the correlation between 8-f TUG and HGS among men (Figure 1A) and women (Figure 1B). The frequency of presarcopenia was 2.6% ($n = 10$), and was more frequent in men (4.5%; $n = 8$) than women (1.0%; $n = 2$). The frequency of sarcopenia and severe sarcopenia was 0.3% ($n = 1$) and 0.5% ($n = 2$) in men and women, respectively. Eight men showed high 8-f TUG and low HGS scores (including severe sarcopenic participants), and 39 women registered high and low scores in both physical tests ($p < 0.001$).

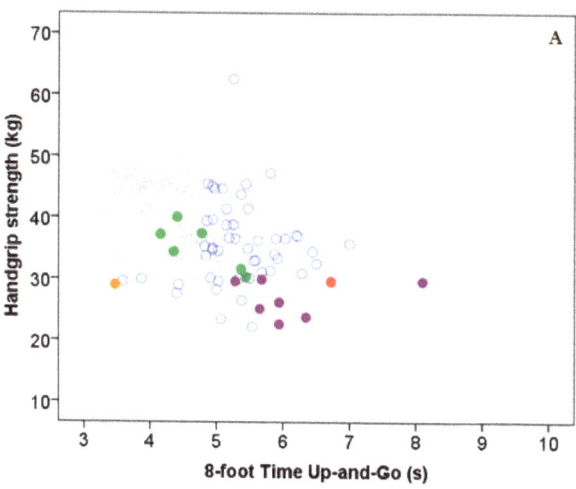

Figure 1. Cont.

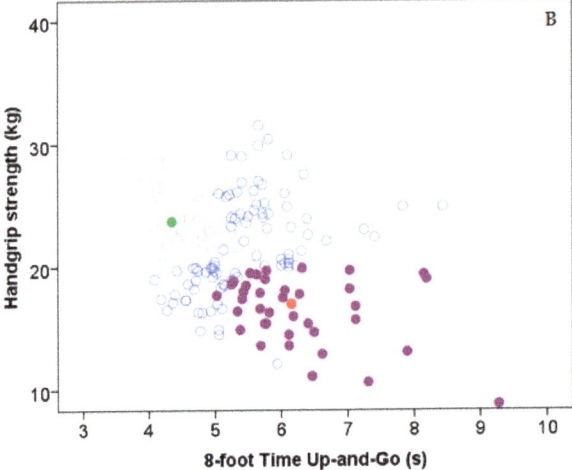

Figure 1. Scatter plot of variables used for diagnosis of sarcopenia: (**A**) men and (**B**) women. Grey open circles denote normal appendicular skeletal muscle index (ASMI, kg/m^2), 8-foot Time Up-and-Go (8-f TUG, s), and handgrip strength (HGS, kg). Grey solid circles denote presarcopenia. Grey open triangles denote high 8-f TUG or low HGS. Grey solid triangles denote high 8-f TUG and low HGS. Black open squares denote sarcopenia, and black solid squares denote severe sarcopenia.

Concerning macronutrients intake (Table 3), women with low HGS had significantly lower intake of calories, total fats, MUFAs, cholesterol, and fiber than women with low HGS, and significantly higher intake of carbohydrates. No differences between groups were observed for protein, PUFA, or SFA intake. No statistically significant differences between low/normal HGS groups were found in macronutrient intake in men. Additionally, no statistically significant differences between high/normal 8-fTUG groups were found in macronutrient intake in both sexes.

Table 3. Energy and macronutrient intake according to low/normal HGS and high/normal 8-f TUG score.

Variables	Maximum HGS			Maximum 8-f TUG		
	Normal (n = 287)	Low (n = 93)	p	Normal (n = 240)	High (n = 140)	p
All (n = 380)						
Energy intake (kcal/day)	1679 (1394–2046)	1547 (1269–1833)	0.007	1708 (1394–2043)	1559 (1277–1844)	0.004
Carbohydrate intake (% total energy)	44.7 (38.2–50.0)	47.3 (41.5–53.6)	0.003	44.9 (38.0–50.0)	46.6 (40.3–51.4)	0.201
Protein intake (% total energy)	16.0 (14.2–18.6)	16.1 (13.4–19.0)	0.738	16.2 (14.4–18.7)	15.8 (13.2–18.8)	0.149
Fat intake (% total energy)	35.0 (30.0–40.0)	32.5 (28.6–37.6)	0.025	34.3 (29.8–39.8)	34.0 (29.4–38.6)	0.520
PUFA (% total energy)	4.2 (3.5–5.1)	4.2 (3.5–5.7)	0.369	4.3 (3.5–5.4)	4.1 (3.3–5.0)	0.084
MUFA (% total energy)	16.0 (13.4–18.6)	14.0 (12.3–16.9)	0.001	15.8 (13.2–18.6)	15.1 (12.7–17.8)	0.254
SFA (% total energy)	10.0 (8.2–12.5)	9.6 (7.3–11.2)	0.058	9.8 (8.0–12.0)	10.1 (8.1–11.9)	0.600
Cholesterol intake (mg/1000 kcal)	261.9 (177.4–383.9)	211.1 (127.3–309.6)	0.054	253.8 (170.4–384.2)	245.7 (160.5–356.5)	0.993
Fiber intake (g/1000 kcal)	65.6 (51.2–82.5)	58.7 (45.3–71.2)	0.006	64.5 (51.3–82.3)	60.5 (45.1–78.1)	0.625
Men (n = 176)	n = 158	n = 18		n = 128	n = 48	
Energy intake (kcal/day)	1926 (1579–2255)	1789 (1527–1892)	0.068	1914 (1606–2202)	1817 (1507–2265)	0.528
Carbohydrate intake (% total energy)	43.8 (37.8–49.6)	43.6 (34.5–53.4)	0.914	44.2 (37.6–49.7)	43.6 (38.5–50.2)	0.847
Protein intake (% total energy)	15.7 (13.9–18.2)	16.0 (14.1–19.7)	0.461	15.9 (14.3–18.5)	14.9 (12.9–18.2)	0.092
Fat intake (% total energy)	34.8 (29.8–39.6)	32.5 (29.6–40.8)	0.907	34.1 (29.6–39.6)	35.6 (31.2–40.1)	0.361
PUFA (% total energy)	4.3 (3.5–5.1)	5.0 (3.6–6.3)	0.160	4.3 (3.5–5.3)	4.2 (3.6–5.0)	0.515
MUFA (% total energy)	16.1 (13.5–18.3)	14.9 (12.9–18.3)	0.646	16.0 (13.2–18.3)	16.0 (13.8–18.3)	0.740
SFA (% total energy)	10.2 (8.2–12.5)	9.5 (7.3–11.6)	0.470	9.8 (7.8–12.2)	10.6 (8.9–13.1)	0.059
Cholesterol intake (mg/1000 kcal)	149.6 (101.7–210.7)	193.4 (94.1–277.3)	0.372	141.2 (101.1–205.9)	158.0 (102.6–220.5)	0.570
Fiber intake (g/1000 kcal)	9.4 (7.2–12.2)	10.2 (7.9–13.8)	0.449	9.8 (7.6–12.7)	8.5 (6.8–10.1)	0.040
Women (n = 204)	n = 129	n = 75		n = 112	n = 92	
Energy intake (kcal/day)	1456 (1236–1721)	1515 (1235–1820)	0.486	1463 (1286–1774)	1486 (1193–1735)	0.525
Carbohydrate intake (% total energy)	46.3 (38.5–51.1)	48.3 (43.4–54.0)	0.018	46.3 (38.9–51.3)	47.4 (41.4–52.8)	0.265
Protein intake (% total energy)	16.7 (14.5–19.5)	16.1 (13.3–18.7)	0.155	16.7 (14.6–19.1)	16.1 (13.4–19.1)	0.374
Fat intake (% total energy)	35.2 (30.3–40.3)	32.5 (28.5–36.8)	0.016	34.7 (30.2–40.2)	33.6 (29.0–37.7)	0.147
PUFA (% total energy)	4.1 (3.4–5.2)	4.2 (3.4–5.3)	0.700	4.3 (3.5–5.5)	4.0 (3.3–5.1)	0.106
MUFA (% total energy)	15.8 (13.4–18.7)	13.7 (12.2–16.5)	0.001	15.6 (13.2–18.6)	14.7 (12.4–17.2)	0.132
SFA (% total energy)	10.0 (8.3–12.1)	9.6 (7.3–11.2)	0.158	9.9 (8.2–11.5)	9.8 (7.7–11.2)	0.567
Cholesterol intake (mg/1000 kcal)	159.6 (119.6–232.0)	123.2 (91.4–179.6)	0.004	147.0 (111.0–202.2)	142.3 (92.9–227.1)	0.613
Fiber intake (g/1000 kcal)	10.9 (8.5–13.6)	11.1 (9.6–14.4)	0.159	11.1 (9.0–13.3)	10.6 (9.0–14.5)	0.779

Abbreviations: HGS, handgrip strength; 8-f TUG, 8-foot time up-and-go. Values are expressed as median (interquartile range, IQR). Significant differences in nutrient medians between low and normal HGS and 8-f TUG score were tested by Mann-Whitney U test.

4. Discussion

The main findings of this study were that maximum HGS was lower among older participants, non-overweight women, inactive men, and men with abdominal obesity. Moreover, 24.5% of the participants had low maximum HGS and this risk increased in women, adults older than 65 and 67 for men and women, respectively, and decreased in overweight and overfat older adults. The maximum 8-f TUG score was higher among older participants, those with lower education, lower income, and inactive participants, those with abdominal obesity and overfat, and women with a BMI ≥ 27 kg/m^2. Additionally, 36.8% of participants had high 8-f TUG score and this risk increased in women, and overweight, overfat, and abdominal obese participants; and decreased in highly educated participants, those with an income of €900 or more per month, and slightly active and active participants. Presarcopenia, sarcopenia, and severe sarcopenia prevalence was 2.6%, 0.3%, and 0.5% among the studied population, respectively. However, 4.5% of men and 19.1% of women registered low physical condition (assessed by high scores in 8-f TUG and low scores in HGS tests) but not low ASMI.

HGS for men was higher in this study than in a sample of Japanese men ($n = 742$) aged 70 ± 9 years (33.4 kg, SD: 7.5) from the Nomura study, but it was similar for women ($n = 937$) aged 70 ± 8 years (21.3 kg, SD: 4.1) [33]. In a cross-sectional analysis of the baseline data from a cohort study conducted in 2012 that included 1971 functionally-independent, community-dwelling Japanese adults aged 65 years or older (977 men, 994 women), HGS means were 34.8 kg (SD: 6.0) for men and 22.4 kg (SD: 3.9) for women [34]. The Hertfordshire Cohort reported different values of HGS among men (44.3 kg) and women (26.7 kg) older adults [35]. Patiño et al. [8] reported dissimilar HGS and 8-f TUG in community-dwelling persons over 60 years old from a northern Spanish city. These differences between studies are possibly due to difference in muscle strength among different populations [36] and to differences in healthy aging among different populations [37], reflected in the minor but existent differences in HGS.

The prevalence of low HGS (24.5%) and high 8-f TUG (36.8%) scores in this study was lower than reported in a northern Spanish city (13.2% and 13.6%, respectively). Compared to the Patiño et al. findings [8], in which participants with a low HGS had higher body fat (%) than participants with normal HGS, our study revealed a lower prevalence of low maximum HGS among those with a BMI ≥ 27 kg/m^2 and those who showed abdominal obesity and overfat. However, similar to the Patiño et al. findings, in which participants with a high 8-f TUG score had higher body fat (%) than participants with normal test results, our study also revealed that overfat and abdominal obese participants had a higher prevalence of a higher maximum 8-f TUG score. This might be due to the fact that fat affects mobility and balance in older people [38]. A systematic review [39] concluded that although muscle and fat mass are considered important factors of age-related decline in physical function, studies examining the association between fat and muscle mass and functionality have produced inconsistent results.

The frequency of sarcopenia (0.3%) in this study was lower than in a northern Spanish city (2.4%), and unlike this northern Spanish city, women were more prone to being affected (19.1% of women registered low physical condition) [2]. This is reflected positively in the population studied, as the low frequency of sarcopenia implies a decreased risk of adverse health outcomes, including falls, loss of independence, and disability. As such, this decreases the socioeconomic burden in the studied population [40].

To the best of our knowledge, data on the association between sociodemographic characteristics and lifestyle habits, and physical condition in older adults are scarce. Physical activity has a major effect on physical condition [41]. Physical activity behavior is affected by two major components of socioeconomic status (SES): educational level and income. Educational level plays a primary role in the level of physical activity; an age-related decline in physical activity was observed among low-education individuals [42]. Lower education was associated with sarcopenia in the Korean National Health and Nutrition Examination Survey KNHANES [43] and in Invecchiare in Chianti (Aging in the Chianti area Study; InCHIANTI) [44]. Our results showed higher prevalence of high 8-f TUG among participants with lower education. Income plays a major role in determining he physical activity; individuals with higher income were more engaged in physical activity according to several studies [45,46]. Income was reported to be lower among those with sarcopenia [43]. In our study, prevalence of low HGS and high 8-f TUG scores was higher among those with a lower income, despite the lack of significance when OR was sex- and age-adjusted in HGS analysis. Our findings showed that inactive participants had higher 8-f TUG scores than active or slightly active participants. Notably, 8-f TUG assesses the agility and dynamic balance in older people, which is important in tasks that require quick accomplishment, such as alighting from a bus in time [14] that are easier to perform by active people. Finally, being single was also associated with higher prevalence of low HGS (despite the lack of significance when OR was sex- and age-adjusted), which agrees with studies that associated single relationship status with sarcopenia [47,48].

An adequate nutritional intake is an important element of any strategy to preserve muscle mass and strength during aging. Muscle wasting is a multifactorial process. A loss of fast twitch fibers, insulin resistance, glycation of proteins, and lipid deposition in muscle cells play important roles in the loss of muscle strength and development of sarcopenia [49,50]. Protein intake is crucial for muscle health and an intake of 1.0–1.2 g/kg of body weight per day is optimal for older adults [50]. High-fat diets may compromise aged muscle, diminishing overall muscle quality and composition [49]. Along this line, the findings of Charlton et al. [51] provide support regarding the importance of physical activity and adequate dietary protein intake for optimal body composition and the maintenance of strength and physical function. Sarti et al. [52] provided evidence that physical performance declines with advancing age, even in healthy women, and this decline in physical activity could lead to a lower intake of calories, carbohydrates, fats, and proteins. People, as they age, eat less and make different food choices. Lower food intake among the elderly has been associated with lower intakes of calcium, iron, zinc, B vitamins, and vitamin E [53]; this also negatively affects health.

Strengths and Limitations

The main strength of this study is due to its strict protocol through validated measurement tools and the objective measurement of physical condition. The assessment method for sarcopenia according to the EWGSOP can be used in clinical practice and as a screening method in public health [54,55], which supports the reliability and accuracy of our results. Height and weight are frequently used to determine BMI and nutritional status in epidemiological research on older adults; however, BMI is an imperfect measure of overweight and obesity. Overfat and abdominal obesity (measured by WHtR that may be the single best clinical indicator of health risk) were also assessed in the present study [56].

However, this study has some limitations. Firstly, the present cross-sectional design limits the ability to elucidate a causal relationship between HGS and 8-f TUG scores and nutrient intake, body composition, sociodemographic characteristics, and lifestyle habits. Secondly, physical activity was not measured objectively, such as using an accelerometer, and sedentary leisure time activities as well as sleep habits were not measured either. Thirdly, height was measured using a stadiometer, which is the established gold standard, but this assessment may not be feasible for studies conducted in elderly populations with mobility limitations [57]. Fourthly, the macronutrient intake was estimated using recall diets instead of food frequency questionnaires that have been questioned in epidemiological studies [58,59]. Two 24-h recall diets tend to underestimate the food intake over a large period compared to food frequency questionnaires, and demonstrate a considerable day-to-day variation in macronutrient intake. Fifth, underreporting was calculated using energy intake/basal metabolic rate and medications types (e.g., antidepressants, influence weight, etc.) that might influence basal metabolic rate, and lifestyle factors and physical activity were not considered in the present study. Finally, the results potentially lack generalizability due to the selecting participants from only two sites as well as the sample size obtained.

5. Conclusions

Overall, 36.8%, 24.5%, and 0.3% of participants had high maximum 8-f TUG score, low maximum HGS, and sarcopenia, respectively. Additionally, 4.5% of men and 19.1% of women registered low physical condition assessed by high and low scores in 8-f TUG and HGS tests, respectively. Prevalence of low maximum HGS differed according to sex, age, weight, and fat status; and high maximum 8-f TUG differed according to sex, educational level, income, presence of extra weight, fat, and abdominal obesity, and LTPA practice. Strategies for early identification of decline in physical condition and appropriate interventions should be adopted to avoid physical impairments.

Author Contributions: M.d.M.B., M.G.-G., and J.A.T. designed the study and wrote the protocol. R.A.-U., C.B., R.P.-C., A.S., J.K., and M.d.M.B. collected data, conducted literature searches, and provided summaries of previous research studies. J.K. and M.d.M.B. conducted the statistical analysis. J.K., M.d.M.B., and J.A.T. wrote the first draft of the manuscript. All authors read and approved the final manuscript.

Funding: This study was supported by the official funding agency for biomedical research of the Spanish government, Institute of Health Carlos III (ISCIII) through the Fondo de Investigación para la Salud (FIS), which is co-funded by the European Regional Development Fund (Projects 11/01791, 14/00636 and 17/01827, Red Predimed-RETIC RD06/0045/1004, and CIBEROBN CB12/03/30038), Grant of support to research groups no. 35/2011 and Grant no. AAEE097/2017 (Balearic Islands Gov.), HERMES EU Program, and EU Cost ACTION CA16112. The funders had no role in study design, data collection and analysis, decision to publish, or preparation of the manuscript.

Acknowledgments: Special thanks to Raquel Seco for technical assistance.

Conflicts of Interest: The authors declare that they have no competing interests.

Availability of Data and Materials: The data analyzed in this paper can be made available to researchers. Requests for access to the dataset used in this paper should be directed to the corresponding author.

Abbreviations

ASMI	appendicular skeletal muscle index
BMI	Body mass index
CI	Confidence interval
EWGSOP	European Working Group on Sarcopenia in Older People
8-f TUG	8-foot time up-and-go test; HGS: handgrip strength test
ISAK	International Society for the Advancement of Kinanthropometry
LTPA	Leisure-time physical activity
OR	Odds ratio
SPSS	Statistical Package for the Social Sciences
WHO	World Health Organization

References

1. Börsch-Supan, A.; Brugiavini, A.; Jürges, H.; Mackenbach, J.; Siegrist, J.; Weber, G. Health, ageing and retirement in Europe. First results from the Survey of Health, Ageing and Retirement in Europe. Manheim: Manheim Research Institute for the Economics of Aging. 2005. Available online: http://www.share-project.org/uploads/tx_sharepublications/SHARE_FirstResultsBookWave1.pdf (accessed on 18 February 2017).
2. Ministerio de Sanidad, Servicios Sociales e Igualdad. Estrategia de Promoción de la Salud y Prevención en el SNS. Documento Consenso sobre Prevención de Fragilidad y Caídas en la Persona Mayor. 2014. Available online: http://www.msssi.gob.es/profesionales/saludPublica/prevPromocion/Estrategia/docs/FragilidadyCaidas_personamayor.pdf (accessed on 18 February 2017).
3. Abellan van Kan, G.; Rolland, Y.; Bergman, H.; Morley, J.E.; Kritchevsky, S.B.; Vellas, B. The I.A.N.A Task Force on frailty assessment of older people in clinical practice. *J. Nutr. Health Aging* **2008**, *12*, 29–37. [CrossRef] [PubMed]
4. Cruz-Jentoft, A.J.; Baeyens, J.P.; Bauer, J.M.; Boirie, Y.; Cederholm, T.; Landi, F.; Martin, F.C.; Michel, J.P.; Rolland, Y.; Schneider, S.M.; et al. Sarcopenia: European consensus on definition and diagnosis: Report of the European Working Group on Sarcopenia in Older People. *Age Ageing* **2010**, *39*, 412–423. [CrossRef] [PubMed]

5. Clegg, A.; Young, J.; Iliffe, S.; Rikkert, M.O.; Rockwood, K. Frailty in elderly people. *Lancet* **2013**, *38*, 752–762. [CrossRef]
6. Bijlsma, A.Y.; Meskers, C.G.M.; Ling, C.H.Y.; Narici, M.; Kurrle, S.E.; Cameron, I.D.; Westendorp, R.G.J.; Maier, A.B. Defining sarcopenia: The impact of different diagnostic criteria on the prevalence of sarcopenia in a large middle aged cohort. *Age* **2013**, *35*, 871–881. [CrossRef] [PubMed]
7. Dupuy, C.; Lauwers-Cances, V.; Guyonnet, S.; Gentil, C.; Abellan van Kan, G.; Beauchet, O.; Schott, A.M.; Vellas, B.; Rolland, Y. Searching for a relevant definition of sarcopenia: Results from the cross-sectional EPIDOS study. *J. Cachexia Sarcopenia Muscle* **2015**, *6*, 144–154. [CrossRef] [PubMed]
8. Patiño Villada, F.A.; Arboleda Franco, S.A.; De Paz Fernández, J.A. Sarcopenia in community-dwelling persons over 60 years of age from a northern Spanish city: Relationship between diagnostic criteria and association with the functional performance. *Nutr. Hosp.* **2015**, *31*, 2154–2160. [PubMed]
9. Legrand, D.; Vaes, B.; Matheï, C.; Adriaensen, W.; Van Pottelbergh, G.; Degryse, J.M. Muscle strength and physical performance as predictors of mortality, hospitalization, and disability in the oldest old. *J. Am. Geriatr. Soc.* **2014**, *62*, 1030–1038. [CrossRef] [PubMed]
10. Aggio, D.A.; Sartini, C.; Papacosta, O.; Lennon, L.T.; Ash, S.; Whincup, P.H.; Wannamethee, S.G.; Jefferis, B.J. Cross-sectional associations of objectively measured physical activity and sedentary time with sarcopenia and sarcopenic obesity in older men. *Prev. Med.* **2016**, *91*, 264–272. [CrossRef] [PubMed]
11. Tseng, L.A.; Delmonico, M.J.; Visser, M.; Boudreau, R.M.; Goodpaster, B.H.; Schwartz, A.V.; Simonsick, E.M.; Satterfield, S.; Harris, T.; Newman, A.B. Body composition explains sex differential in physical performance among older adults. *J. Gerontol. A Biol. Sci. Med. Sci.* **2014**, *69*, 93–100. [CrossRef] [PubMed]
12. Dagan, S.S.; Segev, S.; Novikov, I.; Dankner, R. waist circumference vs. body mass index in assosciation with cardiorespiratory fitness in healthy men and women: A cross sectional analysis of 403 subjects. *Nutr. J.* **2013**, *12*, 12. [CrossRef] [PubMed]
13. Brach, J.S.; Van Swearingen, J.M.; Newman, A.B.; Kriska, A.M. Identifying early decline of physical function in community-dwelling older women: Performance- based and self-report measures. *Phys. Ther.* **2002**, *82*, 320–328. [PubMed]
14. Jones, C.J.; Rikli, R.E. Measuring functional fitness of older adults. *J. Active Aging* **2002**, 24–30.
15. Bibiloni, M.D.M.; Julibert, A.; Argelich, E.; Aparicio-Ugarriza, R.; Palacios, G.; Pons, A.; Gonzalez-Gross, M.; Tur, J.A. Western and Mediterranean Dietary Patterns and Physical Activity and Fitness among Spanish Older Adults. *Nutrients* **2017**, *9*, 704. [CrossRef] [PubMed]
16. Guasch-Ferré, M.; Salas-Salvadó, J.; Ros, E.; Estruch, R.; Corella, D.; Fitó, M.; Martínez-González, M.A.; PREDIMED Investigators. The PREDIMED trial, Mediterranean diet and health outcomes: How strong is the evidence? *Nutr. Metab. Cardiovasc. Dis.* **2017**, *27*, 624–632. [CrossRef] [PubMed]
17. International Society for the Advancement of Kinanthropometry (ISAK). International Standards for Anthropometric Assessment. Underdale, S. Australia: International Society for the Advancement of Kinanthropometry. Available online: http://www.ceap.br/material/MAT17032011184632.pdf (accessed on 18 February 2017).
18. TANITA. BC-418 Segmental Body Composition Analyzer. Available online: https://www.tanita.com/en/bc-418/ (accessed on 7 September 2018).
19. Esquius, M.; Schwartz, S.; López Hellín, J.; Andreu, A.L.; García, E. Anthropometric reference parameters for the aged population. *Med. Clin.* **1993**, *100*, 692–698.
20. Sociedad Española de Nutrición Parenteral y Enteral (SENPE); Sociedad Española de Geriatría y Gerontología (SEGG). *Valoración Nutricional en el Anciano. Recomendaciones Prácticas de los Expertos en Geriatría y Nutrición*; Galénitas-Nigra Trea: Bilbao, Spain, 2007; ISBN 978-84-95364-55-5.
21. Gallagher, D.; Heymsfield, S.B.; Heo, M.; Jebb, S.A.; Murgatroyd, P.R.; Sakamoto, Y. Healthy percentage body fat ranges: An approach for developing guidelines based on body mass index. *Am. J. Clin. Nutr.* **2000**, *72*, 694–701. [CrossRef] [PubMed]
22. Ashwell, M.; Gunn, P.; Gibson, S. Waist-to-height ratio is a better screening tool than waist circumference and BMI for adult cardiometabolic risk factors: Systematic review and meta-analysis. *Obes. Rev.* **2012**, *13*, 275–286. [CrossRef] [PubMed]
23. Baumgartner, R.N.; Koehler, K.M.; Gallagher, D.; Romero, L.; Heymsfield, S.B.; Ross, R.R.; Garry, P.J.; Lindeman, R.D. Epidemiology of sarcopenia among the elderly in New Mexico. *Am. J. Epidemiol.* **1998**, *147*, 755–763. [CrossRef] [PubMed]

24. Exernet Network. Procedures and Questionnaires. Available online: http://www.spanishexernet.com/procedimientos.php/ (accessed on 18 February 2017).
25. Elosua, R.; Marrugat, J.; Molina, L.; Pons, S.; Pujol, E. Validation of the Minnesota Leisure Time Physical Activity Questionnaire in Spanish men. The MARATHOM Investigators. *Am. J. Epidemiol.* **1994**, *139*, 1197–1209. [CrossRef] [PubMed]
26. Elosua, R.; Garcia, M.; Aguilar, A.; Molina, L.; Covas, M.I.; Marrugat, J. Validation of the Minnesota Leisure Time Physical Activity Questionnaire in Spanish Women. Investigators of the MARATDON Group. *Med. Sci. Sports Exerc.* **2000**, *32*, 1431–1437. [CrossRef] [PubMed]
27. Oja, P.; Tuxworth, B. *Eurofit para Adultos. Test Europeo de Aptitud Física. Evaluación de la Aptitud Física en Relación con la Salud*; Ministerio de Educación y Ciencia; Consejo Superior de Deportes: Madrid, Spain, 1998.
28. Rikli, R.; Jones, C.J. *Senior Fitness Test Manual*; Human Kinetics: Champaign, IL, USA, 2001.
29. Rikli, R.E.; Jones, C.J. Development and validation of criterion-referenced clinically relevant fitness standards for maintaining physical independence in later years. *Gerontologist* **2013**, *53*, 255–267. [CrossRef] [PubMed]
30. Gómez, C.; Kohen, V.L.; Nogueira, T.L. *Guía Visual de Alimentos y Raciones*; EDIMSA: Madrid, Spain, 2007.
31. Moreiras, O.; Carbajal, A.; Cabrera, L.; Cuadrado, C. *Tablas de Composición de Alimentos, Guía de Prácticas*, 17th ed.; Piramide: Madrid, Spain, 2015.
32. Black, A.E. Critical evaluation of energy intake using the Goldberg cut-off for energy intake: Basal metabolic rate. A practical guide to its calculation, use and limitations. *Int. J. Obes. Relat. Metab. Disord.* **2000**, *24*, 1119–1130. [CrossRef] [PubMed]
33. Kawamoto, R.; Ninomiya, D.; Kasai, Y.; Kusunoki, T.; Ohtsuka, N.; Kumagi, T.; Abe, M. Handgrip strength is associated with metabolic syndrome among middle-aged and elderly community-dwelling persons. *Clin. Exp. Hypertens.* **2016**, *38*, 245–251. [CrossRef] [PubMed]
34. Ishii, S.; Tanaka, T.; Akishita, M.; Ouchi, Y.; Tuji, T.; Iijima, K.; Kashiwa Study Investigators. Metabolic syndrome, sarcopenia and role of sex and age: Cross-sectional analysis of Kashiwa cohort study. *PLoS ONE* **2014**, *9*, e112718. [CrossRef] [PubMed]
35. Sayer, A.A.; Syddall, H.E.; Dennison, E.M.; Martin, H.J.; Phillips, D.I.; Cooper, C.; Byrne, C.D.; Hertfordshire Cohort. Grip strength and the metabolic syndrome: Findings from the Hertfordshire Cohort Study. *QJM Int. J. Med.* **2007**, *100*, 707–713. [CrossRef] [PubMed]
36. Leong, D.P.; McKee, M.; Yusuf, S.; PURE Investigators. Population Muscle Strength Predicts Olympic Medal Tallies: Evidence from 20 Countries in the PURE Prospective Cohort Study. *PLoS ONE* **2017**, *12*, e0169821. [CrossRef] [PubMed]
37. Fernández-Ballesteros, R.; Robine, J.M.; Walker, A.; Kalache, A. Active Aging: A Global Goal. *Curr. Gerontol. Geriatr. Res.* **2013**, *2013*, 298012. [CrossRef] [PubMed]
38. Marcus, R.L.; Addison, O.; Kidde, J.P.; Dibble, L.E.; Lastayo, P.C. Skeletal muscle fat infiltration: Impact of age, inactivity, and exercise. *J. Nutr. Health Aging* **2010**, *14*, 362–366. [CrossRef] [PubMed]
39. Shin, H.; Panton, L.B.; Dutton, G.R.; Ilich, J.Z. Relationship of Physical Performance with Body Composition and Bone Mineral Density in Individuals over 60 Years of Age: A Systematic Review. *J. Aging Res.* **2011**, *2011*, 191896. [CrossRef] [PubMed]
40. Landi, F.; Calvani, R.; Cesari, M.; Tosato, M.; Martone, A.M.; Ortolani, E.; Savera, G.; Salini, S.; Sisto, A.N.; Picca, A.; et al. Sarcopenia: An overview on current definitions, diagnosis and treatment. *Curr. Protein Pept. Sci.* **2017**. [CrossRef] [PubMed]
41. Warburton, D.E.; Nicol, C.W.; Bredin, S.S. Health benefits of physical activity: The evidence. *Can. Med. Assoc. J.* **2006**, *174*, 801–809. [CrossRef] [PubMed]
42. Shaw, B.A.; Spokane, L.S. Examining the association between education level and physical activity changes during early old age. *J. Aging Health* **2008**, *20*, 767–787. [CrossRef] [PubMed]
43. Go, S.W.; Cha, Y.H.; Lee, J.A.; Park, H.S. Association between Sarcopenia, Bone Density, and Health-Related Quality of Life in Korean Men. *Korean J. Fam. Med.* **2013**, *34*, 281–288. [CrossRef] [PubMed]
44. Volpato, S.; Bianchi, L.; Cherubini, A.; Landi, F.; Maggio, M.; Savino, E.; Bandinelli, S.; Ceda, G.P.; Guralnik, J.M.; Zuliani, G.; et al. Prevalence and clinical correlates of sarcopenia in community-dwelling older people: Application of the EWGSOP definition and diagnostic algorithm. *J. Gerontol. A Biol. Sci. Med. Sci.* **2014**, *69*, 438–446. [CrossRef] [PubMed]
45. Humphreys, B.; Ruseski, J. An economic analysis of participation and time spent in physical activity. *J. Econ. Anal. Policy* **2011**, *11*, 1–38. [CrossRef]

46. Farrell, L.; Shields, M.A. Investigating the economic and demographic determinants of sporting participation in England. *J. R. Stat. Soc. Ser. A* **2002**, *165*, 335–348. [CrossRef]
47. Alexandre Tda, S.; Duarte, Y.A.; Santos, J.L.; Wong, R.; Lebrão, M.L. Prevalence and associated factors of sarcopenia among elderly in Brazil: Findings from the SABE study. *J. Nutr. Health Aging* **2014**, *18*, 284–290. [CrossRef] [PubMed]
48. Lee, S.K.; Lee, J.A.; Kim, J.Y.; Kim, Y.Z.; Park, H.S. The risk factors of Sarcopenia among Korean Elderly Men: Based on 2009 Korean National Health and Nutrition Examination Survey Data. *Korean J. Obes.* **2014**, *23*, 23–31. [CrossRef]
49. McGregor, R.A.; Cameron-Smith, D.; Poppitt, S.D. It is not just muscle mass: A review of muscle quality, composition and metabolism during ageing as determinants of muscle function and mobility in later life. *Longev. Healthspan* **2014**, *3*, 9. [CrossRef] [PubMed]
50. Mithal, A.; Bonjour, J.; Dawson-Hughes, B.; IOF CSA Nutrition Working Group. Impact of nutrition on muscle mass, strength, and performance in older adults: Response to Scott and Jones. *Osteoporos. Int.* **2014**, *25*, 793. [CrossRef] [PubMed]
51. Charlton, K.; Batterham, M.; Langford, K.; Lateo, J.; Brock, E.; Walton, K.; Lyons-Wall, P.; Eisenhauer, K.; Green, N.; McLean, C. Lean Body Mass Associated with Upper Body Strength in Healthy Older Adults While Higher Body Fat Limits Lower Extremity Performance and Endurance. *Nutrients* **2015**, *7*, 7126–7142. [CrossRef] [PubMed]
52. Sarti, S.; Ruggiero, E.; Coin, A.; Toffanello, E.D.; Perissinotto, E.; Miotto, F.; Pintore, G.; Inelmen, E.M.; Manzato, E.; Sergi, G. Dietary intake and physical performance in healthy elderly women: A 3-year follow-up. *Exp. Gerontol.* **2013**, *48*, 250–254. [CrossRef] [PubMed]
53. Drewnowski, A.; Shultz, J.M. Impact of aging on eating behaviors, food choices, nutrition, and health status. *J. Nutr. Health Aging* **2001**, *5*, 75–79. [PubMed]
54. Alexandre Tda, S.; Duarte, Y.A.; Santos, J.L.; Wong, R.; Lebrão, M.L. Sarcopenia according to the European Working Group on Sarcopenia in Older People (EWGSOP) versus dynapenia as a risk factor for mortality in the elderly. *J. Nutr. Health Aging* **2014**, *18*, 751–756. [CrossRef] [PubMed]
55. Lourenço, R.A.; Pérez-Zepeda, M.; Gutiérrez-Robledo, L.; García-García, F.J.; Rodríguez Mañas, L. Performance of the European Working Group on Sarcopenia in Older People algorithm in screening older adults for muscle mass assessment. *Age Ageing* **2015**, *44*, 334–338. [CrossRef] [PubMed]
56. Vogel, L. Overweight or overfat? Many Canadians are both. *Can. Med. Assoc. J.* **2017**, *189*, E1202. [CrossRef] [PubMed]
57. Gordon, S.A.; Fredman, L.; Orwig, D.L.; Alley, D.E. Comparison of methods to measure height in older adults. *J. Am. Geriatr. Soc.* **2013**, *61*, 2244–2246. [CrossRef] [PubMed]
58. Schatzkin, A.; Kipnis, V.; Carroll, R.J.; Midthune, D.; Subar, A.F.; Bingham, S.; Schoeller, D.A.; Troiano, R.P.; Freedman, L.S. A comparison of a food frequency questionnaire with a 24-hour recall for use in an epidemiological cohort study: Results from the biomarker-based Observing Protein and Energy Nutrition (OPEN) study. *Int. J. Epidemiol.* **2003**, *32*, 1054–1062. [CrossRef] [PubMed]
59. Freedman, L.S.; Potischman, N.; Kipnis, V.; Midthune, D.; Schatzkin, A.; Thompson, F.E.; Troiano, R.P.; Prentice, R.; Patterson, R.; Carroll, R.; et al. A comparison of two dietary instruments for evaluating the fat-breast cancer relationship. *Int. J. Epidemiol.* **2006**, *35*, 1011–1021. [CrossRef] [PubMed]

© 2018 by the authors. Licensee MDPI, Basel, Switzerland. This article is an open access article distributed under the terms and conditions of the Creative Commons Attribution (CC BY) license (http://creativecommons.org/licenses/by/4.0/).

Article

Performance of Waist-To-Height Ratio, Waist Circumference, and Body Mass Index in Discriminating Cardio-Metabolic Risk Factors in a Sample of School-Aged Mexican Children

Ibiza Aguilar-Morales [1], Eloisa Colin-Ramirez [1,2,*], Susana Rivera-Mancía [1,2], Maite Vallejo [1] and Clara Vázquez-Antona [3]

1. Department of Social Medicine Research, National Institute of Cardiology 'Ignacio Chávez', Juan Badiano 1, Sección XVI, Mexico City C.P. 14080, Mexico; taniaibizaam@gmail.com (I.A.-M.); syriverama@conacyt.mx or yesqfb@yahoo.com.mx (S.R.-M.); maite_vallejo@yahoo.com.mx (M.V.)
2. CONACYT—National Institute of Cardiology 'Ignacio Chávez', Juan Badiano 1, Sección XVI, Mexico City C.P. 14080, Mexico
3. Department of Pediatric Echocardiography, National Institute of Cardiology 'Ignacio Chávez', Juan Badiano 1, Sección XVI, Mexico City C.P. 14080, Mexico; cvazquezant@yahoo.com
* Correspondence: eloisa_colin@yahoo.com.mx or ecolinra@conacyt.mx; Tel.: +52-55-55732911

Received: 24 October 2018; Accepted: 20 November 2018; Published: 1 December 2018

Abstract: The most common tools used to screen for abdominal obesity are waist circumference (WC) and waist-to-height ratio (WHtR); the latter may represent a more suitable tool for the general non-professional population. The objective of this study was to evaluate the association of WHtR, WC, and body mass index with lipidic and non-lipidic cardio-metabolic risk factors and the prediction capability of each adiposity indicator in a sample of school-aged Mexican children. Overall, 125 children aged 6 to 12 years were analyzed. Anthropometric, biochemical, and dietary parameters were assessed. Receiving operating characteristic (ROC) analysis and univariate and multivariate linear and logistic regression analyses were performed. All the three adiposity indicators showed significant areas under the ROC curve (AURC) greater than 0.68 for high low-density lipoprotein cholesterol (LDL-c), triglycerides, and atherogenic index of plasma, and low high-density lipoprotein cholesterol (HDL-c). A significant increased risk of having LDL-c $\geq$ 3.4 mmol/L was observed among children with WHtR $\geq$ 0.5 as compared to those with WHtR < 0.5 (odds ratio, OR: 2.82; 95% confidence interval, CI: 0.75–7.68; $p = 0.003$). Fasting plasma glucose was not associated with any of the adiposity parameters. WHtR performed similarly to WC and z-BMI in predicting lipidic cardio-metabolic risk factors; however, a WHtR $\geq$ 0.5 was superior in detecting an increased risk of elevated LDL-c.

Keywords: waist-to-height ratio; children; obesity; body mass index; waist circumference; cardio-metabolic risk

1. Introduction

Childhood obesity remains a major public health problem worldwide [1], mainly affecting children in low- and middle-income countries [2]. In Mexico, in 2016, 33.2% of children aged between 5 and 11 years were overweight or obese [3]. Increased cardiovascular risk and the early-onset of chronic diseases are among the health consequences of childhood obesity [4,5]. It has been recognized that evaluating weight status by traditional tools such as body mass index (BMI) to screen for cardio-metabolic risks is limited by the fact that BMI does not reflect fat distribution [6]; for instance, accumulation of visceral fat (intra-abdominal obesity), compared to subcutaneous fat (peripheral), has been associated with a greater cardiovascular risk [7–10] and metabolic disorders such as high blood pressure, dyslipidemia, and altered glucose metabolism [11,12].

The most common tools used to screen for abdominal obesity are waist circumference (WC) and waist-to-height ratio (WHtR); nonetheless, it has been reported that people with equal WC but distinct height have different cardiovascular risk [13,14], highlighting the relevance of the WHtR, which incorporates height in its calculation. A WHtR ≥ 0.5 has been proposed as an indicator of abdominal obesity in both adults and children at any age [4,15] and it has been associated with a greater cardiovascular risk and proinflammatory response in pediatric populations [12,16–18]. Additionally, WHtR has the advantage of not being dependent on age or sex-specific percentiles relative to a reference population when used in pediatric population, as BMI or WC are; therefore, it may represent a more practical tool to evaluate abdominal obesity for the general non-professional population [19–21], which might have relevant public health implications.

Despite the utility of WHtR to screen for cardio-metabolic risk factors in children and its practical advantages in measurement and interpretation, its use is still limited to research purposes without a widespread use in the clinical and population settings. In Mexico, few studies have evaluated the utility of this index as a predictor of cardio-metabolic risk factors compared to WC and/or BMI in pediatric population [22–24]; additionally, to our knowledge, there is no study comparing the performance of these three methods in detecting cardio-metabolic risks factors accounting for relevant dietary indicators that may influence this association and contribute to the inconsistences observed regarding the superiority of WHtR over WC in diverse populations [21]. The aim of this study was to evaluate the association of WHtR and WC as indicators of abdominal adiposity, and BMI as an indicator of general adiposity, with lipidic and non-lipidic cardio-metabolic risk factors and their prediction capability, in a sample of school-aged Mexican children, considering the effect of key dietary indicators.

2. Materials and Methods

2.1. Study Population

This cross-sectional analysis included 125 healthy children aged between 6 to 12 years enrolled in a study aimed to evaluate echocardiography abnormalities associated with obesity in school age children. Participants were recruited from a public elementary school in Mexico City between July 2015 and February 2017 thorough informative sessions delivered by research team members to the parents of children in all grades to explain the study objectives and procedures involved; parents interested in the study were provided with further detailed information. children were included if they and their parents or guardians provided written informed consent to take part of the study. children who were underweight and/or had cardiovascular disease, hypertension, diabetes, or any other chronic condition were excluded from the study. For the purpose of this cross-sectional analysis, children with incomplete anthropometric or biochemical data were also excluded from the analysis. The study was approved by the Research and Ethics Committees of the National Institute of Cardiology Ignacio Chávez (Instituto Nacional de Cardiología Ignacio Chávez (INCICh)) (REF. PT-15-009).

2.2. Assessments

Potential participants identified at school were scheduled for a clinical visit at the INCICh to confirm eligibility and undergo clinical and dietary assessments.

2.2.1. Anthropometry and Adiposity Indicators Definition

Weight, height and waist circumference were measured following standardized procedures described by the International Society for the Advancement of Kinanthropometry (ISAK) [25]. All anthropometric measures were taken by the same previously standardized research personnel. Standardization procedures were carried out according to the Habicht method [26].

Participants were asked to use light clothing without shoes. Height was measured to the nearest 0.1 cm using a Seca 220 stadiometer (seca GmbH & Co. KG., Hamburg, Germany). children were barefoot and advised to stand in an upright position, with shoulders and arms relaxed and head in the Frankfort horizontal plane. Weight was determined to the nearest 0.1 kg using a calibrated Seca 700 mechanical column scale. Waist circumference (WC) was measured with a measuring tape made of glass fiber BodyFlex, with length of 150 cm and precision of 1 mm, at the mid-point between the iliac crest and the lower edge of the ribs, with the subject in a relaxed standing position and the tape situated in a horizontal plane directly on the skin after a normal exhalation.

BMI z-score was calculated, as an indicator of general adiposity, and classified according to the World Health Organization (WHO) age- and gender-specific growth standards with the WHO Anthro Plus software [27]. Normal weight was defined as a BMI z-score between −2 standard deviations (SD) and 1 SD; overweight as z-score > 1 SD; and obesity as z-score > 2 DE [28]. Abdominal obesity was defined by means of WC and WHtR. A WC $\geq$ 90 percentile for gender, age and height, specific for Mexican children [29], was considered to indicate abdominal obesity. WHtR was calculated by dividing WC by height in cm. A WHtR $\geq$ 0.5 was considered as an indicator of abdominal obesity [4].

2.2.2. Biochemical Analysis and Cardio-Metabolic Risk Factors

Fasting blood samples (16 mL) were collected. For the purpose of the biochemical determinations employed in this sub-analysis, 3.5 mL were processed at the central laboratory of the INCICh to determine serum levels of glucose, triglycerides (TGs), low-density lipoprotein cholesterol (LDL-c), high-density lipoprotein cholesterol (HDL-c), and total cholesterol (TC). Elevated fasting plasma glucose (FPG) was defined according to the American Diabetes Association criteria as FPG $\geq$ 5.6 mmol/L [30]. Serum lipid levels were classified according to the criteria endorsed by the Expert Panel on Integrated Guidelines for Cardiovascular Health and Risk Reduction in children and Adolescents [31] as follows: high TC, $\geq$5.2 mmol/L; high LDL-c, $\geq$3.4 mmol/L; high TG, $\geq$1.1 mmol/L for 0–9 years and $\geq$1.5 mmol/L for 10–19 years; low HDL-c, <1 mmol/L.

Additionally, two atherogenic indexes were calculated. The atherogenic index of plasma (AIP) was calculated as Log10 (TG/HDL-c), where a value <0.11 has been suggested as an indicator of low risk, 0.11–0.21 for intermediate risk and >0.21 for increased risk [32]. The atherogenic index (AI) was calculated as LDL-c/HDL-c; an elevated AI was defined as a value >3 for women and >2.5 for men [33].

2.2.3. Dietary Intake

It was assessed with a multiple-pass 24-h food recall with parental assistance taken by a trained research dietitian [34]. children and parents were asked to provide detailed information on the food and beverages consumed by the children the day before. Three-dimensional food models were used to assist in defining food type and portion sizes. Information collected in the 24-h food recall was analyzed by trained personnel with a nutrient software program (ESHA Food Processor SQL v.11.4.0; ESHA Research, Salem, OR, USA). Additional food items were added to the ESHA database when needed to account for local foods and better reflect the actual food consumed by the children. Intake of energy and macronutrients (protein, carbohydrates and lipids) was estimated.

2.3. Statistical Analysis

Descriptive statistics were expressed as mean ± standard deviation (SD) or median with 25th and 75th percentiles for continuous variables, depending on whether or not variables were normally distributed as evaluated by the Kolmogorov–Smirnoff test. Comparison of variables between boys and girls was performed by using the Student's *t*-test or Mann–Whitney U test, as applicable. The receiving operating characteristic (ROC) analysis was employed to test the ability of all adiposity indicators (z-BMI, WC and WHtR) to discriminate children with cardio-metabolic risk factors from those with normal values through the areas under the ROC curve (AURC), for which 95% confidence intervals

(CIs) were constructed. ROC curves for each cardio-metabolic risk factor were compared among the three adiposity indicators.

Univariate and multivariate linear regression analyses were performed to test the linear association between each adiposity indicator with each cardio-metabolic risk marker. Regression coefficients (β), 95% CI for β and standardized β were estimated for all linear models. In the case of WHtR, it was introduced in the linear models as the quotient of WHtR divided by 10, so the β indicated the increase in each cardio-metabolic risk marker per increase of 0.1 units in WHtR.

Binary logistic regression analyses were used to evaluate the influence of excess general (z-BMI > 1 SD) and abdominal (WC ≥ 90 percentile or WHtR ≥ 0.5) adiposity on each cardio-metabolic risk marker as dichotomous variables based on previously described cut-off points. Odds ratios (OR) and 95% CI were estimated for all logistic models. Both liner and binary logistic multivariate models were adjusted for age, sex and dietary variables, as applicable. Additionally, the Firth logistic regression method was applied to test the associations of abdominal adiposity by WHtR (≥0.5) with high LDL-c and by WC (≥90 percentile) with high AIP, due to quasi-complete separation of the data that led to an infinite maximum likelihood estimate for these associations [35,36]. These two multivariate Firth logistic regression models were adjusted for the same covariates.

All analyses were performed using SPSS Version 23.0 (SPSS, Inc., Chicago, IL, USA), except for the comparison of the AURC among the three adiposity indicators, which was performed applying the roccomp command in Stata v.14. For the Firth logistic regression, the IBM SPSS Statistics—Integration Plug-in for R was used. A p value < 0.05 was considered as significant.

3. Results

A total of 142 subjects were enrolled in the study, 17 of them had missing data; therefore, 125 were included in the analysis. The median (25th–75th percentile) age was 9 (8–10) years old, and 58% were girls. Anthropometric, biochemical and dietary intake variables stratified by gender are shown in Table 1. There were no significant differences between genders except for energy intake, that was higher in boys than girls (2081 ± 692.6 vs. 1831 ± 524.4, p = 0.030).

Table 1. Characteristics of the sample by gender [1].

Characteristic	All	Boys (n = 52)	Girls (n = 73)	p [2]
Age (years)	9 (8–10)	9 (8–10)	9 (8–10)	0.564
z-BMI (SD)	1.43 ± 1.19	1.52 ± 1.24	1.35 ± 1.15	0.407
Waist circumference (cm)	73.42 ± 12.79	72.95 ± 13.62	73.76 ± 12.25	0.726
Waist-to-height ratio	0.52 ± 0.07	0.52 ± 0.07	0.52 ± 0.07	0.803
Systolic BP (mmHg)	96.83 ± 8.99	97.51 ± 8.88	96.35 ± 9.10	0.481
Diastolic BP (mmHg)	64.13 ± 6.68	64.19 ± 7.80	64.09 ± 5.8	0.934
Fasting plasma glucose (mmol/L)	5.05 (4.89–5.22)	5.05 (4.90–5.22)	5.05 (4.83–5.22)	0.534
Total cholesterol (mmol/L)	4.21 ± 0.68	4.24 ± 0.67	4.20 ± 0.69	0.745
LDL cholesterol (mmol/L)	2.66 ± 0.64	2.65 ± 0.62	2.66 ± 0.65	0.927
HDL cholesterol (mmol/L)	1.27 (1.12–1.54)	1.30 (1.13–1.59)	1.24 (1.10–1.49)	0.200
Triglycerides (mmol/L)	1.01 (0.74–1.40)	1.01 (0.69–1.35)	1.01 (0.79–1.49)	0.321
AI	1.98 (1.61–2.44)	1.95 (1.59–2.39)	2.01 (1.61–2.59)	0.595
AIP	0.25 ± 0.26	0.21 ± 0.26	0.28 ± 0.26	0.163
Energy intake (kcal/day)	1935 ± 610.2	2081 ± 692.6	1831 ± 524.4	0.030
Protein (g/day)	76.95 ± 26.07	78.44 ± 28.5	75.88 ± 24.31	0.590
Total fat (g/day)	62.9 (48.1–82.5)	63.13 (49.81–105.93)	62.9 (47.5–81.0)	0.256
Saturated fat (g/day)	23.8 (15.3–30.18)	25.58 (15.9–31.8)	22.5 (14.7–29.8)	0.348
Carbohydrates (g/day)	236.9 (186–319)	260.14 (191–346)	231.61 (181–294)	0.564

SD: standard deviation; z-BMI: z-score body mass index; BP: blood pressure; LDL: low-density lipoprotein; HDL: high-density lipoprotein; AI: atherogenic index; AIP: atherogenic index of plasma. [1] Values are mean ± standard deviation or median (25th–75th percentiles). [2] For comparison between boys vs. girls by using Student's t-test for independent samples or Mann–Whitney U test.

Table 2 shows the proportion of children with excess adiposity by each of the three anthropometric indexes among those with cardio-metabolic risk factors. It is worth noting that all children ($n = 12$) with high LDL-c had a WHtR ≥ 0.5.

Table 2. Proportion of children with obesity by the three adiposity indicators among those with cardio-metabolic risk factors.

Cardio-Metabolic Risk Marker	WHtR ≥ 0.5 n (%)	WC $\geq$ 90 Percentile n (%)	BMI z-Score > 1 SD n (%)
LDL-c ≥ 3.4 mmol/L ($n = 12$)	12 (100)	7 (58.3)	11 (91.6)
HDL-c < 1 mmol/L ($n = 15$)	14 (93.3)	10 (66.6)	14 (93.3)
TGs ≥ 1.1 mmol/L (0–9 years) or ≥ 1.5 mmol/L (10–19 years) ($n = 40$)	37 (92.5)	22 (55)	34 (85)
FPG ≥ 5.6 mmol/L ($n = 6$)	3 (50)	3 (50)	3 (50)
TC ≥ 5.2 mmol/L ($n = 11$)	10 (90.9)	5 (45.45)	9 (81.8)
AIP > 0.11 ($n = 92$)	70 (76)	44 (47.8)	71 (77.1)
AI > 3 for women and > 2.5 for men ($n = 27$)	26 (96.2)	17 (62.9)	25 (92.6)

WHtR: waist-to-height ratio; WC: waist circumference; z-BMI: z-score body mass index; CI: confidence interval; LDL: low-density lipoprotein; HDL: high-density lipoprotein; TGs: triglycerides; TC: total cholesterol; AI: atherogenic index; AIP: atherogenic index of plasma.

Table 3 shows the areas under the ROC curves with 95% CI for each adiposity indicator tested for each cardio-metabolic risk marker. The AURC for high TC was statistically significant only for WHtR, while those for high LDL-c, low HDL-c, high TG, and high AIP were significant for all the three adiposity indicators, meaning that all of these anthropometric indexes were able to distinguish children with each lipidic risk factor from those without them. The WHtR showed the largest AURC for high LDL-c (0.742), low HDL-c (0.733), high TGs (0.734), and high TC (0.689), while z-BMI displayed the largest AURC for high AIP (0.831). It is important to highlight that AURC for high FPG and high AI were not statistically significant for any of the three adiposity indicators. When the AURC for each cardio-metabolic risk marker was compared among the anthropometric indicators, no statistical significance was found, except for FPG, although none of the AURCs for FPG was statistically significant, as previously described.

Estimates from linear regression models are shown in Table 4. The three adiposity indicators (predictors) were positively associated with LDL-c, TGs, AIP, and AI, and inversely associated with HDL-c in both univariate and adjusted models. All the three adiposity indexes were stronger associated with the AI and TG. The adjusted regression coefficients (β) showed that per each 0.1 unit increase in WHtR, TGs increased 0.34 mmol/L (95% CI: 0.22, 0.45; $p = 0.000$), and per 1 unit increase in WC and z-BMI, TGs increased 0.02 mmol/L (95% CI: 0.02, 0.03; $p = 0.000$) and 0.21 mmol/L (95% CI: 0.14, 0.29; $p = 0.000$), respectively.

Table 5 shows the ORs for the associations of excess general (z-BMI > 1 SD) and abdominal (WC $\geq$ 90 percentile or WHtR ≥ 0.5) adiposity with cardio-metabolic risk factors defined according to the criteria previously specified. All the adiposity indicators exhibited a significant association with low HDL and high TG, AIP and AI in both the univariate and multivariate models. Overall, higher raw and adjusted ORs were seen for the association between WHtR ≥ 0.5 and elevated TG. Those with a WHtR ≥ 0.5 had a 17.36-fold increased risk of having elevated TGs compared to those with a WHtR < 0.5, adjusted for energy intake (kcal), saturated fat (g) and carbohydrates (g), age and gender. Additionally, LDL-c was significantly associated only with WHtR when the Firth correction was applied; an increased risk (OR: 2.82; 95% CI: 0.75, 7.68; p = 0.003) of having LDL $\geq$ 3.4 mmol/L was observed among children with WHtR $\geq$ 0.5 compared to those with WHtR <0.5.

Table 3. Association of each adiposity indicator and cardio-metabolic risk factors using receiver operating characteristic curves.

Cardio-Metabolic Risk Marker	WHtR AURC (95% CI) p Value	WC AURC (95% CI) p Value	z-BMI AURC (95% CI) p Value	p *
LDL-c $\geq$ 3.4 mmol/L	0.742 (0.63, 0.86) 0.006	0.685 (0.54, 0.83) 0.035	0.687 (0.55, 0.82) 0.034	0.1511
HDL-c < 1 mmol/L	0.733 (0.60, 0.87) 0.004	0.719 (0.59, 0.85) 0.006	0.704 (0.57, 0.83) 0.011	0.8124
TGs $\geq$ 1.1 mmol/L (0–9 years) or $\geq$1.5 mmol/L (10–19 years)	0.734 (0.65, 0.82) 0.000	0.690 (0.59, 0.79) 0.001	0.730 (0.64, 0.82) 0.000	0.2382
FPG $\geq$ 5.6 mmol/L	0.507 (0.21, 0.80) 0.954	0.627 (0.32, 0.93) 0.293	0.574 (0.29, 0.86) 0.544	0.003
TC $\geq$ 5.2 mmol/L	0.689 (0.55, 0.83) 0.039	0.630 (0.47, 0.80) 0.155	0.655 (0.50, 0.81) 0.090	0.3034
AIP > 0.11	0.811 (0.73, 0.89) 0.000	0.825 (0.75, 0.90) 0.000	0.831 (0.75, 0.91) 0.000	0.7050
AI > 3 for women and >2.5 for men	0.699 (0.46, 0.94) 0.335	0.681 (0.56, 0.80) 0.381	0.652 (0.39, 0.92) 0.461	0.2392

WHtR: waist-to-height ratio; WC: waist circumference; z-BMI: z-score body mass index; CI: confidence interval; LDL: low-density lipoprotein; HDL: high-density lipoprotein; TGs: triglycerides; TC: total cholesterol; AI: atherogenic index; AIP: atherogenic index of plasma. * p value for comparison among ROC curves.

Table 4. Univariate and multivariate linear association of adiposity indicators and cardio-metabolic risk factors.

Cardio-Metabolic Risk Marker	WHtR (Per Increase of 0.1 Units) *				WC (cm) *				z-BMI (SD)			
	β	95% CI	Standardized β	p	β	95% CI	Standardized β	p	β	95% CI	Standardized β	p
LDL-c (mmol/L) Unadjusted model	0.27	0.12, 0.41	0.31	0.000	0.01	0.00, 0.02	0.24	0.007	0.13	0.03, 0.21	0.24	0.008
Adjusted model [1]	0.24	0.09, 0.38	0.28	0.002	0.01	0.00, 0.02	0.29	0.005	0.12	0.02, 0.21	0.22	0.015
HDL-c (mmol/L) Unadjusted model	−0.21	−0.27, −0.14	−0.49	0.000	−0.01	−0.02, −0.01	−0.53	0.000	−0.12	−0.16, −0.08	−0.45	0.000
Adjusted model [2]	−0.21	−0.27, −0.14	−0.49	0.000	−0.01	−0.02, −0.01	−0.56	0.000	−0.12	−0.17, −0.08	−0.47	0.000
TGs (mmol/L) Unadjusted model	0.34	0.23, 0.46	0.47	0.000	0.02	0.02, 0.03	0.54	0.000	0.20	0.13, 0.27	0.45	0.000
Adjusted model [2]	0.34	0.22, 0.45	0.47	0.000	0.02	0.02, 0.03	0.55	0.000	0.21	0.14, 0.29	0.48	0.000
TC (mmol/L) Unadjusted model	0.13	−0.03, 0.29	0.14	0.108	0.00	−0.01, 0.01	0.07	0.424	0.06	−0.05, 0.16	0.10	0.277
Adjusted model [1]	0.10	−0.06, 0.27	0.11	0.217	0.01	−0.01, 0.02	0.11	0.299	0.05	−0.06, 0.15	0.08	0.386
FPG (mmol/L) Unadjusted model	0.03	−0.04, 0.10	0.07	0.421	0.00	−0.00, 0.01	0.15	0.089	0.03	−0.02, 0.07	0.11	0.237
Adjusted model [3]	0.02	−0.06, 0.10	0.05	0.597	0.00	−0.00, 0.01	0.14	0.119	0.02	−0.02, 0.07	0.09	0.328
AIP Unadjusted model	0.20	0.14, 0.25	0.54	0.000	0.01	0.01, 0.016	0.62	0.000	0.12	0.08, 0.15	0.52	0.000
Adjusted model [4]	0.20	0.14, 0.25	0.55	0.000	0.01	0.01, 0.016	0.63	0.000	0.12	0.09, 0.16	0.55	0.000
AI Unadjusted model	0.47	0.33, 0.63	0.49	0.000	0.03	0.02, 0.036	0.47	0.000	0.25	0.15, 0.35	0.41	0.000
Adjusted model [4]	0.48	0.33, 0.64	0.50	0.000	0.03	0.02, 0.035	0.46	0.000	0.26	0.16, 0.36	0.43	0.000

WHtR: waist-to-height ratio; WC: waist circumference; z-BMI: z-score body mass index; SD: standard deviation; CI: confidence interval; LDL: low-density lipoprotein; HDL: high-density lipoprotein; TGs: triglycerides; TC: total cholesterol; AIP: atherogenic index of plasma; AI: atherogenic index. [1] Adjusted for total energy (kcal) and saturated fat (g); [2] Adjusted for total energy (kcal), saturated fat (g) and carbohydrates (g); [3] Adjusted for total energy (kcal) and carbohydrates (g); [4] Adjusted for total energy (kcal), total fat (g) and carbohydrates (g). All multivariate models for WHtR and WC were further adjusted for age and gender. * Adjusted for age and gender.

Table 5. Logistic regression analyses for the association of excess general (z-BMI > 1 SD) and abdominal (WC ≥ 90 percentile or WHtR ≥ 0.5) adiposity and cardio-metabolic risk factors.

Cardio-Metabolic Risk Marker	WHtR ≥ 0.5 *			WC ≥ 90 Percentile			BMI z-Score > 1 SD		
	OR	95% CI	p	OR	95% CI	p	OR	95% CI	p
LDL-c ≥ 3.4 mmol/L Unadjusted model	2.91 ¥	0.84, 7.78	0.002	3.12	0.93, 10.51	0.066	7.01	0.86, 56.25	0.067
Adjusted model [1]	2.82 ¥	0.75, 7.68	0.003	3.39	0.97, 11.81	0.055	6.47	0.79, 52.83	0.081
HDL-c < 1 mmol/L Unadjusted model	11.02	1.41, 86.34	0.022	4.88	1.54, 15.39	0.007	9.33	1.18, 73.54	0.034
Adjusted model [2]	11.05	1.36, 89.77	0.025	5.20	1.60, 16.90	0.006	11.06	1.37, 89.43	0.024
TGs ≥ 1.1 mmol/L for 0–9 years and ≥ 1.5 mmol/L for 10–19 years Unadjusted model	13.90	3.99, 48.49	0.000	3.97	1.79, 8.84	0.001	4.80	1.83, 12.64	0.001
Adjusted model [2]	17.36	4.65, 64.77	0.000	4.44	1.93, 10.23	0.000	5.32	1.94, 14.58	0.001
TC ≥ 5.2 mmol/L Unadjusted model	7.60	0.95, 60.89	0.056	2.60	0.74, 9.08	0.134	2.73	0.56, 13.21	0.213
Adjusted model [1]	6.83	0.82, 56.89	0.076	2.67	0.76, 9.41	0.126	2.54	0.51, 12.55	0.253
FPG ≥ 5.6 mmol/L Unadjusted model	0.59	0.12, 3.06	0.532	2.05	0.40, 10.63	0.392	0.55	0.11, 2.82	0.470
Adjusted model [3]	0.52	0.09, 3.00	0.464	2.07	0.40, 10.77	0.388	0.47	0.09, 2.57	0.383
AIP ≥ 0.11 Unadjusted model	12.16	4.65, 31.79	0.000	4.00 ¥	2.00, 8.85	0.000	9.02	3.64, 22.35	0.000
Adjusted model [4]	14.16	4.86, 41.25	0.000	4.16 ¥	2.14, 9.02	0.000	10.22	3.85, 27.11	0.000
AI > 3 for women and < 2.5 for men Unadjusted model	11.06	2.48, 49.26	0.002	4.96	2.00, 12.25	0.001	9.77	2.19, 43.56	0.003
Adjusted model [4]	12.39	2.71, 56.65	0.001	5.11	2.02, 12.94	0.001	10.78	2.33, 49.78	0.002

WHtR: waist-to-height ratio; WC: waist circumference; z-BMI: z-score body mass index; CI: confidence interval; LDL: low-density lipoproteins; HDL: high-density lipoproteins; TGs: triglycerides; TC: total cholesterol; AIP: atherogenic index of plasma; AI: atherogenic index. [1] Adjusted for total energy (kcal) and saturated fat (g); [2] Adjusted for total energy (kcal), saturated fat (g) and carbohydrates (g); [3] Adjusted for total energy (kcal) and carbohydrates (g); [4] Adjusted for total energy (kcal), total fat (g) and carbohydrates (g). ¥ Estimated by the penalized Firth logistic regression method. * All adjusted models for WHtR were further adjusted for age and gender.

4. Discussion

Results of our study confirmed that WHtR performed similarly to WC and z-BMI in predicting lipidic cardio-metabolic risk factors in this sample of school-aged Mexican children, as all the three adiposity indicators showed significant AURCs greater than 0.68 for high LDL-c, low HDL-c, high TG, and high AIP. Additionally, a cut-off of 0.5 for WHtR was useful to detect significant increased risk of having lipidic cardio-metabolic risk factors, similar to that observed for a z-BMI > 1 SD and a WC $\geq$ 90 percentile. However, a WHtR $\geq$ 0.5 showed to be superior in detecting a significant increased risk of elevated LDL-c, even after adjustment for key variables. Importantly, none of the three adiposity indicators were able to discriminate high FPG in this study population.

The high prevalence of childhood obesity worldwide has guided us to search for alternatives to measure and predict the cardiovascular risk entailed in a better and faster way. Central obesity has a stronger association with an adverse cardio-metabolic risk profile in children either in the short and long term, compared to general obesity as determined by whole body fat [37–40]. Therefore, evaluation of abdominal obesity should be given sufficient importance in routine clinical practice during well child visits to improve the process of care. The use of a tool that is simple to measure and interpret as WHtR represents an advantageous alternative to screen for lipidic cardio-metabolic risk factors not only in the clinical setting, but also at the population level.

Diverse imaging techniques have been considered more accurate to evaluate fat content, such as bioimpedance analysis, dual energy X-ray absorptiometry (DEXA), air-displacement plethysmography (ADP), magnetic resonance imaging, etc. [41,42]; however, these are expensive methods, requiring more time and trained personal, and some of them imply radiation exposure. Thus, the utility of alternative easy to use and low-cost anthropometric indexes such as z-BMI, WC, and WHtR in assessing adiposity has been extensively evaluated. A recent systematic review of studies in children aged between 7 and 10 years old showed that BMI and WC were strongly correlated to body fat as measured by bioelectrical impedance or skinfolds, and that there was a moderate positive correlation with percent body fat as calculated by DEXA, ADP, or isotope dilution. However, in the case of WHtR, only a moderate positive correlation with body fat, as estimated by ADP and skinfolds, was reported [43]. In contrast, a study in children aged 8 to 18 years old concluded that WHtR was better than WC and BMI at predicting adiposity in this pediatric population, since it explained 80% of percent body fat variance, accounting for age and gender, as compared with 72% for WC and 68% for BMI [44]; in addition, a systematic review and meta-analysis reported that body fat measured by DEXA was strongly correlated with both BMI and WHtR, thus highlighting the utility of these two indexes to define obesity when more sophisticated techniques are not available [45]. Nonetheless, the relevance of the WHtR does not only rely on its ability to predict total body fat, but mainly on its potential superiority as a more practical tool to assess abdominal adiposity and to screen for cardio-metabolic risk [16,46].

In this regard, a meta-analysis of 34 studies in pediatric populations [21], including two in Mexican children and adolescents [23,24], reported that WHtR had significantly better screening power for elevated TGs compared to BMI and for high metabolic risk score compared to WC. Although WHtR was not superior for all the outcomes studied, authors highlighted its practical advantage in terms of measurement and interpretation for the screening of cardio-metabolic risk factors in children. The results of this present study extend the existing evidence base by reporting a similar good performance of the WHtR, WC, and BMI in the ROC analysis to discriminate children with lipidic cardio-metabolic risk factors from those with normal values, since all the three adiposity indicators exhibited significant AURCs greater than 0.68 for high LDL-c, low HDL-c, high TG, and high AIP; however, WHtR was the only one showing a significant AURC for high TC (0.689). Some other recent studies not included in the previous meta-analysis have also shown a similar performance of the WHtR compared to BMI or WC in identifying cardio-metabolic risk factors in pediatric population [47,48]. Importantly, in our study neither the AURCs for elevated FPG, nor the linear or logistic models constructed for this metabolic marker, were statistically significant for any of the three adiposity indicators. Similar findings were previously reported by other authors. In the meta-analysis by

Lo et al. [21], two of three studies evaluating hyperglycemia reported no significant AURC for WHtR, WC, and BMI, and although the pooled AURC values for all indexes were statistically significant, they were just above 0.5 (0.57). In a more recent study among Korean children and adolescents, these same three adiposity indicators did not show a significant AURC for high fasting plasma glucose (FPG), defined as FPG $\geq$ 6.1 mmol/L, when stratified by gender [48]. Thus, it may be possible that other non-adiposity factors have a greater influence on glycemic status in pediatrics, such as genetics, intrauterine exposure, and environmental and lifestyle-related factors [49,50], which need to be further studied in order to address this metabolic alteration in early life.

It has been largely suggested that a cut-off point of 0.5 for WHtR is an effective indicator for health risks associated to obesity regardless of sex, age and ethnicity [19,51] and a recent meta-analysis concluded that this value is an appropriate cut-off for classifying cardio-metabolic risk in children and adolescents [21]. Nonetheless, diverse studies in children have suggested different cut-off points due to a higher predictive efficacy as compared to the traditional cut-off of 0.5 [16,23,24,48,52]. In Mexico, a cross-sectional study evaluating the utility of WHtR to predict metabolic syndrome in children between 6 and 12 years old, identified a value of 0.59 for WHtR as a strong predictor of this condition, whereas a cut-off of 0.5 showed very poor specificity (22.7%); we need to consider that most of the children (82%) in this study were overweight or obese, thus limiting the generalizability of the data. [23]. Similarly, another study in Mexican obese adolescents suggested that a WHtR $\geq$ 0.6 is a better predictor for metabolic syndrome compared to WC or BMI [24]. In our study, we tested the utility of the traditional cut-off for WHtR of 0.5 to evaluate the risk of presenting cardio-metabolic risk factors by logistic regression models adjusted by key dietary variables, as well as age and gender when applicable, since all these covariates were thought to influence such association. Our results showed that all the adiposity indicators had a significant association with low HDL and high TG, AIP, and AI in both the univariate and multivariate models; however, WHtR was the only of these indicators associated with LDL-C, showing a significant increased risk of elevated LDL-c ($\geq$3.4 mmol/L) among children with WHtR $\geq$ 0.5 (OR: 2.82; 95% CI: 0.75, 7.68; p = 0.003) compared to those with a WHtR < 0.5, after adjustment for total energy (kcal), saturated fat (g), age, and gender.

Pediatric obesity is a public health problem worldwide, with rates in Latin America being among the highest in the world. Considering this, over the last few years diverse strategies and regulations aimed to prevent childhood obesity have been implemented in the Latin America region [53,54]. Here, as in all prevention strategies, monitoring is essential in order to document progress; in this regard, an effective and practical method to screen for obesity and its associated cardio-metabolic complications, as WHtR, may be of relevance. Additionally, the practicality of this method, as it does not require tables or graphics to be interpreted, makes of this an ideal approach for auto-screening at the population level to detect excess abdominal adiposity and its potential metabolic risk, and thus raising awareness among families regarding the need of searching for medical care and making life-style changes to improve children weight status and prevent further complications.

This study has some relevant limitations. Firstly, the small sample size may have led to the complete separation of data observed for the association between WHtR $\geq$ 0.5 and high LDL-c and between WC $\geq$ 90 percentile and high AIP, thus hindering parameter estimation during binomial logistic regression analyses; nonetheless, the estimates were able to be computed by applying the Firth correction [35]. Secondly, this is a cross-sectional design, and therefore a causal relationship between adiposity indicators and cardio-metabolic risk factors was not proved. Further longitudinal studies are still needed for this purpose. Thirdly, there are no well-established cut-off points for AIP and AI for the pediatric population, so we employed those used for adult population. Establishing cut-offs for these lipidic indexes and testing their usefulness as cardiovascular risk markers in pediatric population is necessary. Finally, dietary intake was measured by a single 24-h recall, which does not reflect the day-to-day variation in food intake; however, this method has been proven as valid for assessing the dietary intake in children as young as 8 years old without parental assistance [55].

In our study, we conducted this assessment with parental assistant to improve accuracy and quality of data collected.

In conclusion, we confirmed that WHtR, WC, and z-BMI performed similarly in predicting lipidic cardio-metabolic risk factors in this sample of school-aged Mexican children, while a cut-off of 0.5 for WHtR showed to be superior in detecting a significant increased risk of elevated LDL-c, even after adjustment for key variables. Importantly, none of the three adiposity indicators were able to discriminate high FPG, suggesting that other non-adiposity factors may have a greater influence on glucose metabolism in this pediatric population. Due to the increasing prevalence of obesity in early life and the cardio-metabolic risk associated with this weight condition, it is highly recommended to consider the use of the WHtR as a practical tool for auto-screening for abdominal obesity and cardio-metabolic risk at the population level for timely detection and management of increased cardio-metabolic risk in the pediatric population.

Author Contributions: Conceptualization, I.A.-M., E.C.-R., S.R.-M.; Methodology, E.C.-R., I.A.-M., S.R.-M.; Validation, E.C.-R.; Formal Analysis, I.A.-M., E.C.-R.; Investigation, I.A.-M., S.R.M, C.V.-A.; Resources, M.V., C.V.-A., E.C.-R.; Data Curation, I.A.-M.; Writing—Original Draft Preparation, I.A.-M., E.C.-R.; Writing—Review and Editing, S.R.M., C.V.-A., M.V.; Visualization, S.R.-M., I.A.-M., E.C.-R.; Supervision, E.C.-R.; Project Administration, C.V.A.; E.C.-R., M.V.

Funding: This research received no external funding.

Acknowledgments: We want to thank the Central Lab of the National Institute of Cardiology for their support for blood specimen collection and analysis.

Conflicts of Interest: The authors declare no conflict of interest.

References

1. WHO. Childhood Overweight and Obesity. Available online: http://www.who.int/dietphysicalactivity/childhood/en/ (accessed on 23 November 2013).
2. World Health Organization. *Commission on Ending Childhood Obesity*; Report of the Commission on Ending Childhood Obesity; World Health Organization: Geneva, Switzerland, 2016; ISBN 978-92-4-151006-6.
3. Instituto Nacional de Salud Pública. *Encuesta Nacional de Salud y Nutrición de Medio Camino 2016*; Informe Final de Resultados; Instituto Nacional de Salud Pública: Cuernavaca, Mexico, 2016.
4. Yoo, E.-G. Waist-to-height ratio as a screening tool for obesity and cardiometabolic risk. *Korean J. Pediatr.* **2016**, *59*, 425. [CrossRef] [PubMed]
5. Skinner, A.C.; Perrin, E.M.; Moss, L.A.; Skelton, J.A. Cardiometabolic Risks and Severity of Obesity in children and Young Adults. *N. Engl. J. Med.* **2015**, *373*, 1307–1317. [CrossRef] [PubMed]
6. Vorwieger, E.; Kelso, A.; Steinacker, J.M.; Kesztyüs, D.; Kesztyüs, D. Cardio-metabolic and socio-environmental correlates of waist-to-height ratio in German primary schoolchildren: A cross-sectional exploration. *BMC Public Health* **2018**, *18*. [CrossRef] [PubMed]
7. Daniels, S.R.; Morrison, J.A.; Sprecher, D.L.; Khoury, P.; Kimball, T.R. Association of Body Fat Distribution and Cardiovascular Risk Factors in children and Adolescents. *Circulation* **1999**, *99*, 541–545. [CrossRef] [PubMed]
8. Mokha, J.S.; Srinivasan, S.R.; DasMahapatra, P.; Fernandez, C.; Chen, W.; Xu, J.; Berenson, G.S. Utility of waist-to-height ratio in assessing the status of central obesity and related cardiometabolic risk profile among normal weight and overweight/obese children: The Bogalusa Heart Study. *BMC Pediatr.* **2010**, *10*. [CrossRef] [PubMed]
9. Cho, S.-A.; Joo, H.J.; Cho, J.-Y.; Lee, S.H.; Park, J.H.; Hong, S.J.; Yu, C.W.; Lim, D.-S. Visceral Fat Area and Serum Adiponectin Level Predict the Development of Metabolic Syndrome in a Community-Based Asymptomatic Population. *PLoS ONE* **2017**, *12*, e0169289. [CrossRef] [PubMed]
10. Arnaoutis, G.; Georgoulis, M.; Psarra, G.; Milkonidou, A.; Panagiotakos, D.B.; Kyriakou, D.; Bellou, E.; Tambalis, K.D.; Sidossis, L.S. Association of Anthropometric and Lifestyle Parameters with Fitness Levels in Greek Schoolchildren: Results from the EYZHN Program. *Front. Nutr.* **2018**, *5*, 10. [CrossRef] [PubMed]

11. Aristizabal, J.; González-Zapata, L.; Estrada-Restrepo, A.; Monsalve-Alvarez, J.; Restrepo-Mesa, S.; Gaitán, D. Concentrations of Plasma Free Palmitoleic and Dihomo-Gamma Linoleic Fatty Acids Are Higher in children with Abdominal Obesity. *Nutrients* **2018**, *10*, 31. [CrossRef] [PubMed]
12. Schwandt, P. Defining central adiposity in terms of clinical practice in children and adolescents. *Int. J. Prev. Med.* **2011**, *2*, 1–2. [PubMed]
13. Hsieh, S.D.; Yoshinaga, H. Do people with similar waist circumference share similar health risks irrespective of height? *Tohoku J. Exp. Med.* **1999**, *188*, 55–60. [CrossRef] [PubMed]
14. Schneider, H.J.; Klotsche, J.; Silber, S.; Stalla, G.K.; Wittchen, H.-U. Measuring Abdominal Obesity: Effects of Height on Distribution of Cardiometabolic Risk Factors Risk Using Waist Circumference and Waist-to-Height Ratio. *Diabetes Care* **2011**, *34*, e7. [CrossRef] [PubMed]
15. McCarthy, H.D.; Ashwell, M. A study of central fatness using waist-to-height ratios in UK children and adolescents over two decades supports the simple message—'keep your waist circumference to less than half your height'. *Int. J. Obes.* **2006**, *30*, 988–992. [CrossRef] [PubMed]
16. Jiang, Y.; Dou, Y.; Xiong, F.; Zhang, L.; Zhu, G.; Wu, T.; Zhang, Y.; Yan, W. Waist-to-height ratio remains an accurate and practical way of identifying cardiometabolic risks in children and adolescents. *Acta Paediatr.* **2018**. [CrossRef] [PubMed]
17. Gamboa, E.M.; Domínguez, C.L.; Quintero, D.C. Waist-To-Height Ratio and its relation with cardiometabolic risk factors in children from Bucaramanga, Colombia. *Nutr. Hosp.* **2017**. [CrossRef] [PubMed]
18. Mendes, E.L.; Andaki, A.C.R.; Brito, C.J.; Guedes, J.M.; Santos, M.P.M.; Mota, J. Waist circumference to height ratio predicts inflammatory risk in children. *Ann. Hum. Biol.* **2017**, *44*, 303–308. [CrossRef] [PubMed]
19. Ashwell, M.; Hsieh, S.D. Six reasons why the waist-to-height ratio is a rapid and effective global indicator for health risks of obesity and how its use could simplify the international public health message on obesity. *Int. J. Food Sci. Nutr.* **2005**, *56*, 303–307. [CrossRef] [PubMed]
20. Zhou, D.; Yang, M.; Yuan, Z.-P.; Zhang, D.-D.; Liang, L.; Wang, C.-L.; Zhang, S.; Zhu, H.-H.; Lai, M.-D.; Zhu, Y.-M. Waist-to-Height Ratio: A simple, effective and practical screening tool for childhood obesity and metabolic syndrome. *Prev. Med.* **2014**, *67*, 35–40. [CrossRef] [PubMed]
21. Lo, K.; Wong, M.; Khalechelvam, P.; Tam, W. Waist-to-height ratio, body mass index and waist circumference for screening paediatric cardio-metabolic risk factors: A meta-analysis: Screening cardio-metabolic risk factors. *Obes. Rev.* **2016**, *17*, 1258–1275. [CrossRef] [PubMed]
22. López-González, D.; Miranda-Lora, A.; Klünder-Klünder, M.; Queipo-García, G.; Bustos-Esquivel, M.; Paez-Villa, M.; Villanueva-Ortega, E.; Chávez-Requena, I.; Laresgoiti-Servitje, E.; Garibay-Nieto, N. Diagnostic performance of waist circumference measurements for predicting cardiometabolic risk in mexican children. *Endocr. Pract.* **2016**, *22*, 1170–1176. [CrossRef] [PubMed]
23. Elizondo-Montemayor, L.; Serrano-González, M.; Ugalde-Casas, P.A.; Bustamante-Careaga, H.; Cuello-García, C. Waist-to-height: Cutoff matters in predicting metabolic syndrome in Mexican children. *Metab. Syndr. Relat. Disord.* **2011**, *9*, 183–190. [CrossRef] [PubMed]
24. Rodea-Montero, E.R.; Evia-Viscarra, M.L.; Apolinar-Jiménez, E. Waist-to-Height Ratio Is a Better Anthropometric Index than Waist Circumference and BMI in Predicting Metabolic Syndrome among Obese Mexican Adolescents. *Int. J. Endocrinol.* **2014**, *2014*, 195407. [CrossRef] [PubMed]
25. The International Society for the Advancement in Kinanthropometry (ISAK). *International Standards for Anthropometric Assessment*; ISAK: Underdale, SA, Australia, 2001.
26. Habicht, J.P. Estandarización de métodos epidemiológicos cuantitativos sobre el terreno. (Standardization of anthropometric methods in the field). *PAHO Bull.* **1974**, *76*, 375–384.
27. World Health Organization (WHO). *AnthroPlus for Personal Computers Manual: Software for Assessing Growth of the World's children and Adolescents*; WHO: Geneva, Switzerland, 2009.
28. World Health Organization Growth Chart for children 5–19 Years. Available online: http://www.who.int/growthref/who2007_bmi_for_age/en/ (accessed on 23 November 2018).
29. Klünder-Klünder, M.; Flores-Huerta, S. Waist Circumference Values According to Height Percentiles: A Proposal to Evaluate Abdominal Obesity in Mexican children and Adolescents between 6 and 16 Years of Age. *Arch. Med. Res.* **2011**, *42*, 515–522. [CrossRef] [PubMed]
30. American Diabetes Association Classification and Diagnosis of Diabetes. *Diabetes Care* **2016**, *39*, S13–S22. [CrossRef] [PubMed]

31. Expert Panel on Integrated Guidelines for Cardiovascular Health and Risk Reduction in children and Adolescents; National Heart, Lung, and Blood Institute. Expert panel on integrated guidelines for cardiovascular health and risk reduction in children and adolescents: Summary report. *Pediatrics* **2011**, *128* (Suppl. 5), S213–S256. [CrossRef] [PubMed]
32. Dobiásová, M. [AIP—Atherogenic index of plasma as a significant predictor of cardiovascular risk: From research to practice]. *Vnitr. Lek.* **2006**, *52*, 64–71. [PubMed]
33. Millán, J.; Pintó, X.; Muñoz, A.; Zúñiga, M.; Rubiés-Prat, J.; Pallardo, L.F.; Masana, L.; Mangas, A.; Hernández-Mijares, A.; González-Santos, P.; et al. Lipoprotein ratios: Physiological significance and clinical usefulness in cardiovascular prevention. *Vasc. Health Risk Manag.* **2009**, *5*, 757–765. [PubMed]
34. Johnson, R.K.; Driscoll, P.; Goran, M.I. Comparison of Multiple-Pass 24-Hour Recall Estimates of Energy Intake With Total Energy Expenditure Determined By the Doubly Labeled Water Method in Young children. *J. Am. Diet. Assoc.* **1996**, *96*, 1140–1144. [CrossRef]
35. Heinze, G.; Schemper, M. A solution to the problem of separation in logistic regression. *Stat. Med.* **2002**, *21*, 2409–2419. [CrossRef] [PubMed]
36. Firth, D. Bias reduction of maximum likelihood estimates. *Biometrika* **1993**, *80*, 27–38. [CrossRef]
37. Xi, B.; Mi, J.; Zhao, M.; Zhang, T.; Jia, C.; Li, J.; Zeng, T.; Steffen, L.M.; Public Health Youth Collaborative; Innovative Study Group of Shandong University. Trends in abdominal obesity among U.S. children and adolescents. *Pediatrics* **2014**, *134*, e334–e339. [CrossRef] [PubMed]
38. Fox, C.S.; Massaro, J.M.; Hoffmann, U.; Pou, K.M.; Maurovich-Horvat, P.; Liu, C.-Y.; Vasan, R.S.; Murabito, J.M.; Meigs, J.B.; Cupples, L.A.; et al. Abdominal visceral and subcutaneous adipose tissue compartments: Association with metabolic risk factors in the Framingham Heart Study. *Circulation* **2007**, *116*, 39–48. [CrossRef] [PubMed]
39. Chen, B.; Li, H. Waist circumference as an indicator of high blood pressure in preschool obese children. *Asia Pac. J. Clin. Nutr.* **2011**, *20*, 557–562. [PubMed]
40. Kelishadi, R.; Mirmoghtadaee, P.; Najafi, H.; Keikha, M. Systematic review on the association of abdominal obesity in children and adolescents with cardio-metabolic risk factors. *J. Res. Med. Sci. Off. J. Isfahan Univ. Med. Sci.* **2015**, *20*, 294–307.
41. Kaul, S.; Rothney, M.P.; Peters, D.M.; Wacker, W.K.; Davis, C.E.; Shapiro, M.D.; Ergun, D.L. Dual-energy X-ray absorptiometry for quantification of visceral fat. *Obesity* **2012**, *20*, 1313–1318. [CrossRef] [PubMed]
42. Ross, R. Advances in the application of imaging methods in applied and clinical physiology. *Acta Diabetol.* **2003**, *40* (Suppl. 1), S45–S50. [CrossRef]
43. Jensen, N.S.O.; Camargo, T.F.B.; Bergamaschi, D.P. Comparison of methods to measure body fat in 7-to-10-year-old children: A systematic review. *Public Health* **2016**, *133*, 3–13. [CrossRef] [PubMed]
44. Brambilla, P.; Bedogni, G.; Heo, M.; Pietrobelli, A. Waist circumference-to-height ratio predicts adiposity better than body mass index in children and adolescents. *Int. J. Obes.* **2013**, *37*, 943–946. [CrossRef] [PubMed]
45. Martin-Calvo, N.; Moreno-Galarraga, L.; Martinez-Gonzalez, M.A. Association between Body Mass Index, Waist-to-Height Ratio and Adiposity in children: A Systematic Review and Meta-Analysis. *Nutrients* **2016**, *8*, 512. [CrossRef] [PubMed]
46. Forkert, E.C.O.; Rendo-Urteaga, T.; Nascimento-Ferreira, M.V.; de Moraes, A.C.F.; Moreno, L.A.; de Carvalho, H.B. Abdominal obesity and cardiometabolic risk in children and adolescents, are we aware of their relevance? *Nutrire* **2016**, *41*. [CrossRef]
47. Sardinha, L.B.; Santos, D.A.; Silva, A.M.; Grøntved, A.; Andersen, L.B.; Ekelund, U. A Comparison between BMI, Waist Circumference, and Waist-To-Height Ratio for Identifying Cardio-Metabolic Risk in children and Adolescents. *PLoS ONE* **2016**, *11*, e0149351. [CrossRef] [PubMed]
48. Choi, D.-H.; Hur, Y.-I.; Kang, J.-H.; Kim, K.; Cho, Y.; Hong, S.-M.; Cho, E. Usefulness of the Waist Circumference-to-Height Ratio in Screening for Obesity and Metabolic Syndrome among Korean children and Adolescents: Korea National Health and Nutrition Examination Survey, 2010–2014. *Nutrients* **2017**, *9*, 256. [CrossRef] [PubMed]
49. Kawasaki, M.; Arata, N.; Miyazaki, C.; Mori, R.; Kikuchi, T.; Ogawa, Y.; Ota, E. Obesity and abnormal glucose tolerance in offspring of diabetic mothers: A systematic review and meta-analysis. *PLoS ONE* **2018**, *13*, e0190676. [CrossRef] [PubMed]
50. Pulgaron, E.R.; Delamater, A.M. Obesity and Type 2 Diabetes in children: Epidemiology and Treatment. *Curr. Diab. Rep.* **2014**, *14*. [CrossRef] [PubMed]

51. Maffeis, C.; Banzato, C.; Talamini, G. Waist-to-Height Ratio, a Useful Index to Identify High Metabolic Risk in Overweight children. *J. Pediatr.* **2008**, *152*, 207–213.e2. [CrossRef] [PubMed]
52. Khoury, M.; Manlhiot, C.; McCrindle, B.W. Role of the waist/height ratio in the cardiometabolic risk assessment of children classified by body mass index. *J. Am. Coll. Cardiol.* **2013**, *62*, 742–751. [CrossRef] [PubMed]
53. Cominato, L.; Di Biagio, G.F.; Lellis, D.; Franco, R.R.; Mancini, M.C.; de Melo, M.E. Obesity Prevention: Strategies and Challenges in Latin America. *Curr. Obes. Rep.* **2018**. [CrossRef] [PubMed]
54. Kline, L.; Jones-Smith, J.; Jaime Miranda, J.; Pratt, M.; Reis, R.S.; Rivera, J.A.; Sallis, J.F.; Popkin, B.M. A research agenda to guide progress on childhood obesity prevention in Latin America. *Obes. Rev. Off. J. Int. Assoc. Study Obes.* **2017**, *18* (Suppl. 2), 19–27. [CrossRef] [PubMed]
55. Lytle, L.A.; Nichaman, M.Z.; Obarzanek, E.; Glovsky, E.; Montgomery, D.; Nicklas, T.; Zive, M.; Feldman, H. Validation of 24-hour recalls assisted by food records in third-grade children. The CATCH Collaborative Group. *J. Am. Diet. Assoc.* **1993**, *93*, 1431–1436. [CrossRef]

© 2018 by the authors. Licensee MDPI, Basel, Switzerland. This article is an open access article distributed under the terms and conditions of the Creative Commons Attribution (CC BY) license (http://creativecommons.org/licenses/by/4.0/).

Article

Growth Pattern, Resting Energy Expenditure, and Nutrient Intake of Children with Food Allergies

Enza D'Auria [1], Valentina Fabiano [1,*], Simona Bertoli [2], Giorgio Bedogni [3], Alessandra Bosetti [1], Erica Pendezza [1], Marco Ugo Andrea Sartorio [1], Alessandro Leone [2], Angela Spadafranca [2], Barbara Borsani [1], Francesco Stucchi [1], Alberto Battezzati [2] and Gian Vincenzo Zuccotti [1]

1. Pediatric Department, Vittore Buzzi Children's Hospital, Università degli Studi di Milano, via Castelvetro 32, 20154 Milan, Italy; enza.dauria@unimi.it (E.D.); alessandra.bosetti@asst-fbf-sacco.it (A.B.); erica.pendezza@unimi.it (E.P.); marco.sartorio@unimi.it (M.U.A.S); barbara.borsani@unimi.it (B.B.); francesco.stucchi@studenti.unimi.it (F.S.); gianvincenzo.zuccotti@unimi.it (G.V.Z.)
2. International Center for the Assessment of Nutritional Status (ICANS), Department of Food, Environmental and Nutritional Sciences (DeFENS), Università degli Studi di Milano, Via Sandro Botticelli 21, 20133 Milan, Italy; simona.bertoli@unimi.it (S.B.); alessandro.leone1@unimi.it (A.L.); angela.spadafranca@unimi.it (A.S.); alberto.battezzati@unimi.it (A.B.)
3. Clinical Epidemiology Unit, Liver Research Center, AREA Science park, Strada Statale 14, km 163.5, 34012 Trieste, Italy; giorgiobedogni@gmail.com
* Correspondence: valentina.fabiano@unimi.it; Tel.: +39-025-799-5324

Received: 23 November 2018; Accepted: 15 January 2019; Published: 22 January 2019

Abstract: Growth impairment has been reported in children with food allergies (FA). However, the available data on the dietary intake of FA children are controversial, and no data are available on their resting energy expenditure (REE). The aim of this study was to test whether REE differs between FA and healthy children. In this study, 30 FA children were matched by sex and age, with 31 healthy controls using coarsened exact matching (CEM). Their REE was measured by indirect calorimetry (IC). Energy and macronutrient intake were evaluated using a three-day dietary record. Between-group comparisons were performed by robust median regression using CEM-related weights. The association of REE with allergies was also evaluated using robust median regression models. Anthropometric measurements, REE, and nutrient intake were similar in FA children and matched controls. Taking into account the association of REE with gender and age, a statistically significant but biologically negligible association was detected between median REE and allergy status (+9% in FA children). In conclusion, we did not find any biologically relevant difference in REE, anthropometry, and dietary intake in children with FA compared to healthy children.

Keywords: resting energy expenditure; indirect calorimetry; food allergy; food intake; children

1. Introduction

The prevalence of food allergies (FA) as detected by an oral food challenge is 7–8% in Europe [1] and 8–10% in the USA and Australia [2,3]. The foods most commonly involved in FA are cow's milk, hen's eggs, peanuts, tree nuts, and wheat [4]. The mainstay treatment of FA is the avoidance of culprit food, the so called "avoidance diet", because eating this food may trigger symptoms and, less frequently, produce life-threatening consequences such as anaphylaxis [5].

Recently, much effort has been directed toward a personalized nutritional approach to FA, including advice to avoid unnecessary elimination diets. This is especially important in children because of their sensitivity of growth to nutritional deficiencies. The impact of FA on growth has been investigated by different studies with controversial findings. While some studies have shown growth impairment in FA infants and young children [6–10], other studies found no FA impact on growth [11–13], even in children with multiple food allergies [12]. Such discrepant results may be explained by the different case-mix of patients as well as by the provision of dietary advice given by dieticians in some studies [12,13]. Specific food effects are, however, not easy to rule out. For instance, some studies have shown that the avoidance of cow milk may negatively affect the growth of infants and young children [9,14]. However, a recent retrospective study found no difference in the growth of FA and healthy children, irrespective of the number of foods eliminated, except for the children suffering from cow's milk allergy (CMA) [15]. The effect of atopic co-morbidities on growth and food avoidance has been addressed by only a few studies, focusing mostly on atopic dermatitis [16,17] and asthma [18–21]. Contrasting findings have also been reported on the nutrient intake of FA vs. healthy children, with some studies showing lower energy and protein intake in the former [6,9,22], and other studies showing growth impairment in the former, with energy and protein intake similar to that of the latter [8]. Different hypotheses have been put forward to explain such findings, including nutrient loss due to sustained intestinal or skin inflammation despite the avoidance diet [6,12,23]. The effective nutritional requirements of FA children are presently unknown.

One of the major challenges of modern clinical nutrition is the implementation of tailored nutritional recommendations. In this view, the first step toward a personalized nutritional approach is a reliable knowledge of the patient's energy expenditure. The reference method for measuring resting energy expenditure (REE) is indirect calorimetry (IC) [24,25]. However, IC is often not available in clinical practice because of its cost and the need for trained personnel [26]. For these reasons, REE is often estimated by predictive equations. Such equations are easy to use but have large individual errors and must be employed with caution [27]. Importantly, for the tailored nutritional approach, no study so far has measured REE by IC in FA children.

The aim of this study was therefore to measure REE by IC in FA children and compare it to that of sex- and age-matched children.

2. Materials and Methods

2.1. Study Design

We performed a case-control study where children with FA ("cases") were matched by sex and age to healthy children ("controls").

The FA children were enrolled between May 2017 and October 2018, and were selected from the children who were referred to the allergy unit of the Vittore Buzzi Children's Hospital (Milano, Italy) because of suspected FA. Their FA were definitively diagnosed by an oral food challenge in children with suggestive clinical history and positive prick tests or food-specific immunoglobulins, with the exception of those children with known anaphylaxis. The FA children were eligible for the study if they (1) had a diagnosis of FA by oral food challenge, (2) had been on an avoidance diet for at least 6 months and, (3) were able to perform IC.

Control children were selected from a larger sample of children recruited from the general population between April 2017 and October 2018. Control children were eligible for the study if they (1) did not have FA, (2) were free of known acute (e.g., influenza) or chronic (e.g., diabetes) diseases, and (3) were able to perform IC.

All children underwent IC and anthropometry, and their parents were given a prospective three-day food dietary record as described below.

The study was performed in accordance with the Declaration of Helsinki, and the parents of each child gave their written informed consent. The study protocol was approved by the local ethical committee (2018/ST/267).

2.2. Resting Energy Expenditure

We used an open-circuit ventilated-hood calorimeter (Sensor Medics 29, Anaheim, CA, USA) to measure oxygen consumption (VO_2) and carbon dioxide production (VCO_2). Such measurements were taken in a thermoneutral environment (ambient temperature 24 to 26 °C) devoid of external stimuli. At the beginning of each test, the calorimeter was calibrated with two different gas mixtures (26% O_2 and 74% N_2; 16% O_2, 4% CO_2 and 80% N_2). The children had been fasting for at least 8 h and had had a stable respiratory function for at least 1 h before performing IC. The data collection time was at least 20 min. A run-in time of at least 5 min was used to obtain stable measures and to allow the children to get used to the canopy and the instrument noise. The presence of the steady state was determined by 5 consecutive minutes in which VO_2 and VCO_2 variations were less than 10%. Their REE was estimated using the Weir equation [28].

2.3. Anthropometric Measurements

Anthropometric measurements were collected by trained dietitians following standard guidelines [29]. Body weight was measured to the nearest 100 g with a beam scale, and body height to the nearest 0.1 cm using a vertical stadiometer. BMI was calculated as weight (kg)/height $(m)^2$. The standard deviation scores (SDS) of weight, height, and BMI were calculated using WHO reference data. Biceps, triceps, subscapular, and suprailiac skinfolds were measured using a Tanner-Whitehouse caliper (Holtain Ltd., UK). Each skinfold was measured three times, and the mean value was used for analysis.

2.4. Nutrient Intake

A prospective three-day food dietary record was used to measure nutrient intake. The parents were trained by a dietitian on how to fill in the diary of two working days and one weekend day. Each record consisted of one page, including three main meals (breakfast, lunch, and dinner) and two snacks (mid-morning and mid-afternoon). The parents were asked to report the food consumed; its quantity; and the time of its consumption, including a detailed description (e.g., brand name, ingredients used, recipe, and cooking method) and the amount of each item. They were asked to weigh each single food item, or each ingredient of a homemade recipe, as well as leftovers and to record all the weights in the food diary. When food or beverage weighing was not possible, parents were instructed to use common instruments, such as spoons, graduated cups, or bowls, to quantify them. Energy and macronutrient intake (protein, carbohydrates, and fats) were estimated from the three-day food data using the Metadieta software (Me.Te.Da. S.r.l., San Benedetto Del Tronto, Italy).

2.5. Statistical Analysis

Coarsened exact matching (CEM) was used to match cases to controls on the basis of sex (same) and age (within 1 year) [30]. Descriptive statistics of continuous variables were reported as percentiles because most of them had non-Gaussian distributions.

Between-group comparisons were performed by robust median regression (quantile regression of the 50th percentile) using CEM-related weights [31]. We investigated the association of REE with allergies by using three pre-specified median regression models:

Model (1) an univariable model using allergies as the predictor (discrete; 0 = no, 1 = yes);

Model (2) a multivariable model adding sex (discrete; 0 = female, 1 = male) and age (continuous, years) to the predictor of Model 1 and;

Model (3) a multivariable model adding weight (continuous, kg) to the predictors of model 2.

Model 1 tested whether there is a difference in REE between allergic and non-allergic children; model 2 evaluated the contribution of age and gender independently from allergies; and, lastly, model 3 tested whether allergies added to the most commonly employed predictors of REE, i.e., sex, age, and body weight. The linearity of the association between REE and continuous predictors was tested using fractional polynomials [32]. As post-hoc analyses, we performed quantile regressions of the 25th and 75th percentiles, using the same predictors utilized for the 50th percentile regression (see above). All regression analyses took CEM into account by using CEM-related weights and robust 95%

confidence intervals. Statistical analysis was performed using Stata 15.1 (Stata Corporation, College Station, TX, USA) together with the user-written CEM command [33].

3. Results

Using CEM, we matched 30 FA children with 31 healthy children.

Among the FA children, 10 were allergic to one food, six to two foods, and 14 to more than two foods. The foods most commonly responsible for FA were tree nuts ($n = 20$), eggs ($n = 12$), cow's milk ($n = 11$), fish ($n = 9$), fruits ($n = 7$), peanuts ($n = 5$), legumes ($n = 4$), sesame ($n = 2$), and vegetables ($n = 1$). Among the FA children, six had ongoing and five had previous atopic dermatitis, while nine had ongoing and one had previous asthma.

Table 1 gives the distribution of sex and BMI in control and FA children.

Table 1. Distribution of sex and body mass index (BMI) of the children.

	Controls ($n = 31$)		Food Allergies ($n = 30$)	
	n	%	n	%
Sex				
Female	18	56.7	17	56.7
Male	13	43.3	13	43.3
Total	31	100.0	30	100.0
BMI class according to World Health Organization (WHO) averages				
Underweight	1	3.9	1	3.3
Normal weight	25	82.1	23	76.7
Overweight	0	1.3	3	10.0
Obese	4	12.8	3	10.0
Total	31*	100.0	30	100.0

* Partials do not sum to 31 because of rounding (matching strata).

Table 2 gives the anthropometric measurements, REE, and the nutrient intake of FA and control children.

Table 2. Anthropometric measurements, resting energy expenditure (REE), and nutrient intake of the children.

	Controls ($n = 31$)			Food Allergies ($n = 30$)		
	P_{25}	P_{50}	P_{75}	P_{25}	P_{50}	P_{75}
Age (years)	6	7	9	6	7	9
Weight (kg)	20.7	23.7	37.9	21.2	25.1	31.0
Weight (SDS WHO)	−0.65	0.16	0.74	−0.73	0.08	0.78
Height or length (m)	1.20	1.24	1.38	1.18	1.26	1.34
Height (SDS WHO)	−0.16	0.62	1.17	−0.76	0.14	0.83
BMI (kg/m^2)	14.7	15.4	16.1	14.8	15.7	16.9
BMI (SDS WHO)	−1.01	−0.08	0.31	−0.62	−0.25	0.69
Triceps skinfold (mm)	8	9	12	9	11	14
Biceps skinfold (mm)	5	6	7	6	7	10

Table 2. Cont.

	Controls (n = 31)			Food Allergies (n = 30)		
Subscapular skinfold (mm)	5	5	6	5	6	8
Suprailiac skinfold (mm)	5	6	10	4	6	10
Sum of 4 skinfolds (mm)	26	28	34	25	30	45
REE (kcal/day)	926	1073	1180	984	1103	1251
REE (kcal/kg weight/day)	33	43	45	37	44	49
Energy (kcal/day)	1313	1490	1733	1419	1712	2056
Energy (kcal/kg weight/day)	57	65	72	55	63	79
Proteins (g)	44	52	64	45	56	70
Fats (g)	44	58	69	54	64	71
Carbohydrates (g)	167	197	229	172	226	252
Proteins (% Energy)	12.6	13.3	14.7	12.4	13.8	15.3
Fats (% Energy)	30.0	31.3	35.9	30.3	34.0	38.1
Carbohydrates (% Energy)	49.6	55.6	56.4	47.4	52.6	56.0
Proteins (g/kg weight/day)	1.8	2.1	2.5	1.8	2.2	2.7

Abbreviations: P_{25} = 25th percentile; P_{50} = 50th percentile (median); P_{75}: 75th percentile; SDS = standard deviation score; WHO = World Health Organization; BMI = body mass index; REE = resting energy expenditure.

The anthropometric measurements, REE, and nutrient intake were similar in FA and control children (median regression, $p > 0.05$ for all comparisons).

Table 3 gives the 50th percentile (median) regression models that were used to investigate the association between REE and food allergies.

Table 3. Association between food allergies and resting energy expenditure (REE): 50th percentile (median) regression equations.

	Model 1 (kcal/day)	Model 2 (kcal/day)	Model 3 (kcal/day)
Food allergies (yes)	34 [−132 to 200]	88 * [14 to 163]	99 ** [29 to 168]
Age (years)		59 *** [42 to 77]	12 * [0 to 24]
Sex (male)		114 * [27 to 200]	94 *** [41 to 147]
Weight (kg)			13 *** [10 to 17]
Intercept	1073 *** [939 to 1207]	513 *** [327 to 698]	553 *** [423 to 682]
N	61	61	61

Abbreviations: * $p < 0.05$, ** $p < 0.01$, *** $p < 0.001$. Values are medians and robust CEM-weighted 95% confidence intervals (in brackets). As an instance of how to predict REE using these equations, consider the case of a seven-yr-old allergic boy weighing 25 kg. Using Model 3, his median REE can be estimated as follows: (99 × 1) + (12 × 7) + (94 × 1) + (13 × 25) + 553 = 1155 kcal. (Note that these equations take the matching of FA and control children into account via matching-related weights, see statistical analysis for details).

No association between FA and energy intake was apparent from Model 1. Taking into account the expected association of REE with gender and age as done by Model 2, a statistically significant but biologically negligible association between allergies and REE becomes evident (8% of total REE calculated as 88/1107 kcal, where the denominator is the REE of the whole sample). A similar difference persisted after the expected association with weight was taken into account by Model 3 (9% calculated as 99/1107 kcal, where the denominator is the REE of the whole sample).

Table 4 gives the 25th percentile regression models used to investigate the association between REE and food allergies.

There was no statistically significant association between REE and allergies in any of the models. According to Model 3, allergies accounted for 1% of REE, calculated as 13/950 kcal, where the denominator is the REE of the whole sample.

Table 5 gives the 75th percentile regression models used to investigate the association between REE and food allergies.

Table 4. Association between food allergies and resting energy expenditure (REE): 25th percentile regression equations.

	Model 1 (kcal/day)	Model 2 (kcal/day)	Model 3 (kcal/day)
Food allergies (yes)	58 [−111 to 227]	37 [−92 to 165]	13 [−85 to 111]
Age (years)		68 *** [42 to 94]	23 [−2 to 47]
Sex (male)		120 [−5 to 246]	81 ** [20 to 141]
Weight (kg)			14 *** [9 to 19]
Intercept	926 *** [823 to 1029]	402 ** [153 to 650]	410 *** [252 to 569]
N	61	61	61

Abbreviations: ** $p < 0.01$, *** $p < 0.001$. Values are 25th percentiles and robust CEM-weighted 95% confidence intervals (in brackets).

Table 5. Association between food allergies and resting energy expenditure (REE): 75th percentile regression equations.

	Model 1 (kcal/day)	Model 2 (kcal/day)	Model 3 (kcal/day)
Food allergies (yes)	71 [−123 to 265]	69 [−49 to 187]	115 ** [45 to 185]
Age (years)		49 ** [20 to 79]	9 [−29 to 46]
Sex (male)		26 [−86 to 138]	102 * [18 to 186]
Weight (kg)			13 * [1 to 26]
Intercept	1180 *** [1033 to 1327]	729 *** [496 to 963]	595 *** [381 to 810]
N	61	61	61

Abbreviations: * $p < 0.05$, ** $p < 0.01$, *** $p < 0.001$. Values are 75th percentiles and robust CEM-weighted 95% confidence intervals (in brackets).

According to Model 3, allergies accounted for 9% of REE, calculated as 115/1243 kcal, where the denominator is the 75th percentile REE of the whole sample.

4. Discussion

In this matched case-control study, we found no biologically relevant difference in REE, anthropometry, and nutrient intake of FA compared to control children. It must be pointed out that our FA children were given dietary advice according to Italian dietary guidelines [34] and were regularly followed-up, which may explain why their anthropometric status and nutrient intake did not differ from that of healthy controls. However, our data did not support the hypothesis that REE may differ in FA compared to control children because of the underlying disease.

FA are defined as "an adverse health effect arising from a specific immune response that occurs reproducibly on exposure to a given food" [35] and encompass a range of disorders from IgE-mediated anaphylaxis to delayed cell-mediated reactions affecting the gastrointestinal tract. The mainstay treatment of FA is the avoidance diet. Food exclusion is highly effective but impairs the quality of life of FA patients and puts them at risk of eating an unbalanced diet. A tailored dietary management of FA children is the key to ensure adequate growth [4]. Such management includes the evaluation of REE, which is the main determinant of energy expenditure in physiological conditions [27].

This study is the first one to measure REE in FA compared to healthy children. Our data did not support the hypothesis that REE may be increased in FA children because of the underlying disease, e.g., by the underlying inflammatory status. Albeit statistically significant, the estimate of 9% of REE attributable to allergies, obtained by a multivariable model based on gender, age, and weight, is too low to be biologically relevant, being very close to the measurement error of IC.

Our study had some limitations. The first limitation was its small sample size. This is partly explained by the strict matching criteria, which were nonetheless a point of strength of this study. Despite the strict matching by gender and age, gender and age actually contributed to REE independently from allergies. A second limitation of this study was the lack of data on the physical activity of the children, even if the median SDS of weight and BMI were well within normal limits, and being overweight and obese were similarly common in FA and healthy children. A third limitation was the lack of data on children aged ≤4 years, owing to the fact that is very difficult to perform IC on such children in a reproducible manner. Because most studies of FA were performed on infants and children younger than ours, a direct comparison with previous data may not be possible [6–8,10].

In contrast with previous studies showing growth impairment in children with FA [6–10], we did not observe biologically important differences in anthropometry and nutrient intake between FA and control children. In particular, protein intake was similar in FA and healthy children. These results are in keeping with a previous study of growth and nutrient intake [36] and with previous growth studies [9,12] of FA children. Our FA children were being regularly followed-up and they were given dietary advice following the Italian dietary guidelines [34], which may explain why their anthropometric status and nutrient intake did not differ from that of healthy controls. The same finding was reported by other studies of FA vs. non-FA children [9,12].

As is standard in our clinical practice, the parents of the enrolled children were instructed not only about the foods to avoid but also how to replace them and to avoid unnecessary exclusion diets. For instance, except for one child, all children with CMA were allowed to eat beef, if they were prick by prick negative, because most CMA children can tolerate beef [37]. Likewise, given the low cross-reactivity among legumes, children with clinical evidence of reactivity to peanuts were advised not to routinely avoid other legumes if the corresponding sIgE were negative. When sIgE were positive for legumes, an oral food challenge was performed to exclude a concomitant legume allergy [38]. Even though our understanding of cross-reactivity between different foods is rapidly increasing, unnecessary elimination diets are still very common in clinical practice [39]. Moreover, the diet of CMA children was, in all but three cases, expanded by including heated milk, which allowed them to consume selected baked products and snacks increasing their energy intake [40,41]. These and other dietary personalization strategies are central to the management of FA [42,43].

5. Conclusions

In conclusion, in FA children regularly followed with personalized dietary advice, we did not find any difference in REE, anthropometry, and dietary intake as compared to sex- and age-matched control children. Because this is the only study of the REE of FA children available so far, further studies are certainly needed to better understand energy expenditure in FA.

Author Contributions: Conceptualization, E.D., G.V.Z., and A.B.; Data curation, E.D, A.L., and G.B.; Formal analysis, G.B.; Methodology, E.D., S.B., A.B., E.P., A.L., A.S., B.B., and F.S.; Supervision, G.V.Z. and A.B.; Writing—original draft, E.D., V.F., E.P., M.U.A.S., A.L., and G.B.; Writing—review and editing, E.D., V.F., S.B., E.P., M.U.A.S., A.L., and G.B.

Funding: This research received no external funding.

Conflicts of Interest: The authors declare no conflict of interest.

References

1. Protudjer, J.L.; Vetander, M.; Kull, I.; Hedling, G.; van Hage, M.; Wickman, M.; Bergstrom, A. Food-related symptoms and food allergy in Swedish children from early life to adolesence. *PLoS ONE* **2016**, *11*, 1–13. [CrossRef] [PubMed]
2. Gupta, R.S.; Springston, E.E.; Warrier, M.R.; Smith, B.; Kumar, R.; Pongracic, J.; Holl, J.L. The prevalence, severity, and distribution of childhood food allergy in the United States. *Pediatrics* **2011**, *128*, e9–e17. [CrossRef] [PubMed]
3. Osborne, N.J.; Koplin, J.J.; Martin, P.E.; Gurrin, L.C.; Lowe, A.J.; Matheson, M.C.; Ponsonby, A.L.; Wake, M.; Tang, M.L.; Dharmage, S.C.; et al. Prevalence of challenge-proven IgE-mediated food allergy using population-based sampling and predetermined challenge criteria in infants. *J. Allergy Clin. Immunol.* **2011**, *127*, 668–676.e2. [CrossRef] [PubMed]

4. Venter, C.; Groetch, M.; Netting, M.; Meyer, R. A patient-specific approach to develop an exclusion diet to manage food allergy in infants and children. *Clin. Exp. Allergy* **2018**, *48*, 121–137. [CrossRef] [PubMed]
5. Sova, C.; Feuling, M.B.; Baumler, M.; Gleason, L.; Tam, J.S.; Zafra, H.; Goday, P.S. Systematic review of nutrient intake and growth in children with multiple IgE-mediated food allergies. *Nutr. Clin. Pract.* **2013**, *28*, 669–675. [CrossRef] [PubMed]
6. Isolauri, E.; Sutas, Y.; Salo, M.K.; Isosomppi, R.; Kaila, M. Elimination diet in cow's milk allergy: Risk for impaired growth in young children. *J. Pediatr.* **1998**, *132*, 1004–1009. [CrossRef]
7. Christie, L.; Hine, R.J.; Parker, J.G.; Burks, W. Food allergies in children affect nutrient intake and growth. *J. Am. Diet. Assoc.* **2002**, *102*, 1648–1651. [CrossRef]
8. Flammarion, S.; Santos, C.; Guimber, D.; Jouannic, L.; Thumerelle, C.; Gottrand, F.; Deschildre, A. Diet and nutritional status of children with food allergies. *Pediatr. Allergy Immunol.* **2011**, *22*, 161–165. [CrossRef]
9. Robbins, K.A.; Wood, R.A.; Keet, C.A. Milk allergy is associated with decreased growth in US children. *J. Allergy Clin. Immunol.* **2014**, *134*, 1466–1468.e6. [CrossRef]
10. Vieira, M.C.; Morais, M.B.; Spolidoro, J.V.; Toporovski, M.S.; Cardoso, A.L.; Araujo, G.T.; Nudelman, V.; Fonseca, M.C. A survey on clinical presentation and nutritional status of infants with suspected cow' milk allergy. *BMC Pediatr.* **2010**, *10*, 25. [CrossRef]
11. Meyer, R.; De Koker, C.; Dziubak, R.; Venter, C.; Dominguez-Ortega, G.; Cutts, R.; Yerlett, N.; Skrapak, A.K.; Fox, A.T.; Shah, N. Malnutrition in children with food allergies in the UK. *J. Hum. Nutr. Diet.* **2014**, *27*, 227–235. [CrossRef] [PubMed]
12. Meyer, R.; De Koker, C.; Dziubak, R.; Godwin, H.; Dominguez-Ortega, G.; Chebar Lozinsky, A.; Skrapac, A.K.; Gholmie, Y.; Reeve, K.; Shah, N. The impact of the elimination diet on growth and nutrient intake in children with food protein induced gastrointestinal allergies. *Clin. Transl. Allergy* **2016**, *6*, 25. [CrossRef] [PubMed]
13. Berry, M.J.; Adams, J.; Voutilainen, H.; Feustel, P.J.; Celestin, J.; Jarvinen, K.M. Impact of elimination diets on growth and nutritional status in children with multiple food allergies. *Pediatr. Allergy Immunol.* **2015**, *26*, 133–138. [CrossRef] [PubMed]
14. Tuokkola, J.; Luukkainen, P.; Nevalainen, J.; Ahonen, S.; Toppari, J.; Ilonen, J.; Veijola, R.; Knip, M.; Virtanen, S.M.; Kaila, M. Eliminating cows' milk, but not wheat, barley or rye, increases the risk of growth deceleration and nutritional inadequacies. *Acta Paediatr.* **2017**, *106*, 1142–1149. [CrossRef] [PubMed]
15. Mehta, H.; Ramesh, M.; Feuille, E.; Groetch, M.; Wang, J. Growth comparison in children with and without food allergies in 2 different demographic populations. *J. Pediatr.* **2014**, *165*, 842–848. [CrossRef] [PubMed]
16. Beck, C.; Koplin, J.; Dharmage, S.; Wake, M.; Gurrin, L.; McWilliam, V.; Tang, M.; Sun, C.; Foskey, R.; Allen, K.J. Persistent Food Allergy and Food Allergy Coexistent with Eczema Is Associated with Reduced Growth in the First 4 Years of Life. *J. Allergy Clin. Immunol. Pract.* **2016**, *4*, 248–256. [CrossRef] [PubMed]
17. Jhamnani, R.D.; Levin, S.; Rasooly, M.; Stone, K.D.; Milner, J.D.; Nelson, C.; DiMaggio, T.; Jones, N.; Guerrerio, A.L.; Frischmeyer-Guerrerio, P.A. Impact of food allergy on the growth of children with moderate-severe atopic dermatitis. *J. Allergy Clin. Immunol.* **2018**, *141*, 1526–1529. [CrossRef]
18. Agertoft, L.; Pedersen, S. Effect of long-term treatment with inhaled budesonide on adult height in children with asthma. *N. Engl. J. Med.* **2000**, *343*, 1064–1069. [CrossRef]
19. Kelly, H.W.; Strunk, R.C.; Donithan, M.; Bloomberg, G.R.; McWilliams, B.C.; Szefler, S. Growth and bone density in children with mild-moderate asthma: A cross-sectional study in children entering the Childhood Asthma Management Program (CAMP). *J. Pediatr.* **2003**, *142*, 286–291. [CrossRef]
20. Szefler, S.; Weiss, S.; Tonascia, J.; Adkinson, N.F.; Bender, B.; Cherniack, R.; Donithan, M.; Kelly, H.W.; Reisman, J.; Shapiro, G.G.; et al. Long-term effects of budesonide or nedocromil in children with asthma. *N. Engl. J. Med.* **2000**, *343*, 1054–1063. [CrossRef]
21. Guilbert, T.W.; Mauger, D.T.; Allen, D.B.; Zeiger, R.S.; Lemanske, R.F., Jr.; Szefler, S.J.; Strunk, R.C.; Bacharier, L.B.; Covar, R.; Sorkness, C.A.; et al. Growth of preschool children at high risk for asthma 2 years after discontinuation of fluticasone. *J. Allergy Clin. Immunol.* **2011**, *128*, 956–963. [CrossRef] [PubMed]
22. Tiainen, J.M.; Nuutinen, O.M.; Kalavainen, M.P. Diet and nutritional status in children with cow's milk allergy. *Eur. J. Clin. Nutr.* **1995**, *49*, 605–612. [PubMed]
23. Jarvinen, K.M.; Konstantinou, G.N.; Pilapil, M.; Arrieta, M.C.; Noone, S.; Sampson, H.A.; Meddings, J.; Nowak-Wegrzyn, A. Intestinal permeability in children with food allergy on specific elimination diets. *Pediatr. Allergy Immunol.* **2013**, *24*, 589–595. [CrossRef] [PubMed]

24. Bursztein, S.; Elwyn, H.E.; Askanazi, J.; Kinney, J.M. *Energy Metabolism, Indirect Calorimetry, and Nutrition*; William & Wilkins: Baltimore, MD, USA, 1989.
25. Takala, J.; Meriläinen, P. *Handbook of Gas Exchange and Indirect Calorimetry*; Datex Division Instrumentarium Corp: Helsinki, Finland, 1991.
26. Wooley, J.A. Indirect calorimetry: Applications in practice. *Respir. Care Clin. N. Am.* **2006**, *12*, 619–633. [CrossRef] [PubMed]
27. Da Rocha, E.E.; Alves, V.G.; Silva, M.H.; Chiesa, C.A.; da Fonseca, R.B. Can measured resting energy expenditure be estimated by formulae in daily clinical nutrition practice? *Curr. Opin. Clin. Nutr. Metab. Care* **2005**, *8*, 319–328. [CrossRef] [PubMed]
28. Weir, J.B. New methods for calculating metabolic rate with special reference to protein metabolism. 1949. *Nutrition* **1990**, *6*, 213–221. [PubMed]
29. Lohman, T.G.; Roche, A.F.; Martorell, R. *Anthropometric Standardization Reference Manual*; Human Kinetics Books: Champaign, IL, USA, 1988.
30. Iacus, S.M.; King, G.; Porro, G. Multivariate Matching Methods That Are Monotonic Imbalance Bounding. *J. Am. Stat. Assoc.* **2011**, *106*, 345–361. [CrossRef]
31. Koenker, R. *Quantile Regression*; Cambridge University Press: Cambridge, UK, 2005.
32. Royston, P.; Sauerbrei, W. *Multivariable Model-Building: A Pragmatic Approach to Regression Anaylsis Based on Fractional Polynomials for Modelling Continuous Variables*; John Wiley & Sons: Chichester, UK, 2008.
33. Blackwell, M.; Iacus, S.; King, G.; Porro, G. cem: Coarsened exact matching in Stata. *Stata J.* **2009**, *4*, 524–546. [CrossRef]
34. Guidelines for Healthy Italian Food Habits. Available online: http://www.fao.org/nutrition/education/food-dietary-guidelines/regions/countries/italy/en/ (accessed on 7 January 2019).
35. Sicherer, S.H.; Sampson, H.A. Food allergy: Epidemiology, pathogenesis, diagnosis, and treatment. *J. Allergy Clin. Immunol.* **2014**, *133*, 291–307. [CrossRef]
36. Maslin, K.; Venter, C.; MacKenzie, H.; Vlieg-Boerstra, B.; Dean, T.; Sommer, I. Comparison of nutrient intake in adolescents and adults with and without food allergies. *J. Hum. Nutr. Diet.* **2018**, *31*, 209–217. [CrossRef]
37. Martelli, A.; De Chiara, A.; Corvo, M.; Restani, P.; Fiocchi, A. Beef allergy in children with cow's milk allergy; cow's milk allergy in children with beef allergy. *Ann. Allergy Asthma Immunol.* **2002**, *89*, 38–43. [CrossRef]
38. Sampson, H.A. Utility of food-specific IgE concentrations in predicting symptomatic food allergy. *J. Allergy Clin. Immunol.* **2001**, *107*, 891–896. [CrossRef] [PubMed]
39. D'Auria, E.; Mameli, C.; Piras, C.; Cococcioni, L.; Urbani, A.; Zuccotti, G.V.; Roncada, P. Precision medicine in cow's milk allergy: Proteomics perspectives from allergens to patients. *J. Proteomics* **2018**, *188*, 173–180. [CrossRef]
40. Nowak-Wegrzyn, A.; Bloom, K.A.; Sicherer, S.H.; Shreffler, W.G.; Noone, S.; Wanich, N.; Sampson, H.A. Tolerance to extensively heated milk in children with cow's milk allergy. *J. Allergy Clin. Immunol.* **2008**, *122*, 342–347. [CrossRef] [PubMed]
41. Leonard, S.A.; Caubet, J.C.; Kim, J.S.; Groetch, M.; Nowak-Wegrzyn, A. Baked milk- and egg-containing diet in the management of milk and egg allergy. *J. Allergy Clin. Immunol. Pract.* **2015**, *3*, 13–23. [CrossRef] [PubMed]
42. Muraro, A.; Werfel, T.; Hoffmann-Sommergruber, K.; Roberts, G.; Beyer, K.; Bindslev-Jensen, C.; Cardona, V.; Dubois, A.; duToit, G.; Eigenmann, P.; et al. EAACI food allergy and anaphylaxis guidelines: Diagnosis and management of food allergy. *Allergy* **2014**, *69*, 1008–1025. [CrossRef] [PubMed]
43. Berni Canani, R.; Leone, L.; D'Auria, E.; Riva, E.; Nocerino, R.; Ruotolo, S.; Terrin, G.; Cosenza, L.; Di Costanzo, M.; Passariello, A.; et al. The effects of dietary counseling on children with food allergy: A prospective, multicenter intervention study. *J. Acad. Nutr. Diet.* **2014**, *114*, 1432–1439. [CrossRef]

© 2019 by the authors. Licensee MDPI, Basel, Switzerland. This article is an open access article distributed under the terms and conditions of the Creative Commons Attribution (CC BY) license (http://creativecommons.org/licenses/by/4.0/).

Article

Congruent Validity of Resting Energy Expenditure Predictive Equations in Young Adults

Francisco J. Amaro-Gahete [1,2,*], Guillermo Sanchez-Delgado [2], Juan M.A. Alcantara [2], Borja Martinez-Tellez [2,3], Victoria Muñoz-Hernandez [2], Elisa Merchan-Ramirez [2], Marie Löf [4], Idoia Labayen [5] and Jonatan R. Ruiz [2,*]

1. Departament of Medical Physiology, School of Medicine, University of Granada, 18071 Granada, Spain
2. PROmoting FITness and Health through physical activity research group (PROFITH), Department of Physical Education and Sports, Faculty of Sport Sciences, University of Granada, 18071 Granada, Spain; gsanchezdelgado@ugr.es (G.S.-D.); juanma.alcantara@hotmail.com (J.M.A.A.); borjammt@gmail.com (B.M.-T.); mariavmuher@gmail.com (V.M.-H.); elymerchan@hotmail.com (E.M.-R.)
3. Department of Medicine, division of Endocrinology, and Einthoven Laboratory for Experimental Vascular Medicine, Leiden University Medical Center, Leiden, Post Zone C7Q, P.O. Box 9600, 2300 RC Leiden, The Netherlands
4. Department of Biosciences and Nutrition, Karolinska Institutet, SE-141 83 Huddinge, Sweden; marie.lof@ki.se
5. Institute for Innovation & Sustainable Development in Food Chain (IS-FOOD), Public University of Navarra, 31006 Pamplona, Spain; idoia.labayen@unavarra.es
* Correspondence: amarof@ugr.es (F.J.A.-G.); ruizj@ugr.es (J.R.R.); Tel.: +34-958243540 (F.J.A.-G.)

Received: 26 December 2018; Accepted: 17 January 2019; Published: 22 January 2019

Abstract: Having valid and reliable resting energy expenditure (REE) estimations is crucial to establish reachable goals for dietary and exercise interventions. However, most of the REE predictive equations were developed some time ago and, as the body composition of the current population has changed, it is highly relevant to assess the validity of REE predictive equations in contemporary young adults. In addition, little is known about the role of sex and weight status on the validity of these predictive equations. Therefore, this study aimed to investigate the role of sex and weight status in congruent validity of REE predictive equations in young adults. A total of 132 young healthy adults (67.4% women, 18–26 years old) participated in the study. We measured REE by indirect calorimetry strictly following the standard procedures, and we compared it to 45 predictive equations. The most accurate equations were the following: (i) the Schofield and the "Food and Agriculture Organization of the United Nations/World Health Organization/United Nations" (FAO/WHO/UNU) equations in normal weight men; (ii) the Mifflin and FAO/WHO/UNU equations in normal weight women; (iii) the Livingston and Korth equations in overweight men; (iv) the Johnstone and Frankenfield equations in overweight women; (v) the Owen and Bernstein equations in obese men; and (vi) the Owen equation in obese women. In conclusion, the results of this study show that the best equation to estimate REE depends on sex and weight status in young healthy adults.

Keywords: metabolic rate; basal metabolism; indirect calorimetry; energy balance; obesity

---

1. Introduction

The main component of daily energy expenditure (60%–70%) is resting energy expenditure (REE) [1]. Having valid and reliable REE estimations is crucial to establish reachable goals for dietary and exercise interventions. For the majority of clinics and nutrition centers, it is difficult to get REE measures through indirect calorimetry, because of time constraints and the high cost of the devices. Thus, REE predictive equations are commonly used as an alternative method [2]. REE predictive equations have been used in healthy and unhealthy people, young and old adults of different ethnicities, and in people with a wide range of body weight and body composition characteristics [2–21].

Indirect calorimetry (IC) is considered the reference REE measurement technique [22]. In order to minimise possible estimation errors, the method requires strict measurement conditions and a correct procedure to analyse the IC data [23,24]. REE predictive equations are used in clinical practice, but some of them are specific for certain population groups, including different weight status or different ethnic groups [4,6,16,17,25]. Two predictive equations for young adults were recently validated [4,11], yet little is known about the role of sex and weight status on the validity of these predictive equations. Moreover, most of the REE predictive equations were developed some time ago and, as the body composition of the current population has changed [26], it is highly relevant to assess the validity of REE predictive equations in contemporary young adults.

In the present study, we systemically reviewed the available REE predictive equations including information on age, height, weight, sex, fat mass, and fat free mass. Then, we compared the measured versus estimated REE. Therefore, the purpose of this study was to investigate the role of sex and weight status in congruent validity of REE predictive equations in young adults.

2. Materials and Methods

2.1. Participants

A total of 132 participants (67.4% female) aged 18–26 years old participated in the study. The participants were enrolled in the ACTIBATE study (ClinicalTrials.gov ID:NCT02365129) [27]. The participants reported being engaged in less than 20 minutes on 3 days/week of physical activity, having had a stable weight over the last three months (body weight changes <3 kg), being free of medications or diseases that might interfere with REE measurement, and not being enrolled in a weight-loss program. Each participant provided both oral and written informed consent prior to the initiation of study procedures. The study was in accordance with the Helsinki Declaration and was approved by the Human Research Ethics Committee of both the University of Granada (n° 924) and Servicio Andaluz de Salud (Centro de Granada, CEI-Granada).

2.2. Body Composition

Body weight (± 10 g) and height (± 0.1 cm) were measured using a digital integrating scale (SECA 760, Hamburg, Germany) and a stadiometer (SECA 220, Hamburg, Germany). Body mass index (BMI) was calculated as weight (kg)/height (m^2). The participants were categorized as normal weight (BMI = 18.5–24.9 kg/m^2), overweight (BMI = 25–29.9 kg/m^2), and obese (BMI > 30 kg/m^2) [28]. We determined fat mass and lean mass by dual energy X-ray absorptiometry (Discovery Wi, Hologic, Inc., Bedford, MA, USA).

2.3. Assessment of REE through Indirect Calorimetry

REE was measured through IC strictly following current methodological recommendations [23,24]. The participants were instructed not to engage in any physical activity 48 h before the measurement and to arrive by car or bus at 08.15 in a fasting condition of at least 12 h.

The participants were evaluated in a peaceful and relaxing environment where temperature (22.8 ± 0.9 °C) and humidity ($43.6 \pm 6.6\%$) were controlled. The participants lay on a bed in a supine position and were covered by a sheet. Then, they were instructed to breathe normally, and not to fidget, talk, or sleep. After 30 min of rest, respiratory exchange measurements were determined using a CCM Express system (Med graphics Cardiorespiratory Diagnostic, Saint-Paul, MN, USA) in 59 participants (37 women) and using a CPX Ultima CardiO2 system (Medical Graphics Corp, St Paul, MN, USA) in 73 participants (52 women). Both measurements required the use of a neoprene facemask, equipped with a directconnect™ metabolic flow sensor (Medgraphics Corp, Saint Paul, MN, USA). The measurements took 30 min, and we selected the most stable five-consecutive-minute periods (after discarding the first five minutes) for analysis (Breeze Software, MGC Diagnostic®, Breeze Suite 8.1.0.54 SP7) [29,30]. REE was calculated by the Weir abbreviated equation (assuming negligible protein oxidation) and expressed as Kcal/day [31], as follows: REE = [3.9 (VO2) + 1.1 (VCO2)] * 1.44.

2.4. REE Predictive Equations

We conducted a systematic search for publications reporting REE predictive equations in PubMed and Web of Science. We combined the following keywords in every possible combination: 'energy metabolism', 'basal metabolism', and 'indirect calorimetry', and additional terms ('predict*', 'estimat*', 'equation*', and 'formula*').

We only retrieved equations based on the following criteria: (i) performed in adults; (ii) based on weight, height, age, sex, and/or fat free mass and fat mass. The exclusion criteria included (i) equation derived from patients' or athletes' data, and (ii) small sample size ($n < 50$). A total of 45 predictive equations (see Supplementary material Table S1) were included.

2.5. Statistical Analysis

We conducted analysis of covariance (ANCOVA) to compare measured (by IC) and predicted (by predictive equations) REE, adjusting for metabolic cart (i.e., CCM and MGC). We analysed the BIAS (mean error between measured minus predicted REE), the absolute differences (measured minus predicted in absolute terms), and the 95% limits of agreement. In order to classify participants' under- or overprediction with every REE equation, we considered an accurate estimation when the equation predicted between 90% and 110% of the measured REE [32,33], considering underprediction and overprediction when the estimation was below 90% and above 110% of the measured REE, respectively. We also calculated the percentage of accurate prediction between 95% and 105% of the measured REE. We classified the participants into underprediction or overprediction when the estimation was below 95% and above 105% of the measured REE, respectively.

We also used the repeated measures analysis of variance (ANOVA) to determine differences among the study predictive equation that presented minor absolute differences and measured REE. The heteroscedasticity was examined using the Bland–Altman method [34], which plots the difference between predicted and measured REE versus the mean of predicted and measured REE. The analyses were conducted using the Statistical Package for Social Sciences (SPSS, v. 21.0, IBM SPSS Statistics, IBM Corporation, Armonk, NY, USA), and the level of significance was set at $p < 0.05$.

3. Results

The characteristics of the study sample are shown in Table 1. As expected, men had higher levels of lean mass and REE than women, whereas women had higher levels of fat mass (all $p < 0.001$).

Table 1. Descriptive parameters for the participants in the study.

	Men (n = 43)			Women (n = 79)		
	Normal weight (n = 20)	Overweight (n = 12)	Obese (n = 11)	Normal weight (n = 59)	Overweight (n = 21)	Obese (n = 9)
Age (years)	21.5 (2.0)	23.5 (2.1)	23.0 (2.5)	22.1 (2.1)	22.6 (2.4)	21.6 (2.0)
Weight (kg)	69.0 (7.6)	84.4 (7.6)	109.0 (10.5)	58.9 (7.1)	74.6 (6.5)	84.5 (9.7)
Height (m)	1.75 (0.06)	1.76 (0.06)	1.78 (0.06)	1.64 (0.07)	1.64 (0.06)	1.64 (0.09)
BMI (kg/m^2)	22.4 (1.8)	27.1 (1.4)	34.5 (2.2)	21.8 (1.8)	27.6 (1.2)	31.3 (1.2)
Fat free mass (kg)	50.9 (5.4)	57.2 (4.1)	66.3 (6.5)	37.8 (4.1)	41.7 (4.0)	41.5 (6.0)
Fat mass (kg)	18.1 (4.8)	27.2 (6.8)	42.7 (6.4)	22.1 (4.5)	32.9 (3.6)	39.0 (5.0)
Fat mass (%)	24.9 (5.3)	30.6 (5.9)	37.8 (3.4)	35.2 (4.7)	43.0 (3.0)	45.1 (2.8)
REE (Kcal/day)	1587 (390)	1675 (363)	1870 (251)	1295 (222)	1481 (179)	1470 (203)

Data are expressed as mean (standard deviation). Abbreviations: BMI, body mass index; REE, resting energy expenditure.

Figure 1 shows the percentage of accurate prediction of REE predictive equations and the differences of the mean absolute values between predicted and measured REE in men by BMI categories. In normal weight men, the equations of Schofield [9] and the "Food and Agriculture Organization of the United Nations/World Health Organization/United Nations" (FAO/WHO/UNU) [5] provided

45% prediction accuracy (Figure 1A and Supplementary material Table S2a), 10% underpredictions, and 45% overpredictions (mean BIAS: −142 and −147 Kcal/day, respectively). There were no differences between the most accurate predictive equation (i.e., Schofield [9]) and the rest (Figure 1B, $p = 0.303$).

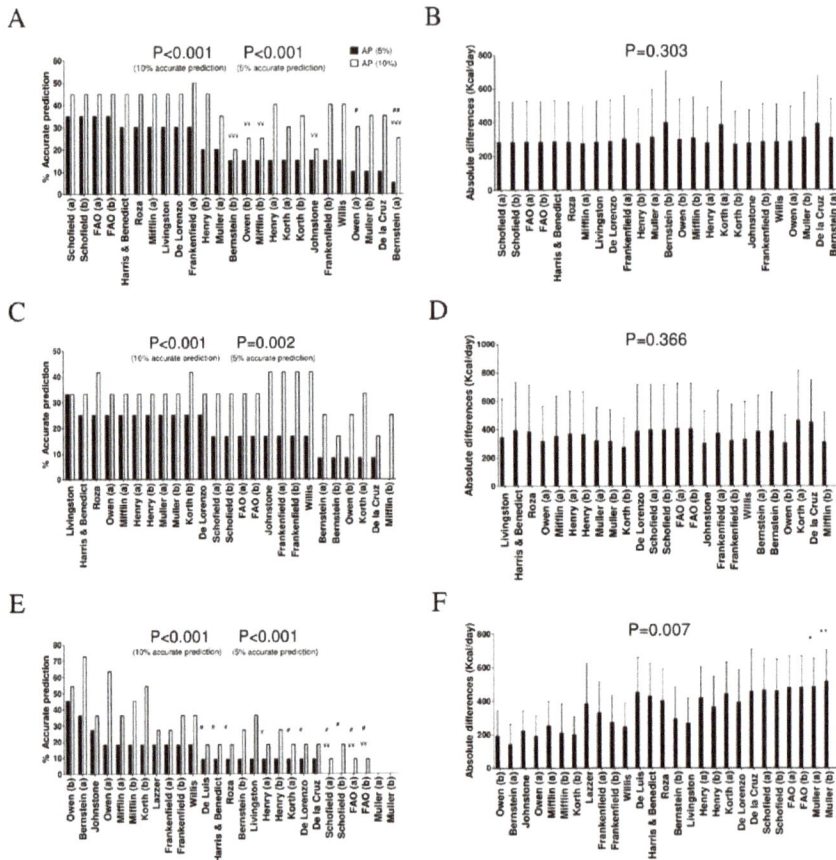

Figure 1. Percentage of accurate prediction of resting energy predictive equations and differences of mean absolute values between predicted and measured resting energy expenditure in men by weight status categories. (**A**) Percentage of accurate prediction at 5% and 10% of measured resting energy expenditure in normal weight men. (**B**) Mean (SD) absolute differences between predicted and measured resting energy expenditure in normal weight men. (**C**) Percentage of accurate prediction at 5% and 10% of resting energy expenditure measured in overweight men. (**D**) Mean (SD) differences between predicted and measured resting energy expenditure in absolute values in overweight young men. (**E**) Percentage of accurate prediction at 5% and 10% of resting energy expenditure measured in obese men. (**F**) Mean (SD) differences between predicted and measured resting energy expenditure in absolute values in obese men. (a) and (b) refer to predictive equations that are proposed by the same author, but require different anthropometry or body composition parameters. p-value of repeated measures analysis of variance (with Bonferroni post-hoc analysis) among the predictive equations. * $p <$ 0.05; ** $p < 0.01$ when compared with the predictive equation that presented minor absolute differences with measured resting energy expenditure. ¥ $p < 0.05$; ¥¥ $p < 0.01$; ¥¥¥ $p < 0.001$ when compared with the

predictive equation that presented the best resting energy expenditure accurate prediction (10%) with measured resting energy expenditure. # $p < 0.05$; ## $p < 0.01$; ### $p < 0.001$ when compared with the predictive equation that presented the best resting energy expenditure accurate prediction (10%) with measured resting energy expenditure. AP: accurate predictions. Abbreviations: FAO, "Food and Agriculture Organization of the United Nations/World Health Organization/United Nations" equation.

In overweight men, five equations [4,10,15,20,35] presented 41.7% of accurate predictions (Figure 1C and Supplementary Materials Table S2b). All of these equations overestimated REE (33%–50% of all participants). However, when we applied a severe accurate estimation (±5% of measured REE), the Livingston and Korth equations [13,20] provided the highest (33% and 25%, respectively) accurate predictions (mean BIAS was −183 and −69 Kcal/day, respectively). There were no differences across predictive equations (Figure 1D, $p = 0.366$). Also, there were no differences between the most accurate predictive equations (i.e., Livingston [13] and Korth [20]) and the rest (Figure 1D, $p = 0.366$).

In obese men, the Bernstein and Owen equations [14,16] provided 72.7% and 54.5% prediction accuracy (±10%), respectively. When applying a severe accurate estimation (±5% of measured REE), these equations presented 36.4% and 45.5% prediction accuracy, respectively (Figure 1E and Supplementary Materials Table S2c). The mean BIAS was 18 and 133 Kcal/day for the Bernstein and Owen predictive equations, respectively. We also observed significant differences ($p = 0.007$) when comparing the estimation of REE by the Bernstein and Owen equations [14,16] with the Muller predictive equation (which is the one that presented less accuracy) [8] (Figure 1F).

Figure 2 shows the percentage of accurate prediction of REE predictive equations, and the differences of the mean absolute values between predicted and measured REE in women by weight status categories. In normal weight women, several REE equations provided >60% prediction accuracy [5,9,13,18,19] (Figure 2A and Supplementary Material Table S2d), yet when we applied a severe accurate estimation (±5% of measured REE), the Mifflin equation [19] showed the highest accuracy (40.7% prediction accuracy, mean BIAS: −50 Kcal/day). There were significant differences in the estimation of REE by the Mifflin equation [19] compared with the Korth [20], Weijs & Vansant [25], de la Cruz [11], Bernstein [16], and Owen [21] predictive equations (Figure 2B).

In overweight women, the Korth [20] and Johnstone [15] equations provided 61.9% and 57.1% prediction accuracy, respectively (Figure 2C and Supplementary material Table S2e). However, when taking into consideration a severe accurate estimation (±5%), the Korth equation presented 23.8% and the Johnstone equation 42.9% prediction accuracy (mean BIAS: −162 and −281 Kcal/day, respectively). There were significant differences between the Johnstone [15] and Frankenfield equations [36], and the Bernstein [16] and Owen equations [21] (both $p = 0.002$) (Figure 2D).

In obese women, the Owen equation [21] provided 66.7% prediction accuracy (mean BIAS: 68 Kcal/day) (Figure 2E and Supplementary material Table S2f). There were no differences between all REE predictive equations ($p = 0.277$).

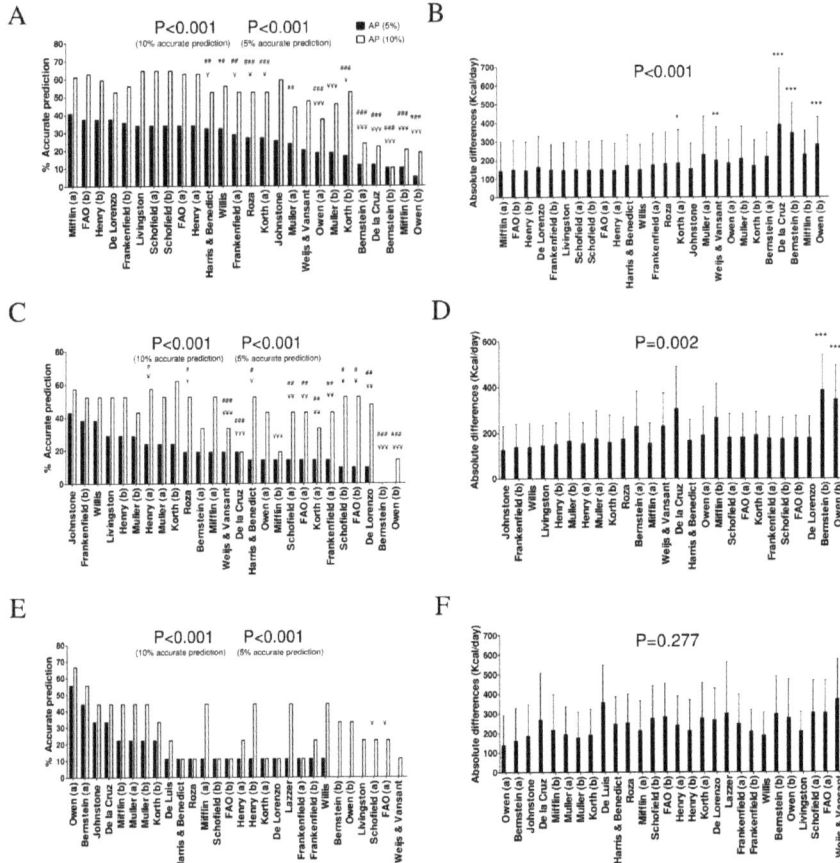

Figure 2. Percentage of accurate prediction of resting energy predictive equations and mean differences between predicted and measured resting energy expenditure in absolute values in women by weight status categories. (**A**) Percentage of accurate prediction at 5% and 10% of resting energy expenditure measured in normal weight women. (**B**) Mean (SD) differences between predicted and measured resting energy expenditure in absolute values in normal weight women. (**C**) Percentage of accurate prediction of several resting energy predictive equations at 5% and 10% of resting energy expenditure measured in overweight women. (**D**) Mean (SD) differences between predicted and measured resting energy expenditure in absolute values in overweight women. (**E**) Percentage of accurate prediction at 5% and 10% of resting energy expenditure measured in obese young women. (**F**) Mean (SD) differences between predicted and measured resting energy expenditure in absolute values in obese women. (a) and (b) refer to predictive equations that are proposed by the same author, but require different anthropometry or body composition parameters. p-value of repeated measures analysis of variance (with Bonferroni post-hoc analysis) among the predictive equations. * $p < 0.05$; ** $p < 0.01$; *** $p < 0.001$ when compared with the predictive equation that presented minor absolute differences with measured resting energy expenditure. ¥ $p < 0.05$; ¥¥ $p < 0.01$; ¥¥¥ $p < 0.001$ when compared with the predictive equation that presented the best resting energy expenditure accurate prediction (10%) with measured resting energy expenditure. # $p < 0.05$; ## $p < 0.01$; ### $p < 0.001$ when compared with the predictive equation that presented the best resting energy expenditure accurate prediction (10%) with measured resting energy expenditure. AP: accurate predictions.

Figure 3 shows Bland–Altman plots for the six selected equations in men and women and by weight status. The limits of agreement were large in all six cases: (i) −836 to 551 Kcal/day in normal weight men (using the Schofield equation [9], see Figure 3A and Supplementary material Table S2a), (ii) −465 to 364 Kcal/day in normal weight women (using the Mifflin equation [19], see Figure 3B and Supplementary material Table S2d), (iii) −998 to 631 Kcal/day in overweight men (using Livingston equation [13], see Figure 3C and Supplementary material Table S2b), (iv) −281 to 361 Kcal/day in overweight women (using the Johnstone equation [15], see Figure 3D and Supplementary material Table S2e), (v) −514 to 273 Kcal/day in obese men (using the Owen equation [14], see Figure 3E and Supplementary material Table S2c), and (vi) −333 to 470 Kcal/day in obese women (using the Owen equation [21], see Figure 3F and Supplementary material Table S2f). There was no interaction effect between any of the REE predicted equations, metabolic cart, and measured REE (all $p > 0.2$).

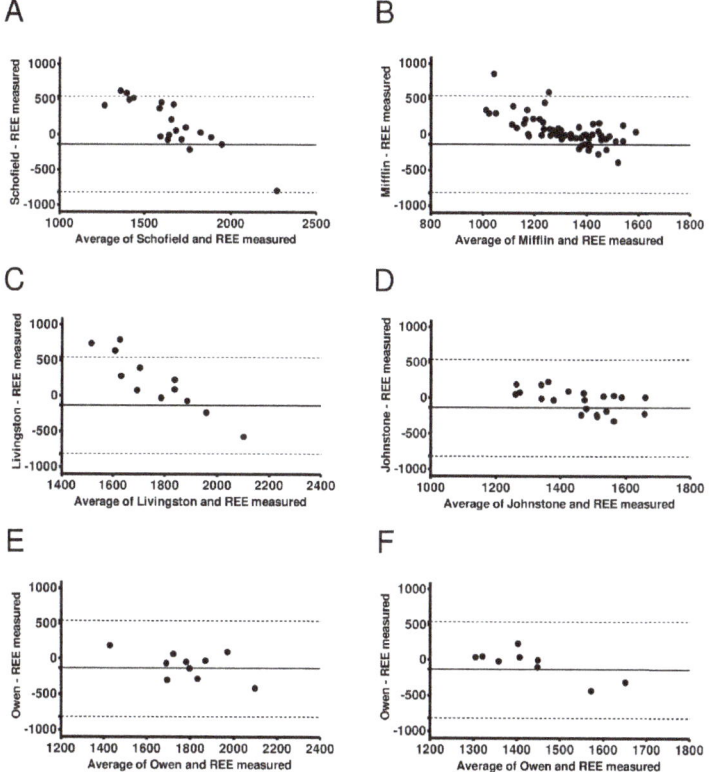

Figure 3. Bland–Altman plots for selected resting energy expenditure (REE) predictive equations. The solid lines represent the mean difference (BIAS) between predicted and measured REE. The upper and lower dashed lines represent the 95% limits of agreement. (**A**) normal weight young men; (**B**) normal weight young women; (**C**) overweight young men; (**D**) overweight young women; (**E**) obese young men; and (**F**) obese young women.

4. Discussion

The results of this study indicate that the most accurate equation to estimate REE differs by sex and weight status in young adults. The most accurate equations are (i) the Schofield [9] and FAO/WHO/UNU [5] equations in normal weight men; (ii) the Livingston [13] and Korth equations [20] in overweight men; (iii) the Owen [21] and Bernstein equations [16] in obese men; (iv) the Mifflin [19] and FAO/WHO/UNU [5] equations in normal weight women; (v) the Johnstone [15] and Frankenfield equations [32] in overweight women; and (vi) the Owen equation [21] in obese women. For practical purposes, we provide a flowchart decision tree to select an energy predictive equation by sex and weight status (see Figure 4).

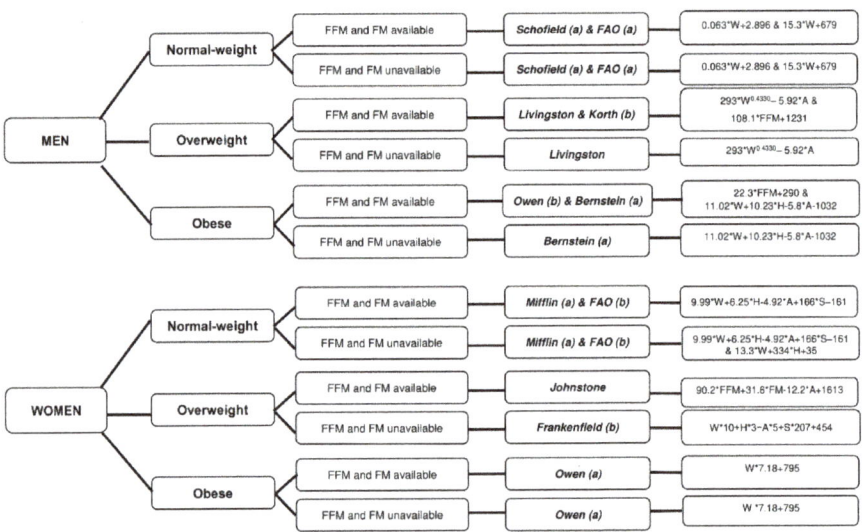

Figure 4. Decision tree to select a resting energy expenditure predictive equation by sex and weight status. (a) and (b) refer to predictive equations that are proposed by the same author but require different anthropometry or body composition parameters. Abbreviations: M: men; F: women; W: weight; H: height; A: age; S (men = 0; women = 1); FFM: fat free mass; FM: fat mass.

4.1. Normal Weight Men

Our results show that the Schofield [9] and FAO/WHO/UNU equations [5] were the most accurate REE equations in young healthy adults, which is in line with previous studies [37–39]. The Schofield equation was derived from a sample of 7173 men and women, which included 4814 participants above the age of 18 and with a BMI between 21 and 24 kg/m^2 (47% Italians). The FAO/WHO/UNU [5] equation was based on the Schofield equation [9] database and extended to 11,000 participants.

Willis et al. [4] recently proposed a predictive equation for young adults, and, although no differences were found between the Schofield and Willis equations, the first showed higher accuracy (45% vs. 40%, mean absolute differences: 280 ± 239 vs. 280 ± 222 Kcal/day, respectively). Of note is that participants' characteristics in the study of Willis et al. [4] were substantially different compared with the participants enrolled in our study: (i) American versus Spanish population; (ii) BMI 28.7 ± 4.7 versus 22.4 ± 1.8 kg/m^2, respectively; and (iii) REE 1866 ± 251 versus 1587 ± 390 Kcal/day, respectively.

4.2. Overweight Men

The results of our study showed that several equations (the Frankenfield, Johnstone, Korth, Livingston, Roza, and Willis equations) overpredicted REE (>50% of the study participants in all cases, mean absolute differences: 317 ± 256, 298 ± 226, 271 ± 205, 342 ± 273, 382 ± 330, and 325 ± 265 Kcal/day, respectively), and previous studies indicated similar trends when these equations were applied in other cohorts with similar characteristics [4,40]. In good agreement with other studies [2,25,32,33], we observed that the inclusion of body composition (fat free mass or fat mass) did not improve the accuracy of REE prediction in these participants, because Frankenfield, Johnstone, Livingston, Roza, and Willis did not include body composition variables. This is especially relevant because age-, weight-, and height-derived equations are more feasible in clinical practice.

4.3. Obese Men

A recent review conducted by an expert panel [32] concluded that the Mifflin equation [19] should be used for overweight and obese participants. Although this conclusion was based on limited data, another review confirmed that both the Mifflin and Owen equations [14,19] were accurate in overweight and obese participants [2]. We observed 45.5% prediction accuracy (mean absolute differences: 210 ± 174 Kcal/day) when we applied the Mifflin equation in our sample of obese men. Moreover, a study conducted in overweight and obese Dutch adults (BMI: 25–40 kg/m^2) obtained higher accuracy when the Lazzer equation [7] was applied (almost 80% prediction accuracy), whereas we had 27.3% prediction accuracy when using this equation. This fact could be explained by the gases collection system and the gas analyser device used to determine REE [41]. In addition, we found 72.7% and 54.5% prediction accuracy (±10% and ±5% of measured REE, respectively) with the Bernstein equation [16]. Of note is that the participants' characteristics in Bernstein's study had a similar BMI compared with our study participants. Previous studies have shown that the estimation of REE is less accurate in obese than in non-obese subjects [25,32,33].

4.4. Normal Weight Women

Our results provide more evidence in the use of the Mifflin equation in normal weight women (61% prediction accuracy, mean absolute differences: 142 ± 157 Kcal/day). Our findings concur with other studies in non-obese individuals (aged 18–78, 82% prediction accuracy) [31], in normal weight European American women (63.7% prediction accuracy) [42], in overweight and obese individuals (aged 19–69 years old, 78% accurate prediction) [32], in extremely obese women (84% prediction accuracy) [43], and in overweight U.S. adults (almost 80% prediction accuracy) [2].

4.5. Overweight Women

In overweight women, the Korth equation (which includes fat free mass) showed the highest accuracy (61.9% prediction accuracy, mean absolute differences: 158 ± 119 Kcal/day). However, others [2,25,32,33] showed that the inclusion of fat free does not improve the accuracy of REE prediction. In our study, the Willis equation [4], which includes weight, age, and sex data of young adults (18–30 years old), showed 52% prediction accuracy (mean absolute differences: 137 ± 103 Kcal/day), which is considered acceptable [32]. However, the prediction accuracy observed in the study by Willis et al. [4] was 70%, which might be partially explained by the inclusion of normal weight and obese individuals as a part of the total sample included in their study.

4.6. Obese Women

Mifflin [19] is the recommended equation in obese women [42], as well as in individuals with different ages, BMI, and ethnicities [2,6,8,32,42]. Our results also revealed an acceptable prediction accuracy (44.4%, mean absolute differences: 176 ± 132 Kcal/day) of the Mifflin equation, but far from being the best predictive equation in this group. As observed in obese men, the highest accuracy equations in obese women were the Owen [14] and Bernstein equations [16] (66.7% and 55.6% prediction accuracy, respectively, and mean absolute differences: 136 ± 156 and 162 ± 166 Kcal/day, respectively). These results could be expected because the Owen equation usually underestimated the REE measure in young adults without considering BMI [4], and the Bernstein equation was proposed based on participants with the same characteristics as those in our study [16,21].

4.7. Limitations

Our study has some limitations. (i) The participants were young healthy adults, and we do not know if these results can be extended to older or unhealthy people. (ii) Our results for overweight men, obese men, and obese women need confirmation because of the small number of women and men in these groups; this fact could have influenced the results obtained, yet it is important to consider that our sample was more homogeneous than other studies conducted in young adults as a result of the strict inclusion criteria and the narrow age range [4]. (iii) The metabolic carts could overestimate or underestimate the REE measure, yet the data collection process and analysis were strictly controlled and standardised, which is certainly a strength.

5. Conclusions

In conclusion, this study shows that there is a wide variation in the accuracy of REE predictive equations depending on sex and BMI index in young adults. Future studies are, however, needed to confirm the results obtained for overweight men, obese men, and obese women because of the relatively small sample size in our study. We provide a decision tree (Figure 4) to select an REE equation depending on sex and BMI in the individuals, taking into account the percentage of accurate prediction applying an accuracy of ±5% and ±5% of measured REE. We also provide an open access Excel sheet that automatically estimates REE using 47 equations considering sex, age, weight, and height, as well as individuals' fat mass and/or fat free mass (if available) (see Supplementary file S1) [44].

Supplementary Materials: The following are available online at http://www.mdpi.com/2072-6643/11/2/223/s1, Table S1: Resting energy expenditure predictive equations, Table S2: Validity of resting energy expenditure (REE) predictive equations in young adults, File S1: Excel sheet that automatically estimates the REE and the total energy expenditure using 45 equations considering anthropometric and/or body composition parameters (if available).

Author Contributions: Conceptualization, F.J.A.-G. and J.R.R.; Data curation, F.J.A.-G., G.S.-D., and J.R.R.; Formal analysis, F.J.A.-G., G.S.-D., and J.R.R.; Funding acquisition, J.R.R.; Investigation, F.J.A.-G., G.S.-D., J.M.A., B.M.-T., V.M.-H., E.M.-R., M.L., I.L., and J.R.R.; Methodology, F.J.A.-G., G.S.-D., J.M.A., B.M.-T., V.M.-H., E.M.-R., and J.R.R.; Project administration, J.R.R.; Resources, J.R.R.; Supervision, M.L., I.L., and J.R.R.; Writing—original draft, F.J.A.-G. and J.R.R.; Writing—review & editing, F.J.A.-G., G.S.-D., J.M.A., B.M.-T., V.M.-H., E.M.-R., M.L., I.L., and J.R.R.

Funding: This study was supported by the Spanish Ministry of Economy and Competitiveness, Fondo de Investigación Sanitaria del Instituto de Salud Carlos III (PI13/01393), Retos de la Sociedad (DEP2016-79512-R), and Fondos Estructurales de la Unión Europea (FEDER); by the Spanish Ministry of Education (FPU 13/04365, FPU14/04172, and FPU15/04059); by the Fundación Iberoamericana de Nutrición (FINUT); by the Redes temáticas de investigación cooperativa RETIC (Red SAMID RD16/0022); by AstraZeneca HealthCare Foundation; by the University of Granada, Plan Propio de Investigación 2016, Excellence actions: Units of Excellence; Unit of Excellence on Exercise and Health (UCEES), and Plan Propio de Investigación 2018, Programa Contratos-Puente; and by Wiemspro®(Malaga, Spain).

Acknowledgments: We are grateful to Carmen Sainz-Quinn for assistance with the English language. This study is part of a Ph.D. Thesis conducted in the Biomedicine Doctoral Studies of the University of Granada, Spain.

Conflicts of Interest: The authors have no conflict of interest that are directly relevant to the content of this article.

References

1. Pinheiro Volp, A.C.; Esteves de Oliveira, F.C.; Duarte Moreira Alves, R.; Esteves, E.A.; Bressan, J. Energy expenditure: Components and evaluation methods. *Nutr. Hosp.* **2011**, *26*, 430–440. [CrossRef] [PubMed]
2. Weijs, P.J.M. Validity of predictive equations for resting energy expenditure in US and Dutch overweight and obese class I and II adults aged 18–65 y. *Am. J. Clin. Nutr.* **2008**, *88*, 959–970. [CrossRef] [PubMed]
3. De Luis, D.A.; Aller, R.; Izaola, O.; Romero, E. Prediction equation of resting energy expenditure in an adult spanish population of obese adult population. *Ann. Nutr. Metab.* **2006**, *50*, 193–196. [CrossRef] [PubMed]
4. Willis, E.A.; Herrmann, S.D.; Ptomey, L.T.; Honas, J.J.; Bessmer, C.T.; Donnelly, J.E.; Washburn, R.A. Predicting resting energy expenditure in young adults. *Obes. Res. Clin. Pract.* **2014**, *8*, 201–208. [CrossRef] [PubMed]
5. FAO/WHO/UNU. *Energy and Protein Requirements*; FAO: Geneva, Switzerland, 1985.

6. Lazzer, S.; Agosti, F.; Silvestri, P.; Derumeaux-Burel, H.; Sartorio, A. Prediction of resting energy expenditure in severely obese Italian women. *J. Endocrinol. Investig.* **2007**, *30*, 20–27. [CrossRef] [PubMed]
7. Lazzer, S.; Agosti, F.; Resnik, M.; Marazzi, N.; Mornati, D.; Sartorio, A. Prediction of resting energy expenditure in severely obese Italian males. *J. Endocrinol. Investig.* **2007**, *30*, 754–761. [CrossRef] [PubMed]
8. Müller, M.J.; Bosy-Westphal, A.; Klaus, S.; Kreymann, G.; Lührmann, P.M.; Neuhäuser-Berthold, M.; Noack, R.; Pirke, K.M.; Platte, P.; Selberg, O.; et al. World Health Organization equations have shortcomings for predicting resting energy expenditure in persons from a modern, affluent population: Generation of a new reference standard from a retrospective analysis of a German database of resting energy expe. *Am. J. Clin. Nutr.* **2004**, *80*, 1379–1390. [CrossRef] [PubMed]
9. Schofield, W.N. Predicting basal metabolic rate, new standards and review of previous work. *Hum. Nutr. Clin. Nutr.* **1985**, *39* (Suppl. 1), 5–41. [PubMed]
10. Roza, A.M.; Shizgal, H.M. The Harris Benedict equation reevaluated: Resting energy requirements and the body cell mass. *Am. J. Clin. Nutr.* **1984**, *40*, 168–182. [CrossRef]
11. de la Cruz Marcos, S.; de Mateo Silleras, B.; Camina Martín, M.A.; Carreño Enciso, L.; Miján de la Torre, A.; Galgani Fuentes, J.E.; Redondo del Río, M.P. Proposal for a new formula for estimating resting energy expenditure for healthy spanish population. *Nutr. Hosp.* **2015**, *32*, 2346–2352. [CrossRef] [PubMed]
12. Harris, J.; Benedict, F. A biometric study of basal metabolism in man. *Proc. Natl. Acad. Sci. USA* **1918**, *4*, 370–373. [CrossRef] [PubMed]
13. Livingston, E.H.; Kohlstadt, I. Simplified resting metabolic rate-predicting formulas for normal-sized and obese individuals. *Obes. Res.* **2005**, *13*, 1255–1262. [CrossRef] [PubMed]
14. Owen, O.E.; Holup, J.L.; D'Alessio, D.A.; Craig, E.S.; Polansky, M.; Smalley, K.J.; Kavle, E.C.; Bushman, M.C.; Owen, L.R.; Mozzoli, M.A. A reappraisal of the caloric requirements of men. *Am. J. Clin. Nutr.* **1987**, *46*, 875–885. [CrossRef] [PubMed]
15. Johnstone, A.M.; Rance, K.A.; Murison, S.D.; Duncan, J.S.; Speakman, J.R. Additional anthropometric measures may improve the predictability of basal metabolic rate in adult subjects. *Eur. J. Clin. Nutr.* **2006**, *60*, 1437–1444. [CrossRef] [PubMed]
16. Bernstein, R.S.; Thornton, J.C.; Yang, M.U.; Wang, J.; Redmond, A.M.; Pierson, R.N.; Pi-Sunyer, F.X.; Van Itallie, T.B. Prediction of the resting metabolic rate in obese patients. *Am. J. Clin. Nutr.* **1983**, *37*, 595–602. [CrossRef]
17. De Lorenzo, A.; Tagliabue, A.; Andreoli, A.; Testolin, G.; Comelli, M.; Deurenberg, P. Measured and predicted resting metabolic rate in Italian males and females, aged 18–59 y. *Eur. J. Clin. Nutr.* **2001**, *55*, 208–214. [CrossRef]
18. Henry, C.J.K. Basal metabolic rate studies in humans: Measurement and development of new equations. *Public Health Nutr.* **2005**, *8*, 1133–1152. [CrossRef]
19. Mifflin, M.D; St Jeor, S.T.; Hill, L.A.; Scott, B.J.; Daugherty, S.A.; Koh, Y.O. A new predictive equation for resting energy expenditure in healthy individuals. *Am. J. Clin. Nutr.* **1990**, *51*, 241–247. [CrossRef]
20. Korth, O.; Bosy-Westphal, A.; Zschoche, P.; Glüer, C.C.; Heller, M.; Müller, M.J. Influence of methods used in body composition analysis on the prediction of resting energy expenditure. *Eur. J. Clin. Nutr.* **2007**, *61*, 582–589. [CrossRef]
21. Owen, O.E.; Kavle, E.; Owen, R.S.; Polansky, M.; Caprio, S.; Mozzoli, M.A.; Kendrick, Z.V.; Bushman, M.C.; Boden, G. A reappraisal of caloric requirements in healthy women. *Am. J. Clin. Nutr.* **1986**, *44*, 1–19. [CrossRef]
22. da Rocha, E.E.M.; Alves, V.G.F.; da Fonseca, R.B.V. Indirect calorimetry: Methodology, instruments and clinical application. *Curr. Opin. Clin. Nutr. Metab. Care* **2006**, *9*, 247–256. [CrossRef] [PubMed]
23. Fullmer, S.; Benson-Davies, S.; Earthman, C.P.; Frankenfield, D.C.; Gradwell, E.; Lee, P.S.P.; Piemonte, T.; Trabulsi, J. Evidence analysis library review of best practices for performing indirect calorimetry in healthy and non-critically ill individuals. *J. Acad. Nutr. Diet.* **2015**, *115*, 1417–1446. [CrossRef] [PubMed]
24. Compher, C.; Frankenfield, D.; Keim, N.; Roth-Yousey, L.; Evidence Analysis Working Group. Best practice methods to apply to measurement of resting metabolic rate in adults: A systematic review. *J. Am. Diet. Assoc.* **2006**, *106*, 881–903. [CrossRef] [PubMed]
25. Weijs, P.J.M.; Vansant, G.A.A.M. Validity of predictive equations for resting energy expenditure in Belgian normal weight to morbid obese women. *Clin. Nutr.* **2010**, *29*, 347–351. [CrossRef] [PubMed]

26. Lof, M.; Hannestad, U.; Forsum, E. Comparison of commonly used procedures, including the doubly-labelled water technique, in the estimation of total energy expenditure of women with special reference to the significance of body fatness. *Br. J. Nutr.* **2003**, *90*, 961. [CrossRef] [PubMed]
27. Sanchez-Delgado, G.; Martinez-Tellez, B.; Olza, J.; Aguilera, C.M.; Labayen, I.; Ortega, F.B.; Chillon, P.; Fernandez-Reguera, C.; Alcantara, J.M.A.; Martinez-Avila, W.D.; et al. Activating brown adipose tissue through exercise (ACTIBATE) in young adults: Rationale, design and methodology. *Contemp. Clin. Trials* **2015**, *45*, 416–425. [CrossRef]
28. World Health Organization. *Obesity: Preventing and Managing the Global Epidemic*; Executive Summary WHO Technical Report Series; WHO: Geneva, Switzerland, 2010; Volume 1997, pp. 5–8.
29. Sanchez-Delgado, G.; Alcantara, J.M.A.; Ortiz-Alvarez, L.; Xu, H.; Martinez-Tellez, B.; Labayen, I.; Ruiz, J.R. Reliability of resting metabolic rate measurements in young adults: Impact of methods for data analysis. *Clin. Nutr.* **2018**, *37*, 1618–1624. [CrossRef]
30. Alcantara, J.M.A.; Sanchez-Delgado, G.; Martinez-Tellez, B.; Merchan-Ramirez, E.; Labayen, I.; Ruiz, J.R. Congruent validity and inter-day reliability of two breath by breath metabolic carts to measure resting metabolic rate in young adults. *Nutr. Metab. Cardiovasc Dis.* **2018**, *28*, 929–936. [CrossRef] [PubMed]
31. Weir, J. New methods for calculating metabolic rate with special reference to protein metabolism. *J. Physiol.* **1949**, *109*, 1–9. [CrossRef] [PubMed]
32. Frankenfield, D.; Roth-Yousey, L.; Compher, C. Comparison of predictive equations for resting metabolic rate in healthy nonobese and obese adults: A systematic review. *J. Am. Diet. Assoc.* **2005**, *105*, 775–789. [CrossRef] [PubMed]
33. Ruiz, J.R.; Ortega, F.B.; Rodríguez, G.; Alkorta, P.; Labayen, I. Validity of resting energy expenditure predictive equations before and after an energy-restricted diet intervention in obese women. *PLoS ONE* **2011**, *6*, e23759. [CrossRef] [PubMed]
34. Bland, J.M.; Altman, D.G. Statistical methods for assessing agreement between two methods of clinical measurement. *Lancet* **1986**, *1*, 307–310. [CrossRef]
35. Frankenfield, D. Bias and accuracy of resting metabolic rate equations in non-obese and obese adults. *Clin. Nutr.* **2013**, *32*, 976–982. [CrossRef] [PubMed]
36. Frankenfield, D.C.; Rowe, W.A.; Smith, J.S.; Cooney, R.N. Validation of several established equations for resting metabolic rate in obese and nonobese people. *J. Am. Diet. Assoc.* **2003**, *103*, 1152–1159. [CrossRef]
37. Lee, S.H.; Kim, E.K. Accuracy of Predictive Equations for Resting Metabolic Rates and Daily Energy Expenditures of Police Officials Doing Shift Work by Type of Work. *Clin. Nutr. Res.* **2012**, *1*, 66. [CrossRef] [PubMed]
38. Ramirez-Zea, M. Validation of three predictive equations for basal metabolic rate in adults. *Public Health Nutr.* **2005**, *8*, 1213–1228. [CrossRef] [PubMed]
39. Wahrlicha, V.; Anjos, L. Validation of predictive equations of basal metabolic rate of women living in Southern Brazil. *Rev. Saúde Pública* **2001**, *35*, 39–45.
40. Song, T.; Venkataraman, K.; Gluckman, P.; Seng, C.Y.; Meng, K.C.; Khoo, E.Y.H.; Leow, M.K.S.; Seng, L.Y.; Shyong, T.E. Validation of prediction equations for resting energy expenditure in Singaporean Chinese men. *Obes. Res. Clin. Pract.* **2014**, *8*, 201–208. [CrossRef]
41. Cooper, J.A.; Watras, A.C.; O'Brien, M.J.; Luke, A.; Dobratz, J.R.; Earthman, C.P.; Schoeller, D.A. Assessing validity and reliability of resting metabolic rate in six gas analysis systems. *J. Am. Diet. Assoc.* **2009**, *109*, 128–132. [CrossRef]
42. Vander Weg, M.W.; Watson, J.M.; Klesges, R.C.; Eck Clemens, L.H.; Slawson, D.L.; McClanahan, B.S. Development and cross-validation of a prediction equation for estimating resting energy expenditure in healthy African-American and European-American women. *Eur. J. Clin. Nutr.* **2004**, *58*, 474–480. [CrossRef]

43. Dobratz, J.R.; Sibley, S.D.; Beckman, T.R.; Valentine, B.J.; Kellogg, T.A.; Ikramuddin, S.; Earthman, C.P. Predicting energy expenditure in extremely obese women. *J. Parenter. Enter. Nutr.* **2007**, *31*, 217–227. [CrossRef] [PubMed]
44. Amaro-Gahete, F.J.; Jurado-Fasoli, L.; De-la-O, A.; Gutierrez, A.; Castillo, M.; Ruiz, J.R. Accuracy and Validity of Resting Energy Expenditure Predictive Equations in Middle-Aged Adults. *Nutrients* **2018**, *10*, 1635. [CrossRef] [PubMed]

© 2019 by the authors. Licensee MDPI, Basel, Switzerland. This article is an open access article distributed under the terms and conditions of the Creative Commons Attribution (CC BY) license (http://creativecommons.org/licenses/by/4.0/).

Article

Nut Consumptions as a Marker of Higher Diet Quality in a Mediterranean Population at High Cardiovascular Risk

Maria del Mar Bibiloni [1,2,3], Alicia Julibert [1,2,3], Cristina Bouzas [1,2,3], Miguel A. Martínez-González [1,4,5], Dolores Corella [1,6], Jordi Salas-Salvadó [1,7], M. Dolors Zomeño [8,9], Jesús Vioque [10,11], Dora Romaguera [1,3], J. Alfredo Martínez [1,12,13], Julia Wärnberg [1,14], José López-Miranda [1,15], Ramón Estruch [1,16], Aurora Bueno-Cavanillas [10,17], Fernando Arós [1,18], Francisco Tinahones [1,19], Lluis Serra-Majem [1,20], Vicente Martín [10,21], José Lapetra [1,22], Clotilde Vázquez [1,23], Xavier Pintó [1,24], Josep Vidal [25,26], Lidia Daimiel [27], Miguel Delgado-Rodríguez [11,28], Pilar Matía [29], Emilio Ros [1,30], Rebeca Fernández-Carrión [1,6], Antonio Garcia-Rios [1,15], M. Angeles Zulet [1,12], Domingo Orozco-Beltrán [10,11], Helmut Schröder [8,11], Montserrat Fitó [1,8], Mónica Bulló [1,7], Josep Basora [1,7], Juan Carlos Cenoz [1,4], Javier Diez-Espino [1,4], Estefanía Toledo [1,4] and Josep A. Tur [1,2,3,*]

1. CIBER Fisiopatología de la Obesidad y Nutrición (CIBEROBN), Instituto de Salud Carlos III (ISCIII), 28029 Madrid, Spain; mar.bibiloni@uib.es (M.d.M.B.); aliciajulibert@gmail.com (A.J.); cristinabouvel@gmail.com (C.B.); mamartinez@unav.es (M.A.M.-G.); dolores.corella@uv.es (D.C.); jordi.salas@urv.cat (J.S.-S.); mariaadoracion.romaguera@ssib.es (D.R.); jalfmtz@unav.es (J.A.M.); jwarnberg@uma.es (J.W.); jlopezmir@gmail.com (J.L.-M.); restruch@clinic.cat (R.E.); aborau@secardiologia.es (F.A.); fjtinahones@hotmail.com (F.T.); lluis.serra@uplgc.es (L.S.-M.); jlapetra@ono.com (J.L.); cvazquezma@gmail.com (C.V.); xpinto@bellvitgehospital.cat (X.P.); eros@clinic.cat (E.R.); rebeca.fernandez@uv.es (R.F.-G.); angariaros2004@yahoo.es (A.G.-R.); mazulet@unav.es (M.A.Z.); mfito@imim.es (M.F.); monica.bullo@urv.cat (M.B.); jbasora.tgn.ics@gencat.cat (J.B.); jc.cenoz.osinaga@cfnavarra.es (J.C.C.); javierdiezesp@ono.com (J.D.-E.); etoledo@unav.es (E.T.)
2. Research Group on Community Nutrition and Oxidative Stress, University of Balearic Islands, 07122 Palma de Mallorca, Spain
3. Health Research Institute of the Balearic Islands (IdISBa), 07120 Palma de Mallorca, Spain
4. Department of Preventive Medicine and Public Health, University of Navarra-IDISNA, 31008 Pamplona, Spain
5. Department of Nutrition, Harvard T. H. Chan School of Public Health, Boston, MA 02115, USA
6. Department of Preventive Medicine, University of Valencia, 46010 Valencia, Spain
7. Human Nutrition Unit, Biochemistry and Biotechnology Department, IISPV, Universitat Rovira i Virgili, 43201 Reus, Spain
8. Cardiovascular Risk and Nutrition Research Group (CARIN), Hospital del Mar Medical Research Institute (IMIM), 08003 Barcelona, Spain; mzomeno@imim.es (M.D.Z.); hschroeder@imim.es (H.S.)
9. Human Nutrition Unit, Blanquerna-Ramon Llull University, 08022 Barcelona, Spain
10. Miguel Hernandez University, ISABIAL-FISABIO, 46020 Alicante, Spain; vioque@umh.es (J.V.); abueno@ugr.es (A.B.-C.); vicente.martin@unileon.es (V.M.); dorozcobeltran@gmail.com (D.O.-B.)
11. CIBER Epidemiología y Salud Pública (CIBERESP), Instituto de Salud Carlos III (ISCIII), 28029 Madrid, Spain; mdelgado@ujaen.es
12. Department of Nutrition, Food Sciences, and Physiology, Center for Nutrition Research, University of Navarra, 31008 Pamplona, Spain
13. Cardiometabolics Nutrition Group, IMDEA Food, CEI UAM + CSIC, 28049 Madrid, Spain
14. School of Nursing, School of Health Sciences, University of Málaga-IBIMA, 29010 Málaga, Spain
15. Lipids and Atherosclerosis Unit, Department of Internal Medicine, Maimonides Biomedical Research Institute of Cordoba (IMIBIC), Reina Sofia University Hospital, University of Cordoba, 14004 Córdoba, Spain
16. Department of Internal Medicine, IDIBAPS, Hospital Clinic, University of Barcelona, 08036 Barcelona, Spain
17. Department of Preventive Medicine, University of Granada, 18016 Granada, Spain
18. Department of Cardiology, OSI ARABA, University Hospital Araba, University of the Basque Country UPV/EHU, 01006 Vitoria-Gasteiz, Spain

[19] Department of Endocrinology, Virgen de la Victoria Hospital, University of Málaga, 29010 Málaga, Spain
[20] Institute for Biomedical Research, University of Las Palmas de Gran Canaria, 35001 Las Palmas, Spain
[21] Institute of Biomedicine (IBIOMED), University of León, 24071 León, Spain
[22] Department of Family Medicine, Research Unit, Distrito Sanitario Atención Primaria Sevilla, 41013 Sevilla, Spain
[23] Department of Endocrinology, Fundación Jiménez-Díaz, 28040 Madrid, Spain
[24] Lipids and Vascular Risk Unit, Internal Medicine, Hospital Universitario de Bellvitge, Hospitalet de Llobregat, 08907 Barcelona, Spain
[25] Department of Endocrinology, IDIBAPS, Hospital Clinic, University of Barcelona, 08036 Barcelona, Spain; jovidal@clinic.cat
[26] CIBER Diabetes y Enfermedades Metabólicas (CIBERDEM), Instituto de Salud Carlos III (ISCIII), 28029 Madrid, Spain
[27] Nutritional Genomics and Epigenomics Group, IMDEA Food, CEI UAM + CSIC, 28049 Madrid, Spain; lidia.daimiel@imdea.org
[28] Department of Health Sciences, University of Jaen, 23071 Jaen, Spain
[29] Department of Endocrinology and Nutrition, Instituto de Investigación Sanitaria Hospital Clínico San Carlos (IdISSC), 28040 Madrid, Spain; pilar.matia@gmail.com
[30] Lipid Clinic, Department of Endocrinology and Nutrition, Institut d'Investigacions Biomèdiques August Pi Sunyer (IDIBAPS), Hospital Clínic, 08036 Barcelona, Spain
* Correspondence: pep.tur@uib.es

Received: 13 February 2019; Accepted: 28 March 2019; Published: 30 March 2019

Abstract: Background: Nut consumption has been associated with improved nutrient adequacy and diet quality in healthy adult populations but this association has never been explored in individuals at high cardiovascular risk. Objective: to assess the associations between consumption of nuts and nutrient adequacy and diet quality in a Mediterranean population at high cardiovascular risk. Design: baseline assessment of nutritional adequacy in participants ($n = 6060$, men and women, with ages 55–75 years old, with overweight/obesity and metabolic syndrome) in the PREDIMED-PLUS primary cardiovascular prevention randomized trial. Methods: nut intake was assessed using a validated food frequency questionnaire. Participants who reported consuming zero quantity of nuts were classified as 'non-nut consumers'. 'Nut consumers' were participants who reported consuming any quantity of nuts. Nineteen micronutrients were examined (vitamins B1, B2, B3, B6, B12, A, C, D, E and folic acid; Ca, K, P, Mg, Fe, Se, Cr, Zn, and iodine). The proportion of micronutrient inadequacy was estimated using the estimated average requirements (EAR) or adequate intake (AI) cut-points. Diet quality was also assessed using a 17-item Mediterranean dietary questionnaire (Mediterranean diet score, MDS), a carbohydrate quality index (CQI) and a fat quality index (FQI). Results: eighty-two percent of participants were nut consumers (median of nut consumption 12.6 g/day; interquartile range: 6.0–25.2). Nut consumers were less likely to be below the EAR for vitamins A, B1, B2, B6, C, D, E, folic acid, and Ca, Mg, Se and Zn than non-nut consumers. Nut consumers were also more likely to be above the AI for K and Cr than non-nut consumers. Nut consumers had lower prevalence of inadequate micronutrient intakes, but also higher CQI, higher FQI, and better scores of adherence to the Mediterranean diet (Mediterranean diet score, MDS). Conclusions: nut consumers had better nutrient adequacy, diet quality, and adherence to the MedDiet than those non-nut consumers.

Keywords: nut consumption; nutrient adequacy; diet quality; Mediterranean diet; cardiovascular risk disease

1. Introduction

The Mediterranean diet (MedDiet) is a pattern with high nutritional quality. It has been demonstrated that higher levels of adherence to a Mediterranean dietary pattern are associated with a reduced risk of inadequate nutrient intake [1,2]. Recently, nut consumption (i.e., peanuts, almonds, hazelnuts, walnuts, pine nuts, pistachios, Brazil nuts, macadamia and cashews), a key food of the MedDiet, has been reported to be associated with an improvement in nutrient intakes but also with better overall nutrient adequacy and diet quality in adult populations [3–6]. In particular, in the National Health and Nutrition Examination Survey (NHANES) 1999–2004 data, the diets of tree nut consumers contained greater amounts of dietary fiber, vitamin E, Ca, Mg and K and lower amounts of Na compared to non-consumers [3]. In addition, in the NHANES 2005–2010, using the Healthy Eating Index-2005, diet quality was found to be higher in nut consumers [6]. In the New Zealand Adult Nutrition Survey (NZANS) 2008/09 data, the diets of whole nut consumers contained greater energy and percentage of energy total fat, monounsaturated fatty acids (MUFA) and polyunsaturated fatty acids (PUFA), and greater amounts of dietary fiber, vitamin E, folate, Cu, Mg, K, P and Zn, whereas energy from saturated fatty acid (SFA) and carbohydrate, and intakes of cholesterol and vitamin B_{12} were significantly lower compared with non-whole nut consumers [6].

Nuts have high content of MUFA and PUFA, soluble fiber, vitamins (e.g., folate and vitamin E), minerals (e.g., Ca, Mg, Cu, Zn, Se and K) and bioactive compounds (e.g., phytosterols, antioxidants and phenolic compounds), which independently or jointly confer health benefits, and frequent consumption was associated to a lower risk of all-cause and cause-specific mortality, with the strongest reduction for coronary heart disease mortality [7]. Frequent nut consumption could play a role in reducing the risk of cardiovascular risk disease [8–11]. However, a limited number of studies have examined associations between nut consumption and nutrient intakes or diet quality [3–6]. None have investigated these associations in a Mediterranean population at high cardiovascular risk. Our hypothesis is that consumption of nuts is going to increase nutrient adequacy, diet quality and adherence to Mediterranean diet. Then, our aim was to assess the associations between consumption of nuts and nutrient adequacy and diet quality in a Mediterranean population at high cardiovascular risk.

2. Materials and Methods

2.1. Study Design

The present study was a cross-sectional analysis on baseline data within the frame of the PREDIMED-PLUS study, a six-year multicentre, parallel-group, randomised trial conducted in Spain to assess the effect on cardiovascular disease morbimortality of an intensive weight loss intervention programme based on an energy-restricted traditional MedDiet (erMedDiet), physical activity promotion and behavioural support, in comparison with an usual care intervention only with energy-unrestricted MedDiet (control group). Details on the study protocol can be found elsewhere [12] and at http://predimedplus.com/. The trial was registered in 2014 at the International Standard Randomized Controlled Trial (ISRCT; http://www.isrctn.com/ISRCTN89898870) with number 89898870.

2.2. Participants, Recruitment and Randomization

Eligible participants were community-dwelling adults (aged 55–75 in men; 60–75 in women), who were overweight or obese (body mass index (BMI) $\geq$ 27 and <40 kg/m^2) and met at least three criteria for the metabolic syndrome (MetS) according to the updated harmonized criteria of the International Diabetes Federation and the American Heart Association and National Heart, Lung and Blood Institute [13].

From 5 September 2013 to 31 October 2016, a total of 6874 participants were recruited in 23 Spanish centres (universities, hospitals and research institutes).

All participants provided written informed consent, and the study protocol and procedures were approved according to the ethical standards of the Declaration of Helsinki by all the participating institutions.

2.3. Dietary Assessment

Registered dietitians collected data on dietary intake at baseline with a semiquantitative 137-item food frequency questionnaire (FFQ), repeatedly validated in Spain [14]. Detailed information about the development, reproducibility and validity of FFQ in the PREDIMED cohort has been previously reported [15,16]. For each item, a typical portion size was included and consumption frequencies were registered in nine categories that ranged from "never or almost never" to "≥6 times/day". Energy and nutrient intakes were calculated as frequency multiplied by nutrient composition of specified portion size for each food item, using a computer program based on available information in Spanish food composition tables [17–19]. We also considered for the total nutrient intake the average intake of micronutrients from dietary supplements, declared by participants in the FFQ. Participants reporting extreme total energy intakes (<500 or >3.500 kcal/day in women or <800 or >4.000 kcal/day in men) or outliers for micronutrient intake (at three or more standard deviations (SD) from both sides of the mean) were excluded from the analysis [2]. The final sample in the present study included 6060 subjects (3118 men and 2942 women) who had available data on nutrient intake.

2.4. Determination of Nut Consumption

For the purpose of this study, nut consumption was assessed using the FFQ data, and total nut consumption comprised of the following four categories: almonds, pistachios, walnuts, and other nuts. Participants who reported consuming zero quantity of nuts in their FFQ were classified as 'non-nut consumers' (n = 1091), and 'nut-consumers' (n = 4969) were participants who reported consuming any quantity of nuts. 'Nut-consumers' were also categorized into quintiles (Q1: <4.2 g/day, n = 911; Q2: 4.2–8.3 g/day, n = 1058; Q3: 8.4–14.5 g/day, n = 868; Q4: 14.6–29.3, n = 1093; Q5: ≥29.4 g/day, n = 1039).

2.5. Determination of Micronutrients Intake

The micronutrients examined were vitamins B1, B2, B3, B6, B12, C, A, D, E and folic acid, and Zn, iodine, Se, Fe, Ca, K, P, Mg, and Cr. We used the dietary references intakes (DRIs) values proposed by Institute of Medicine [17], that are quantitative estimates of nutrient intakes to be used for assessing and planning diets for healthy people and included four different values: estimated average requirements (EAR), recommended daily allowances (RDA), adequate intake (AI) (i.e., values for nutrients having undetermined RDA), and tolerable upper level (UL) values. We estimated the prevalence of inadequate micronutrients intake according to sex and age by using the EAR cut-point, except for K and Cr intakes, whose prevalence was evaluated based on AI cut-point [18,19].

The carbohydrate (CHO) quality index (CQI) and the fat quality index (FQI) were calculated as previously described [2,20]. Briefly, the CQI was defined summing up quintiles of the following four criteria: dietary fiber intake (g per day, positively weighted), glycemic index (negatively weighted), ratio whole grains/total grains (positively weighted), and finally, ratio solid CHO/(solid CHO + liquid CHO) (positively weighted). Solid CHO intake included all CHO containing solid foods, and liquid CHO intake included sugar-sweetened beverages and fruit juice. For each of these four components, we categorized participants into quintiles and received a value (ranging from one to five) according to each quintile (for GI, those in the fifth quintile received one point and those in the first quintile received five points). Finally, we constructed the CQI summing all values. All criteria had the same weighting, and the CQI ranged from four to 20. On the other hand, the FQI was calculated using the ratio (MUFA + PUFA)/(SFA + trans fatty acid [TFA]) as a continuous variable.

Registered dietitians also administered a 17-item Mediterranean dietary questionnaire, a modified version of the previously validated questionnaire used in the PREDIMED trial [21], designed to assess adherence to the Mediterranean diet. Compliance with each of the 17 food habits reflecting a Mediterranean diet was scored with one point, and zero points otherwise. Therefore, a score ranging from 0–17 points, with 0 meaning no adherence and 17 meaning maximum adherence to the Mediterranean diet (Mediterranean diet score (MDS)) was developed.

2.6. Physical Activity

Physical activity was measured using the validated Minnesota-REGICOR short physical activity questionnaire [22–24] and the validated Spanish version of the nurses' health study questionnaire to assess sedentary behaviours [25]. In dietary assessment according to physical activity variables, participants who had not responded to all of the physical activity questionnaires ($n = 14$) and participants reporting outliers for total physical activity expressed as MET·min/week (at three or more SD from the mean for each sex) were excluded and 5742 participants were included in the analysis (2981 men and 2761 women).

2.7. Anthropometric and Blood Pressure Measurements

Anthropometric variables were measured by trained personnel according to the PREDIMED-PLUS protocol. Weight and height were measured with high-quality electronic calibrated scales and a wall-mounted stadiometer, respectively. The body mass index was calculated as weight in kilograms divided by the square of height in meters. Waist circumference was measured halfway between the last rib and the iliac crest by using an anthropometric tape. Blood pressure was measured in triplicate with a validated semi-automatic oscillometer (Omron HEM-705CP, the Netherlands) after five minutes of rest in-between measurements while the participant was in a seated position. All anthropometric variables were determined in duplicate, except for blood pressure (in triplicate).

2.8. Blood Collection and Analysis

Blood samples were collected after an overnight fast and biochemical analyses were performed on fasting plasma glucose, total cholesterol, high density lipoprotein (HDL)-cholesterol and triglyceride concentrations in local laboratories using standard enzymatic methods.

2.9. Other Health Variables

Information related to individual medical history, current medication use and smoking status were also obtained.

2.10. Statistical Analyses

Analyses were performed with the SPSS statistical software package version 25.0 (SPSS Inc., Chicago, IL, USA). Data are shown as mean, standard deviation (SD) or, median and interquartile range (IQR). Difference in means between the two comparison groups were tested by an unpaired Students' *t*-test. Differences in means between the quintiles of nut consumption were tested by one-way ANOVA with Bonferroni post-hoc test. The difference in prevalence across nut consumers and non-nut consumers was examined using χ^2 (all *p* values are two-tailed). We have also defined the cut-off ≥ 6 and ≥ 8 unmet DRI according to the number of nutrients unmet. Thus, six and eight unmet DRI of all nutrients examined as previously described. Logistic regression analyses with the calculation of corresponding odds ratio (OR) and the 95% confidence interval (95% CI) were used to examine the association between unmet DRI in ≥ 6 or ≥ 8 items (dependent variables) and nut consumption (independent variable). Univariate analysis was first carried out for the two different cut-offs (crude OR). Secondly, results were adjusted for sex, energy intake (continuous variable) and physical activity (continuous variable, expressed as MET·min/week) to control for potential confounding. Thirdly, results were adjusted for sex, energy intake (continuous variable), total fat intake (continuous variable, expressed as % of total energy intake), MDS (continuous variable) and physical activity (continuous variable, expressed as MET·min/week). Results were considered statistically significant if *p*-value (two-tailed) <0.05.

3. Results

Overall, 82.0% of participants were nut consumers (83.6% of men and 80.3% of women, $p = 0.001$); the median of nut consumption was 12.6 g/day (IQR: 6.0, 25.2). Table 1 shows the comparison of diet quality and lifestyle characteristics between the two study groups. Nut consumers had higher intakes of energy, solid CHO, total fat, PUFA, MUFA, cholesterol and fibre intake, but lower intakes of total CHO than non-nut consumers. No statistically significant differences were found in intakes of liquid CHO, SFA and TFA. Usual intake of fruits, vegetables, legumes, olive oil, total fish and total meat were all higher in nut consumers compared with non-nut consumers. Nut consumers had also lower usual intake of dairy products than non-nut consumers. No statistically significant differences were found in usual intake of total cereals, cookies and alcohol between the two comparison groups. Nut consumers had lower glycaemic index and higher CQI and FQI than non-nut consumers. They also had a higher MDS (even when nuts were not included in the MDS: 7.7 ± 2.6 g/day for non-nut consumers and 8.1 ± 2.5 g/day for not consumers, $p < 0.001$; data not shown). On the other hand, nut consumers had lower BMI and reported higher total physical activity (expressed as MET·min/week). Statistically significant differences in smoking habit were also found between the two nut groups. Finally, no statistically significant differences in MetS components were found between the two groups.

Table 2 shows usual intake of vitamins and minerals. Nut consumers had higher intakes of all vitamins (B1, B2, B3, B6, B12, C, A, D, E and folic acid) and minerals (Zn, Se, Fe, Ca, K, P, Mg, and Cr) examined in the present study, except for iodine. Table 2 also shows that nut consumers were less likely to be below the EAR for vitamins A, B1, B2, B6, C, D, E and folic acid, Ca, Mg, Se and Zn than non-nut consumers. Furthermore, results showed a percent below the EAR equal or below 10% for vitamins B1, B2, B3, B6, B12 and C, and P, Fe, Se, Zn and iodine (only in nut consumers); a prevalence between 11 and 20% for vitamin A and Mg in nut consumers, and for iodine in non-nut consumers; a prevalence above 21% for vitamin D, vitamin E, folic acid and Ca in both groups, and for vitamin A and Mg in non-nut consumers. Nut consumers were also more likely to be above the AI for K and Cr than non-nut consumers. No statistically significant differences in vitamin B3, vitamin B12, P or Fe were found between the two groups.

Usual intake of vitamins and minerals of the nut consumers as per quintiles of nut consumption were also assessed (Table 3). Intakes of all vitamins and minerals (except for iodine) increased when increased quintiles of nut consumption. Participants in the highest quintile of nut consumption were less likely to be below the EAR for vitamins A, B1, B2, B6, C, D, E and folic acid, Ca, Mg, and Zn. Participants in the highest quintile of nut consumption were also more likely to be above the AI for K and Cr. No statistically significant differences in vitamins B3 and B12, P, Fe, Se and iodine were found between the quintiles of nut consumption.

Finally, the average number of nutrients for which the DRIs were unmet was 4.4 (SD: 1.7) in nut-consumers and 5.2 (SD: 2.0) in non-nut consumers ($p < 0.001$) (difference = 0.9, 95% CI: 0.7, 1.0). Moreover, the average number of nutrients for which the DRIs were unmet was also lower for participants in the fifth quintile (Q5, $n = 1039$) of nut consumption (3.6, SD: 1.3) than for participants in the first quintile (Q1, $n = 911$) of nut consumption (5.0, SD: 1.9) (difference = 1.4, 95% CI: 1.2, 1.5) (Figure 1). Nut consumers were also less likely to have unmet DRI ≥ 6 and ≥ 8 than non-nut consumers in crude and multivariable-adjusted analyses (except for DRI ≥ 8 analysis when results were adjusted for sex, energy intake, MDS, and physical activity; $p = 0.132$) (Table 3). The nut consumption median for unmet ≥ 6 and ≥ 8 DRIs was 8.0 (IQR: 4.0, 14.6) in both cases; and for unmet <6 and <8 DRIs was 12.6 g/day in both cases (IQR: 6.0, 27.4 and 6.0, 25.2, respectively) (Table 4).

Table 1. Lifestyle and dietary characteristics according to nut consumption.

	Non-Nut Consumers (n = 1091)		Nut Consumers (n = 4969)		p
	Mean (SD)	Median (IQR)	Mean (SD)	Median (IQR)	
Subject characteristics					
Age (years) †	65.2 (4.9)	65.0 (61.0, 69.0)	65.0 (4.9)	65.0 (61.0, 69.0)	0.222
Body mass index (kg/m²)	33.2 (3.5)	32.9 (30.4, 35.8)	32.6 (3.4)	32.2 (29.9, 34.9)	<0.001
Total physical activity (MET·min/week) *,†	2074 (1845)	1573 (707, 3019)	2487 (1952)	2014 (1007, 3476)	<0.001
Males †	2402 (2079)	1958 (888, 3357)	2837 (2174)	2294 (1147, 4091)	<0.001
Females †	1780 (1552)	1386 (559, 2587)	2093 (1577)	1734 (839, 2946)	<0.001
Smoking habit ‡					<0.001
Current smoker	173 (16.2)		567 (11.7)		
Former smoker	432 (40.4)		2128 (43.8)		
Never smoked	463 (43.4)		2167 (44.6)		
Nutrients					
Energy intake (kcal/day) †	2141 (555)	2096 (1729, 2495)	2360 (518)	2333 (1996, 2692)	<0.001
Carbohydrate intake (% total energy)	42.3 (7.6)	42.2 (37.3, 47.6)	40.5 (6.6)	40.5 (35.9, 45.0)	<0.001
Solid carbohydrate (g/day)	200.6 (69.1)	191.0 (152.1, 243.0)	214.6 (64.9)	209.6 (166.3, 254.5)	<0.001
Liquid carbohydrate (g/day)	8.6 (13.8)	1.6 (0.0, 11.4)	8.9 (12.4)	3.3 (0.0, 12.3)	0.641
Glycemic index	53.7 (5.6)	54.1 (50.5, 57.7)	53.3 (5.1)	53.7 (50.1, 57.0)	0.015
Protein intake (% total energy)	16.8 (3.1)	16.6 (14.7, 18.6)	16.5 (2.7)	16.3 (14.6, 18.1)	0.002
Fat intake (% total energy)	37.6 (7.1)	37.2 (32.7, 42.3)	39.9 (6.3)	39.9 (35.5, 44.2)	<0.001
PUFA (% total energy)	5.1 (1.3)	5.0 (4.3, 5.7)	6.6 (1.7)	6.3 (5.3, 7.5)	<0.001
MUFA (% total energy)	19.3 (4.7)	19.0 (15.8, 22.4)	20.9 (4.5)	20.7 (17.6, 23.8)	<0.001
SFA (% total energy)	9.9 (2.2)	9.8 (8.5, 11.3)	9.9 (1.9)	9.8 (8.6, 11.1)	0.543
Trans fatty acid (g/d)	0.6 (0.4)	0.5 (0.3, 0.7)	0.6 (0.4)	0.5 (0.3, 0.8)	0.901
Cholesterol (mg/d)	352.9 (114.5)	341.2 (278.9, 422.1)	374.9 (106.7)	365.8 (304.1, 433.4)	<0.001
Fibre intake (g/d)	21.9 (7.4)	21.2 (16.8, 26.3)	25.9 (7.8)	24.8 (20.3, 30.4)	<0.001
Food groups					
Fruits (g/day) †	309.4 (189.9)	281.3 (175.2, 414.1)	352.5 (186.2)	326.6 (217.6, 456.2)	<0.001
Vegetables (g/day) †	291.7 (129.6)	269.8 (202.1, 365.5)	322.0 (128.8)	304.4 (230.2, 398.1)	<0.001
Legumes (g/day) †	18.9 (11.2)	16.4 (12.1, 24.8)	20.3 (10.1)	16.8 (16.1, 24.8)	<0.001
Olive oil (g/day) †	38.0 (17.5)	35.0 (25.0, 50.0)	40.4 (16.8)	50.0 (25.0, 50.0)	<0.001
Nuts (g/day) †	0.0 (0.0)	0.0 (0.0, 0.0)	17.1 (15.8)	12.6 (6.0, 25.2)	<0.001
Total fish (g/day) †	89.1 (44.4)	84.6 (56.6, 119.0)	101.0 (44.2)	96.1 (68.1, 128.6)	<0.001
Total cereals (g/day) †	144.6 (80.1)	114.9 (87.4, 202.0)	148.1 (74.4)	122.1 (91.8, 204.3)	0.182
Dairy products (g/day) †	346.7 (195.0)	306.9 (220.6, 518.7)	331.3 (182.3)	298.0 (216.6, 418.1)	0.017
Total meat (g/day) †	138.9 (58.3)	134.1 (101.6, 171.9)	144.9 (54.6)	139.6 (109.2, 177.2)	0.002
Cookies (g/day) †	26.5 (31.3)	14.6 (4.2, 39.4)	26.6 (29.1)	17.4 (6.7, 37.8)	0.938
Alcohol (g/day) †	10.9 (16.0)	4.3 (0.0, 12.9)	11.0 (14.8)	5.0 (0.7, 14.7)	0.826

Table 1. Cont.

		Non-Nut Consumers (n = 1091)		Nut Consumers (n = 4969)		p
		Mean (SD)	Median (IQR)	Mean (SD)	Median (IQR)	
Diet Quality Measures (units)						
17-item MDS †		7.7 (2.6)	8.0 (6.0, 10.0)	8.6 (2.6)	9.0 (7.0, 10.0)	<0.001
CQI †		11.1 (3.4)	11.0 (8.0, 14.0)	12.1 (3.4)	12.0 (9.0, 15.0)	<0.001
FQI †		2.5 (0.6)	2.4 (2.1, 2.8)	2.8 (0.6)	2.7 (2.3, 3.1)	<0.001
MetS components: n (%)						
High blood pressure ‡		1012 (92.8)		4577 (92.1)		0.469
Hyperglycemia ‡		839 (76.9)		3738 (75.2)		0.244
Hypertriglyceridemia ‡		613 (56.2)		2781 (56.0)		0.895
Low HDL-cholesterol ‡		459 (42.1)		2130 (42.9)		0.631
Abdominal obesity ‡		1053 (96.5)		4771 (96.0)		0.438
Males ‡		476 (93.0)		2424 (93.0)		0.969
Females ‡		577 (99.7)		2347 (99.3)		0.490

Abbreviations: MDS, Mediterranean diet score; CQI, carbohydrates quality index; FQI, fat quality index; HDL-cholesterol, high density lipoprotein cholesterol; MET, metabolic equivalent of task. * Participants who have not responded the physical activity questionnaires and participants reporting outliers for total physical activity expressed as MET·min/week (at 3 or more standard deviations from the mean) were excluded from the analysis (i.e., 79 participants 'non-nut consumers' and 239 participants 'nut consumers'). † Difference in means between non-nut consumers and nut consumers were tested by unpaired Students' t-test. ‡ The difference in prevalence across the two comparison groups was examined using χ^2.

Table 2. Usual intake and percentage of population below the estimated average requirement (EAR) or above adequate intake (AI) in nut-consumers (n = 4969) compared with non-nut consumers (n = 1091).

Variable	Group	Usual Intake		Percentile						EAR	% Below EAR	
		Mean (SD)	p[1]	10	25	50	75	90			%	p[2]
Vitamin A RAE (µg/day)	Non-nut consumers	940.6 (517.0)	<0.001	439.7	564.9	783.6	1171.9	1692.4		M: 625.0 µg/day	23.9	<0.001
	Nut-consumers	1064.0 (533.6)		521.2	662.6	913.2	1387.2	1826.7		W: 500.0 µg/day	15.1	
Vitamin B1 (mg/day)	Non-nut consumers	1.4 (0.4)	<0.001	1.0	1.2	1.4	1.7	1.9		M: 1.0 mg/day	8.7	<0.001
	Nut-consumers	1.6 (0.4)		1.2	1.4	1.6	1.8	2.1		W: 0.9 mg/day	2.5	
Vitamin B2 (mg/day)	Non-nut consumers	1.8 (0.5)	<0.001	1.2	1.4	1.7	2.1	2.5		M: 1.1 mg/day	4.5	<0.001
	Nut-consumers	1.9 (0.5)		1.3	1.6	1.9	2.3	2.6		W: 0.9 mg/day	2.0	
Vitamin B3 NE (mg/day)	Non-nut consumers	36.3 (9.1)	<0.001	25.2	30.1	35.6	42.3	48.0		M: 12.0 mg/day	0.0	1.000
	Nut-consumers	39.8 (8.8)		28.8	33.7	39.6	45.7	51.4		W: 11.0 mg/day	0.0	
Vitamin B6 (mg/day)	Non-nut consumers	2.0 (0.5)	<0.001	1.4	1.7	2.0	2.4	2.7		M: 1.4 mg/day	6.2	<0.001
	Nut-consumers	2.3 (0.5)		1.7	1.9	2.3	2.6	3.0		W: 1.3 mg/day	2.6	

Table 2. Cont.

Variable	Group	Usual Intake Mean (SD)	P^1	Percentile 10	25	50	75	90	EAR	%	% Below EAR P^2
Vitamin B12 (μg/day)	Non-nut consumers	8.7 (3.8)	<0.001	4.5	5.9	8.0	10.9	14.1	M: 2.0 μg/day	0.4	0.088
	Nut-consumers	9.7 (3.8)		5.3	6.7	9.0	12.0	15.1	W: 2.0 μg/day	0.1	
Folic acid (μg/day)	Non-nut consumers	303.7 (86.7)	<0.001	200.2	242.0	295.0	354.3	419.1	M: 320.0 μg/day	60.6	<0.001
	Nut-consumers	345.8 (89.4)		238.8	283.0	335.5	400.9	470.2	W: 320.0 μg/day	42.5	
Vitamin C (mg/day)	Non-nut consumers	175.0 (74.6)	<0.001	85.5	120.8	165.6	217.3	277.3	M: 75.0 mg/day	4.6	<0.001
	Nut-consumers	197.5 (76.6)		108.4	142.5	184.4	243.5	304.0	W: 60.0 mg/day	1.9	
Vitamin D (μg/day)	Non-nut consumers	5.2 (3.2)	<0.001	1.9	3.0	4.3	6.8	10.2	M: 10.0 μg/day	89.6	0.001
	Nut-consumers	6.1 (3.2)		2.6	3.8	5.1	8.8	10.8	W: 10.0 μg/day	85.7	
Vitamin E (mg/day)	Non-nut consumers	8.3 (2.7)	<0.001	5.3	6.5	7.9	9.5	11.5	M: 12 mg/day	91.8	<0.001
	Nut-consumers	10.6 (3.2)		6.9	8.3	10.0	12.3	15.0	W: 12 mg/day	71.9	
Ca (mg/day)	Non-nut consumers	950.9 (325.3)	<0.001	572.7	708.8	909.9	1144.1	1391.5	M 51–70 y-o: 800.0 mg/day M >70 y-o: 1000.0 mg/day	50.6	<0.001
	Nut-consumers	1008.4 (306.1)		637.7	789.4	977.0	1208.7	1418.4	W: 1000.0 mg/day	40.2	
Mg (mg/day)	Non-nut consumers	344.4 (86.2)	<0.001	245.4	284.7	331.1	393.7	461.7	M: 350.0 mg/day	36.7	<0.001
	Nut-consumers	402.9 (94.5)		288.9	333.8	394.8	463.2	533.8	W: 265.0 mg/day	18.8	
P (mg/day)	Non-nut consumers	1580.8 (388.3)	<0.001	1109.0	1291.8	1541.2	1827.1	2099.9	M: 580.0 mg/day	0.2	0.086
	Nut-consumers	1728.7 (374.9)		1253.3	1465.5	1714.3	1985.1	2225.5	W: 580.0 mg/day	0.0	
Fe (mg/day)	Non-nut consumers	14.6 (3.6)	<0.001	10.2	12.1	14.3	16.8	19.5	M: 6.0 mg/day	0.2	0.086
	Nut-consumers	16.4 (3.6)		12.0	13.9	16.2	18.8	21.3	W: 5.0 mg/day	0.0	
Se (μg/day)	Non-nut consumers	106.1 (32.1)	<0.001	66.9	83.1	102.7	126.8	148.8	M: 45.0 μg/day	1.4	<0.001
	Nut-consumers	116.5 (30.5)		78.7	94.8	114.9	136.1	157.0	W: 45.0 μg/day	0.3	
Zn (mg/day)	Non-nut consumers	12.0 (3.1)	<0.001	8.4	9.8	11.7	13.9	16.3	M: 9.4 mg/day	9.4	<0.001
	Nut-consumers	13.1 (3.0)		9.4	11.0	12.9	15.0	17.1	W: 6.8 mg/day	5.0	
Iodine (μg/day)	Non-nut consumers	282.5 (153.8)	0.213	92.9	176.4	252.2	328.0	531.0	M: 95.0 μg/day	10.4	0.577
	Nut-consumers	276.1 (143.5)		95.5	181.5	258.2	298.2	531.9	W: 95.0 μg/day	9.8	
K (g/day)	Non-nut consumers	4.0 (1.0)	<0.001	2.9	3.3	3.9	4.6	5.4	M: 4.7 g/day	23.5	<0.001
	Nut-consumers	4.4 (1.0)		3.3	3.8	4.4	5.1	5.7	W: 4.7 g/day	37.7	
Cr (μg/day)	Non-nut consumers	76.6 (46.1)	<0.001	37.4	46.7	61.4	89.7	140.1	M: 30.0 μg/day	98.8	0.046
	Nut-consumers	83.8 (44.2)		42.1	51.8	70.6	103.7	144.5	W: 20.0 μg/day	99.4	

Abbreviations: EAR, estimated average requirement; AI, adequate intake; SD, standard deviation; RAE, retinol activity equivalents; NE, niacin equivalents; vitamin E (i.e., α-tocopherol); M: men; W: women; Ca, calcium; Mg, magnesium; P, phosphorous; Fe, iron; Se, selenium; Zn, zinc; K, potassium; Cr, chromium; y-o: years-old. [1] Difference in means between non-nut consumers and nut consumers were tested by unpaired Students' t-test. [2] The difference in prevalence across the two comparison groups was examined using χ^2.

Table 3. Usual intake of vitamins and minerals of the nut consumers (n = 4969).

Variables	Q1 (n = 1182)	Q2 (n = 980)	Quintiles of Nut Consumption Q3 (n = 848)	Q4 (n = 987)	Q5 (n = 972)	p *
Vitamin A RAE (µg/day)						
Mean ± SD	980.5 ± 520.2 [a,b,c,d]	1055.1 ± 519.9 [a,g]	1069.9 ± 532.6 [b,h,i]	1096.2 ± 525.9 [c]	1136.8 ± 558.2 [d,h,i]	<0.001
% below EAR	20.8	13.2	14.6	13.3	12.1	<0.001
Vitamin B1 (mg/day)						
Mean ± SD	1.5 ± 0.4 [a,b,c,d]	1.6 ± 0.4 [a,f,g]	1.6 ± 0.4 [b,h,i]	1.7 ± 0.3 [c,f,h,j]	1.8 ± 0.3 [d,g,i,j]	<0.001
% below EAR	4.7	2.9	2.5	1.3	0.4	<0.001
Vitamin B2 (mg/day)						
Mean ± SD	1.8 ± 0.5 [b,c,d]	1.9 ± 0.5 [f,g]	1.9 ± 0.5 [b,h,i]	2.0 ± 0.5 [c,f,h,j]	2.1 ± 0.5 [d,g,i,j]	<0.001
% below EAR	3.2	1.9	2.0	1.2	1.4	0.009
Vitamin B3 NE (mg/day)						
Mean ± SD	37.8 ± 8.8 [a,b,c,d]	39.3 ± 8.7 [a,f,g]	39.3 ± 8.6 [b,h,i]	41.0 ± 8.6 [c,f,h]	42.1 ± 8.6 [d,g,i]	<0.001
% below EAR	0.0	0.0	0.0	0.0	0.0	1.000
Vitamin B6 (mg/day)						
Mean ± SD	2.1 ± 0.5 [a,b,c,d]	2.2 ± 0.5 [a,f,g]	2.3 ± 0.5 [b,h,i]	2.4 ± 0.5 [c,f,h,j]	2.5 ± 0.5 [d,g,i,j]	<0.001
% below EAR	6.6	2.6	1.8	1.0	0.3	<0.001
Vitamin B12 (µg/day)						
Mean ± SD	9.2 ± 3.8 [a,c,d]	9.7 ± 3.8 [a]	9.6 ± 3.8	10.0 ± 3.9 [c]	10.0 ± 3.9 [d]	<0.001
% below EAR	0.1	0.1	0.2	0.2	0.0	0.590
Folic acid (µg/day)						
Mean ± SD	316.6 ± 83.9 [a,b,c,d]	332.1 ± 87.5 [a,f,g]	340.5 ± 82.4 [b,h,i]	358.3 ± 86.7 [c,f,h,j]	387.1 ± 89.1 [d,g,i,j]	<0.001
% below EAR	57.3	48.1	45.4	35.1	24.2	<0.001
Vitamin C (mg/day)						
Mean ± SD	181.5 ± 75.5 [a,b,c,d]	194.3 ± 77.2 [a,g]	195.2 ± 73.1 [b,i]	202.6 ± 74.4 [c,j]	216.9 ± 78.1 [d,g,i,j]	<0.001
% below EAR	3.8	1.4	1.9	1.2	0.9	<0.001
Vitamin D (µg/day)						
Mean ± SD	5.5 ± 3.1 [a,b,c,d]	6.0 ± 3.1 [a,f,g]	5.9 ± 3.1 [b,h,i]	6.5 ± 3.3 [c,f,h]	6.6 ± 3.3 [d,g,i]	<0.001
% below EAR	89.1	87.6	88.1	82.1	81.1	<0.001
Vitamin E (mg/day)						
Mean ± SD	8.9 ± 2.7 [a,b,c,d]	9.9 ± 2.5 [a,f,g]	10.0 ± 2.6 [b,h,i]	11.4 ± 2.7 [c,f,h,j]	13.1 ± 3.7 [d,g,i,j]	<0.001
% below EAR	89.0	84.8	80.8	62.5	39.7	<0.001

135

Table 3. Cont.

Variables	Quintiles of Nut Consumption					p *
	Q1 (n = 1182)	Q2 (n = 980)	Q3 (n = 848)	Q4 (n = 987)	Q5 (n = 972)	
Ca (mg/day)						
Mean ± SD	961.6 ± 296.8 b,c,d	983.4 ± 295.5 g	1000.4 ± 310.9 b,i	1027.3 ± 307.2 c,f,j	1078.6 ± 308.6 d,g,i,j	<0.001
% below EAR	46.7	43.4	41.4	38.2	30.3	<0.001
Mg (mg/day)						
Mean ± SD	355.7 ± 83.5 a,b,c,d	379.1 ± 84.6 a,e,f,g	392.5 ± 81.8 b,e,h,i	424.5 ± 87.0 c,f,h,j	471.7 ± 88.9 d,g,i,j	<0.001
% below EAR	32.4	23.0	18.5	12.5	4.7	<0.001
P (mg/day)						
Mean ± SD	1609.6 ± 358.8 a,b,c,d	1671.7 ± 358.8 a,f,g	1706.7 ± 360.7 b,h,i	1785.8 ± 367.9 c,f,h,j	1891.9 ± 361.9 d,g,i,j	<0.001
% below EAR	0.1	0.0	0.0	0.0	0.0	0.524
Fe (mg/day)						
Mean ± SD	15.2 ± 3.5 a,b,c,d	16.0 ± 3.5 a,f,g	16.2 ± 3.4 b,h,i	16.9 ± 3.4 c,f,h,j	18.0 ± 3.4 d,g,i,j	<0.001
% below EAR	0.1	0.0	0.0	0.0	0.0	0.524
Se (µg/day)						
Mean ± SD	111.3 ± 31.5 b,c,d	114.8 ± 29.8 f,g	115.6 ± 30.6 b,i	119.2 ± 29.7 c,f	122.7 ± 29.54 d,g,i	<0.001
% below EAR	0.5	0.4	0.4	0.2	0.0	0.251
Zn (mg/day)						
Mean ± SD	12.4 ± 3.0 a,b,c,d	12.8 ± 3.0 a,f,g	12.9 ± 3.0 b,h,i	13.4 ± 2.9 c,f,h,j	13.9 ± 2.8 d,g,i,j	<0.001
% below EAR	7.4	5.3	5.4	4.4	1.9	<0.001
Iodine (µg/day)						
Mean ± SD	280.7 ± 144.9	266.4 ± 135.5	279.4 ± 146.8	274.4 ± 145.1	279.3 ± 144.8	0.148
% below EAR	10.2	9.0	10.0	9.5	10.2	0.862
K (g/day)						
Mean ± SD	4135.7 ± 927.2 a,b,c,d	4290.8 ± 923.2 a,e,f,g	4424.5 ± 891.3 b,e,h,i	4597.0 ± 957.3 c,f,h,j	4855.8 ± 954.2 d,g,i,j	<0.001
% above AI	25.2	30.7	36.1	43.9	55.1	<0.001
Cr (µg/day)						
Mean ± SD	77.4 ± 44.0 c,d	79.3 ± 41.8 f,g	82.7 ± 42.2 h,i	88.8 ± 45.3 c,f,h	92.2 ± 45.6 d,g,i	<0.001
% above AI	98.7	99.6	99.4	99.5	99.8	0.020

Abbreviations: AI: adequate intake. EAR: estimated average requirements. Nut consumption range in each of the quintiles: Q1: <4.2 g/day, n = 911; Q2: 4.2–8.3 g/day, n = 1058; Q3: 8.4–14.5 g/day, n = 868; Q4: 14.6–29.3 g/day, n = 1093; Q5: ≥29.4 g/day, n = 1039. * Differences in means between quintiles were tested by one-way ANOVA with Bonferroni's post-hoc test. Different letters indicate statistically significant differences between quintile groups.

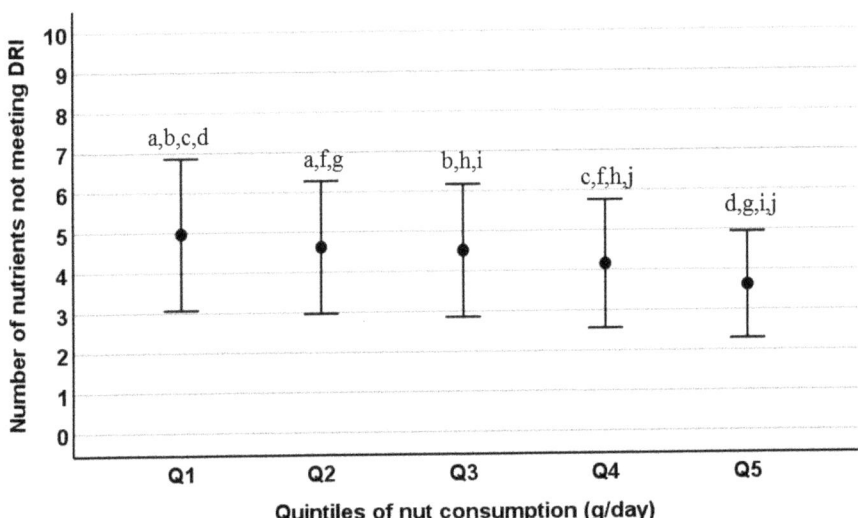

Figure 1. Mean (with standard deviation (SD)) number of nutrients with intakes not meeting the recommended levels across quintiles of nut consumption (g/day). Nut consumption range in each of the quintiles: Q1: <4.2 g/day, n = 911; Q2: 4.2–8.3 g/day, n = 1058; Q3: 8.4–14.5 g/day, n = 868; Q4: 14.6–29.3, n = 1093; Q5: ≥29.4 g/day, n = 1039. DRI, dietary reference intake; Q, quintile. Differences in means between quintiles were tested by one-way ANOVA ($p < 0.001$) with Bonferroni's post-hoc test. Different letters indicate statistically significant differences between quintile groups.

Table 4. Unmet dietary reference intakes (DRI) ≥6 and ≥8 number of nutrients in nut-consumers (n = 4969) compared with non-nut consumers as reference value (n = 1091).

Unmet DRI	Non-Nut Consumers (n = 1091)	Nut Consumers (n = 4969)	p [1]
Failing to meet 6 or more recommendations			
<6	64.4	80.6	<0.001
≥6	35.6	19.4	
Crude OR [2] (95% CI)	1.00 (ref.)	0.44 (0.38, 0.50) **	
Adjusted OR [3] (95% CI)	1.00 (ref.)	0.58 (0.49, 0.69) **	
Adjusted OR [4] (95% CI)	1.00 (ref.)	0.59 (0.49, 0.71) **	
Failing to meet 8 or more recommendations			
<8	89.2	95.0	<0.001
≥8	10.8	5.0	
Crude OR [2] (95% CI)	1.00 (ref.)	0.43 (0.34, 0.54) **	
Adjusted OR [3] (95% CI)	1.00 (ref.)	0.73 (0.55, 0.97) *	
Adjusted OR [4] (95% CI)	1.00 (ref.)	0.80 (0.59, 1.07) NS	

Abbreviations: OR, odds ratio; CI, confidence interval; ref., reference. Values are expressed as n (%) and OR (95% CI). [1] Significant differences in prevalence were calculated by means of χ^2. [2] Logistic regression analysis comparing the two different cut-offs (independent variables) between nut-consumers and non-nut consumers as reference value (dependent variable). [3] Logistic regression analysis after adjustment for sex, energy intake (continuous variable) and total physical activity (continuous variable, expressed as MET·min/week). [4] Logistic regression analysis after additional adjustment for total fat intake (continuous variable, expressed as % of total energy intake), and Mediterranean diet score (MDS) (continuous variable). [3,4] Participants who not responded the physical activity questionnaires and participants reporting outliers for total physical activity expressed as MET·min/week (at 3 or more standard deviations from the mean) were excluded from the analysis (i.e., 79 participants 'non-nut consumers' and 239 participants 'nut consumers'). * $p < 0.05$; ** $p < 0.001$; NS: no significant.

4. Discussion

In the present study nutrient adequacy and diet quality was better in nut consumers than in non-consumers. This study also confirmed that nut consumption was associated with better adherence to the MedDiet (MDS) than that observed in their non-consumers counterparts. Furthermore, nut consumers had lower BMI [26], were more likely to be physically active and less likely to smoke than non-nut consumers. A novelty of the present study is that it investigated these associations in a Mediterranean population at high cardiovascular risk. Moreover, nut consumers (82%) were higher in this study than in previous reports, such as the NHANES 2005–2010 (n = 14386; nut consumers: 5.2%) [4], the NHANES 2001–2010 (n = 24,808; almond consumers: 1.6%) [5] and the NZANS 2008/09 (n = 4721; nut consumers: 28.9%) [6]; however, the median of nut consumption was only 12.6 g/day (IQR: 6.0, 25.2).

This study showed that nut consumers were less likely to be below the EAR for some nutrients and above the AI for others than non-nut consumers. Moreover, higher nut consumers showed better compliance with the nutritional recommendations for micronutrients. Previously, Roman–Viñas et al. [27] analyzed the prevalence of inadequate intakes of several micronutrients (vitamins B_{12}, C, and D; folic acid, Ca, Fe, Se, iodine and Cu) in European adult (19–64 years) and elderly (>64 years) populations. In their study, Roman–Viñas et al. [27] showed a prevalence of inadequacy equal or below 10% for Zn, Fe, and vitamin B12 (only in the elderly population); prevalence between 11–20% for Cu in the adult and elderly populations, for vitamin B_{12} in the adult population, and for vitamin C in the elderly Europeans; and a prevalence above 21% for vitamin D, vitamin C (only in the adult population), folic acid, Ca, Se, and iodine [27]. Nevertheless, to our knowledge, only two studies conducted by O'Neil et al. [4,5] using NHANES data have previously examined associations between nut consumption and nutrient adequacy.

O'Neil et al. [4] analyzing data from the NHANES 2005–2010 found a lower prevalence of inadequacy for vitamins A, C and E, folate, Ca, Mg, Fe, Zn and K in nut-consumers than in non-nut consumers. Lately, O'Neil et al. [5] also examined the prevalence of inadequate intakes of a number of micronutrients between almond and non-almond consumers from the NHANES 2001–2010 and found a lower prevalence of inadequacy for vitamins A, B_2, C and E, Ca, Mg, P, Zn and Cu in almond consumers than in non-almond consumers [5]. Accordingly, in our study the prevalence of inadequate intakes of vitamins A, B1, B_2, B_6, C, D and E, folate, Ca, Mg, Se and Zn were lower in nut consumers than in non-nut consumers.

Nuts are rich in vitamin E, folate, Ca and Mg, and in our study the proportions of inadequate intakes for these four micronutrients were high, especially in non-nut consumers, in which the proportions with intakes below the EAR were 37–92%, in comparison with nut consumers, in which the proportions were 20–72%. Accordingly, O'Neil et al. [6] also found a high proportion of non-nut consumers with intakes below the EAR for vitamin E, Ca and Mg (i.e., 94.2%, 44.3% and 60.1%, respectively) in comparison with nut consumers (37.7%, 26.9% and 8.2%, respectively). Previously, Serra-Majem et al. [28], assessing the relationship between nutrient adequacy and a posteriori defined Mediterranean and Western dietary pattern in the Seguimiento Universidad de Navarra (SUN) cohort, also found that 89–94% of participants did not comply with recommended vitamin E intakes. Moreover, the proportions of inadequate intakes for folic acid and Mg were also higher in the first quintile of adherence to the Mediterranean dietary pattern (19% and 21%, respectively) than in the fifth quintile (10% and 2%, respectively) [27]. Recently, Zazpe et al. [2] also found an inverse association between the risk of failing to meet ≥4 DRIs and deciles of adherence to the MedDiet (Mediterranean diet score, MDS) in participants of the SUN cohort.

Most species of nuts have high contents of K (e.g., almonds, pine nuts, pecans). While O'Neil et al. [4,5] studies found a proportion of inadequate intake for K below 12% in both nut and non-nut consumers, in our study the prevalence of inadequacy for K was above 21% in both groups. However, K intake is still below the recommended intakes in our population [17]. Moreover, not only nuts but also fruits, vegetables and dairy products, which were more frequently consumed by nut consumers than non-nut consumers, are high K foods.

Nuts are poor sources of vitamin D. However, in Mediterranean countries, it can be obtained from conversion through the skin stimulated by UV radiation. Therefore, the proportion that should be obtained from food is unknown [1,29]. According to O'Neil's studies [4,5], its prevalence of inadequacy was also exceptionally very high in both groups (i.e., 86% in nut consumers and 90% in non-nut consumers).

Finally, nut consumers had lower prevalence of inadequate micronutrient intakes (≥ 6 and ≥ 8 DRI), but also higher CQI, adherence to the MedDiet (Mediterranean diet score, MDS) and FQI than non-nut consumers. In this line, Sánchez–Tainta et al. [2] have also recently reported lower prevalence of inadequate micronutrient intakes (≥ 8 DRI) in the highest quintile of CQI or adherence to the MedDiet (Mediterranean Diet Score, MDS), and in the lowest quintile of FQI. Nevertheless, in Spain there is a general thought that nuts can decrease the cardiovascular risk, and nut consumers may also be more conscious of having a MedDiet. Nevertheless, the median consumption of nuts for which the DRIs were unmet <6 and <8 was only 12.6 g/day in both cases (IQR: 6.0, 27.4 and 6.0, 25.2, respectively).

5. Strengths and Limitations of the Study

The strengths of this study are that it used a large Mediterranean sample at high cardiovascular risk and that, the contribution of supplements to micronutrient intake was considered. The main limitation of this study is that it is a cross-sectional study; thus, we fully acknowledge that causal inferences cannot be drawn but only observations. A second limitation is that all nutritional data presented here is self-reported, as well as most of nutritional assessment methods. Another limitation is that the same source of information was used to assess nut intake and nutritional adequacy. Moreover, the self-reported FFQ could overestimate the intake of certain food groups even having been validated. Nevertheless, it is likely to be similar in both compared groups and therefore could only contribute to the increase of the measurement error and to dilute the true differences. Furthermore, in order address such a possible error and avoid information bias we excluded participants with energy or micronutrient intake out of predefined ranges [2]. Previously, in the PREDIMED study, 827 participants who had extreme values for total energy intake or any micronutrient intake out of the predefined values were also excluded in the nutritional adequacy analysis [2]. Nonetheless, plasma concentrations of vitamins and micronutrients were not determined in our study. Finally, nut consumers may simply be more health conscious than non-nut consumers [6]. Nevertheless, this is a cross-sectional study and therefore we acknowledge that we are not able to draw causal conclusions but only observations.

6. Conclusions

In conclusion, a high proportion of individuals at high cardiovascular risk consumed nuts. The rate was higher than in previous similar studies; however, the average amount of daily nut consumption was low among them. Nevertheless, consumption of nuts was associated with nutrient adequacy, better diet quality, and higher adherence to the MedDiet (Mediterranean diet score, MDS) than those seen in non-nut consumers. Nuts contributed to these results and to an overall healthier diet. Thus, consumption of nuts should be encouraged by health professionals, including registered dietitians. Moreover, nutrition education programs that increase awareness, health benefits, and consumption of nuts should be designed for the general adult population at high cardiovascular risk to attain nutrient adequacy. This study also raises the possibility that future research should include a categorized nut consumption amount to assess health benefits in interventional programs encouraging nut consumption.

Author Contributions: All authors contributed to obtain data from the participants recruited in the PREDIMEDPLUS survey. J.A.T., M.M.B., A.J. and C.B. wrote the first draft of the manuscript and all other authors gave additional suggestions. All authors approve final version of the manuscript.

Funding: The PREDIMED-Plus trial was supported by the official funding agency for biomedical research of the Spanish government, ISCIII through the Fondo de Investigación para la Salud (FIS), which is co-funded by the European Regional Development Fund (four coordinated FIS projects led by Jordi Salas-Salvadó and Josep Vidal, including the following projects: PI13/00673, PI13/00492, PI13/00272, PI13/01123, PI13/00462, PI13/00233, PI13/02184, PI13/00728, PI13/01090, PI13/01056, PI14/01722, PI14/00636, PI14/00618, PI14/00696, PI14/01206, PI14/01919, PI14/00853, PI14/01374, PI16/00473, PI16/00662, PI16/01873, PI16/01094, PI16/00501,

PI16/00533, PI16/00381, PI16/00366, PI16/01522, PI16/01120, PI17/00764, PI17/01183, PI17/00855, PI17/01347, PI17/00525, PI17/01827, PI17/00532, PI17/00215, PI17/01441, PI17/00508, PI17/01732, PI17/00926, the Especial Action Project entitled: Implementación y evaluación de una intervención intensive sobre la actividad física Cohorte PREDIMED-PLUS grant to Jordi Salas-Salvadó, the European Research Council (Advanced Research Grant 2013–2018; 340918) grant to Miguel Ángel Martínez–Gonzalez, the Recercaixa grant to Jordi Salas–Salvadó (2013ACUP00194), the grant from the Consejería de Salud de la Junta de Andalucía (PI0458/2013; PS0358/2016), the PROMETEO/2017/017 grant from the Generalitat Valenciana, the SEMERGEN grant, and CIBEROBN and FEDER funds (CB06/03), ISCIII. Josep A. Tur, Maria del Mar Bibiloni, Alicia Julibert and Cristina Bouzas are granted by Grant of support to research groups no. 35/2011 (Balearic Islands Gov.; FEDER funds) and EU-COST ACTION CA16112. None of the funding sources took part in the design, collection, analysis or interpretation of the data, or in the decision to submit the manuscript for publication. The corresponding authors had full access to all the data in the study and had final responsibility to submit for publication.

Acknowledgments: The authors especially thank the PREDIMED-Plus participants for their enthusiastic collaboration, the PREDIMED-Plus personnel for their outstanding support, and the personnel of all associated primary care centers for their exceptional effort. Centros de Investigación Biomédica en Red: Obesidad y Nutrición (CIBEROBN), Centros de Investigación Biomédica en Red: Epidemiología y Salud Pública (CIBERESP) and Centros de Investigación Biomédica en Red: Diabetes y Enfermedades Metabólicas asociadas (CIBERDEM) are initiatives of Instituto de Salud Carlos III (ISCIII), Madrid, Spain. Food companies, Hojiblanca and Patrimonio Comunal Olivarero, donated extra-virgin olive oil and Almond Board of California, American Pistachio Growers and Paramount Farms donated nuts for the pilot study. We thank the PREDIMED-Plus Biobank Network as a part of the National Biobank Platform of the ISCIII for storing and managing the PREDIMED-Plus biological samples.

Conflicts of Interest: J.S.-S. reports serving on the board of and receiving grant support through his institution from International Nut and Dried Fruit Council; receiving consulting personal fees from Danone, Font Vella Lanjaron, Nuts for Life, and Eroski; and receiving grant support through his institution from Nut and Dried Fruit Foundation and Eroski. ER reports grants, non-financial support, and other fees from California Walnut Commission and Alexion; personal fees and non-financial support from Merck, Sharp and Dohme; personal fees, non-financial support and other fees from Aegerion, and Ferrer International; grants and personal fees from Sanofi Aventis; grants from Amgen and Pfizer and; personal fees from Akcea, outside of the submitted work. X.P. reports serving on the board of and receiving consulting personal fees from Sanofi Aventis, Amgen, and Abbott laboratories; receiving lecture personal fees from Esteve, Lacer and Rubio laboratories. M.D.-R. reports receiving grants from the Diputación Provincial de Jaén and the Caja Rural de Jaén. L.D. reports grants from Fundación Cerveza y Salud. All other authors declare no competing interests.

Abbreviations

AI	Adequate intake
CHO	Carbohydrate
CQI	Carbohydrate quality index
EAR	Estimated average requirements
erMedDiet	Energy-restricted traditional MedDiet
FFQ	Food frequency questionnaire
FQI	Fat quality index
MedDiet	Mediterranean diet
MET	Metabolic equivalents
MetS	Metabolic syndrome
NHANES	National Health and Nutrition Examination Survey
NE	Niacin equivalents
NZANS	New Zealand Adult Nutrition Survey
RAE	Retinol activity equivalents
RAPA	Rapid assessment of physical activity questionnaire
RDA	Recommended daily allowances
DRI	Dietary reference intake
TFA	Trans fatty acid
UL	Tolerable upper level

References

1. Castro-Quezada, I.; Román-Viñas, B.; Serra-Majem, L. The Mediterranean diet and nutritional adequacy: A review. *Nutrients* **2014**, *6*, 231–248. [CrossRef] [PubMed]

2. Sánchez-Tainta, A.; Zazpe, I.; Bes-Rastrollo, M.; Salas-Salvadó, J.; Bullo, M.; Sorlí, J.V.; Corella, D.; Covas, M.I.; Arós, F.; Gutierrez-Bedmar, M.; et al. PREDIMED studyinvestigators. Nutritional adequacy according to carbohydrates and fat quality. *Eur. J. Nutr.* **2016**, *55*, 93–106. [CrossRef]
3. O'Neil, C.E.; Keast, D.R.; Fulgoni, V.L., 3rd; Nicklas, T.A. Tree nut consumption improves nutrient intake and diet quality in US adults: An analysis of National Health and Nutrition Examination Survey (NHANES) 1999–2004. *Asia Pac. J. Clin. Nutr.* **2010**, *19*, 142–150.
4. O'Neil, C.E.; Nicklas, T.A.; Fulgoni, V.L., 3rd. Tree nut consumption is associated with better nutrient adequacy and diet quality in adults: National Health and Nutrition Examination Survey 2005–2010. *Nutrients* **2015**, *7*, 595–607. [CrossRef]
5. O'Neil, C.E.; Nicklas, T.A.; Fulgoni, V.L., 3rd. Almond Consumption Is Associated with Better Nutrient Intake, Nutrient Adequacy, and Diet Quality in Adults: National Health and Nutrition Examination Survey 2001–2010. *Food Nutr. Sci.* **2016**, *7*, 504–515.
6. Brown, R.C.; Tey, S.L.; Gray, A.R.; Chisholm, A.; Smith, C.; Fleming, E.; Parnell, W. Nut consumption is associated with better nutrient intakes: Results from the 2008/09 New Zealand Adult Nutrition Survey. *Br. J. Nutr.* **2016**, *115*, 105–112. [CrossRef] [PubMed]
7. Chen, C.G.; Zhang, R.; Martínez-González, M.A.; Zhang, Z.L.; Bonaccio, M.; van Dam, R.M.; Qin, L.Q. Nut consumption in relation to all-cause and cause-specific mortality: A meta-analysis 18 prospective studies. *Food Funct.* **2017**, *8*, 3893–3905. [CrossRef] [PubMed]
8. Ros, E. Nuts and, C.V.D. *Br. J. Nutr.* **2015**, *113* (Suppl. 2), S111–S120. [CrossRef]
9. Kim, Y.; Keogh, J.B.; Clifton, P.M. Benefits of Nut Consumption on Insulin Resistance and Cardiovascular Risk Factors: Multiple Potential Mechanisms of Actions. *Nutrients* **2017**, *9*, 1271. [CrossRef]
10. Relja, A.; Miljković, A.; Gelemanović, A.; Bošković, M.; Hayward, C.; Polašek, O.; Kolčić, I. Nut Consumption and Cardiovascular Risk Factors: A Cross-Sectional Study in a Mediterranean Population. *Nutrients* **2017**, *9*, 1296. [CrossRef]
11. Guasch-Ferré, M.; Liu, X.; Malik, V.S.; Sun, Q.; Willett, W.C.; Manson, J.E.; Rexrode, K.M.; Li, Y.; Hu, F.B.; Bhupathiraju, S.N. Nut Consumption and Risk of Cardiovascular Disease. *J. Am. Coll. Cardiol.* **2017**, *70*, 2519–2532. [CrossRef]
12. Martínez-González, M.A.; Buil-Cosiales, P.; Corella, D.; Bulló, M.; Fitó, M.; Vioque, J.; Romaguera, D.; Martínez, J.A.; Wärnberg, J.; López-Miranda, J.; et al. Cohort Profile: Design and methods of the PREDIMED-PLUS randomised trial. *Int. J. Epidemiol.* **2018**. [CrossRef]
13. Alberti, K.G.; Eckel, R.H.; Grundy, S.M.; Zimmet, P.Z.; Cleeman, J.I.; Donato, K.A. Harmonizing the metabolic syndrome: A joint interim statement of the International Diabetes Federation Task Force on Epidemiology and Prevention; National Heart, Lung, and Blood Institute; American Heart Association; World Heart Federation; International. *Circulation* **2009**, *120*, 1640–1645. [CrossRef]
14. Fernández-Ballart, J.D.; Piñol, J.L.; Zazpe, I.; Corella, D.; Carrasco, P.; Toledo, E.; Perez-Bauer, M.; Martínez-González, M.A.; Salas-Salvadó, J.; Martín-Moreno, J.M. Relative validity of a semi-quantitative food-frequency questionnaire in an elderly Mediterranean population of Spain. *Br. J. Nutr.* **2010**, *103*, 1808–1816. [CrossRef]
15. Martin-Moreno, J.M.; Boyle, P.; Gorgojo, L.; Maisonneuve, P.; Fernandez-Rodriguez, J.C.; Salvini, S.; Willett, W.C. Development and validation of a food frequency questionnaire in Spain. *Int. J. Epidemiol.* **1993**, *22*, 512–519. [CrossRef] [PubMed]
16. De la Fuente-Arrillaga, C.; Ruiz, Z.V.; Bes-Rastrollo, M.; Sampson, L.; Martinez-González, M.A. Reproducibility of an FFQ validated in Spain. *Public Health Nutr.* **2010**, *13*, 1364–1372. [CrossRef]
17. The National Academies of Sciences Engineering Medicine, Institute of Medicine (US), Food and Nutrition Board. Dietary Reference Intakes (DRIs): Estimated Average Requirements Values. Available online: http://nationalacademies.org/hmd/Activities/Nutrition/SummaryDRIs/DRI-Tables.aspx (accessed on 9 April 2018).
18. Institute of Medicine (US) Committee to Review Dietary Reference Intakes for Vitamin D and Calcium. *Dietary Reference Intakes for Calcium and Vitamin, D*; National Academies Press (US): Washington, DC, USA, 2011. Available online: https://www.ncbi.nlm.nih.gov/books/NBK56070/ (accessed on 9 April 2018).

19. Institute of Medicine (US) Subcommittee on Interpretation and Uses of Dietary Reference Intakes; Institute of Medicine (US) Standing Committee on the Scientific Evaluation of Dietary Reference Intakes. *DRI Dietary Reference Intakes: Applications in Dietary Assessment*; National Academies Press (US): Washington, DC, USA, 2000. Available online: https://www.ncbi.nlm.nih.gov/books/NBK222872/ (accessed on 9 April 2018).
20. Zazpe, I.; Sánchez-Taínta, A.; Santiago, S.; de la Fuente-Arrillaga, C.; Bes-Rastrollo, M.; Martínez, J.A.; Martínez-González, M.Á. SUN Project Investigators. Association between dietary carbohydrate intake quality and micronutrient intake adequacy in a Mediterranean cohort: The SUN (Seguimiento Universidad de Navarra) Project. *Br. J. Nutr.* **2014**, *111*, 2000–2009. [CrossRef] [PubMed]
21. Schröder, H.; Fitó, M.; Estruch, R.; Martínez-González, M.A.; Corella, D.; Salas-Salvadó, J.; Lamuela-Raventós, R.; Ros, E.; Salaverría, I.; Fiol, M.; et al. A short screener is valid for assessing Mediterranean diet adherence among older Spanish men and women. *J. Nutr.* **2011**, *141*, 1140–1145. [CrossRef]
22. Molina, L.; Sarmiento, M.; Peñafiel, J.; Donaire, D.; Garcia-Aymerich, J.; Gomez, M.; Ble, M.; Ruiz, S.; Frances, A.; Schröder, H.; et al. Validation of the Regicor Short Physical Activity Questionnaire for the Adult Population. *PLoS ONE* **2017**, *12*, e0168148. [CrossRef] [PubMed]
23. Elosua, R.; Garcia, M.; Aguilar, A.; Molina, L.; Covas, M.I.; Marrugat, J. Validation of the Minnesota Leisure Time Physical Activity Questionnaire in Spanish Women. Investigators of the MARATDON Group. *Med. Sci. Sports Exerc.* **2000**, *32*, 1431–1437. [CrossRef]
24. Elosua, R.; Marrugat, J.; Molina, L.; Pons, S.; Pujol, E. Validation of the Minnesota Leisure Time Physical Activity Questionnaire in Spanish men. The MARATHOM Investigators. *Am. J. Epidemiol.* **1994**, *139*, 1197–1209. [CrossRef] [PubMed]
25. Martínez-González, M.A.; López-Fontana, C.; Varo, J.J.; Sánchez-Villegas, A.; Martinez, J.A. Validation of the Spanish version of the physical activity questionnaire used in the Nurses' Health Study and the Health Professionals' Follow-up Study. *Public Health Nutr.* **2005**, *8*, 920–927. [CrossRef] [PubMed]
26. Celis-Morales, C.; Livingstone, K.M.; Affleck, A.; Navas-Carretero, S.; San-Cristobal, R.; Martinez, J.A.; Marsaux, C.F.M.; Saris, W.H.M.; O'Donovan, C.B.; Forster, H.; et al. Food4Me Study. Correlates of overall and central obesity in adults from seven European countries: Findings from the Food4Me Study. *Eur. J. Clin. Nutr.* **2018**, *72*, 207–219. [CrossRef] [PubMed]
27. Roman Viñas, B.; Ribas Barba, L.; Ngo, J.; Gurinovic, M.; Novakovic, R.; Cavelaars, A.; de Groot, L.C.; van't Veer, P.; Matthys, C.; Serra Majem, L. Projected prevalence of inadequate nutrient intakes in Europe. *Ann. Nutr. Metab.* **2011**, *59*, 84–95. [CrossRef]
28. Serra-Majem, L.; Bes-Rastrollo, M.; Román-Viñas, B.; Pfrimer, K.; Sánchez-Villegas, A.; Martínez-González, M.A. Dietary patterns and nutritional adequacy in a Mediterranean country. *Br. J. Nutr.* **2009**, *101* (Suppl. 2), S21–S28. [CrossRef]
29. Mensink, G.B.; Fletcher, R.; Gurinovic, M.; Huybrechts, I.; Lafay, L.; Serra-Majem, L.; Szponar, L.; Tetens, I.; Verkaik-Kloosterman, J.; Baka, A.; et al. Mapping low intake of micronutrients across Europe. *Br. J. Nutr.* **2013**, *110*, 755–773. [CrossRef] [PubMed]

© 2019 by the authors. Licensee MDPI, Basel, Switzerland. This article is an open access article distributed under the terms and conditions of the Creative Commons Attribution (CC BY) license (http://creativecommons.org/licenses/by/4.0/).

Article

Body Shape Index Is a Stronger Predictor of Diabetes

Hiba Bawadi *, Merna Abouwatfa, Sara Alsaeed, Abdelhamid Kerkadi and Zumin Shi

Department of Nutrition, College of Health Sciences, QU-Health, Qatar University, Doha P.O. Box 2713, Qatar; a1409072@student.qu.edu.qa (M.A.); ma1403220@student.qu.edu.qa (S.A.); abdel.hamid@qu.esdu.qa (A.K.); zumin@qu.edu.qa (Z.S.)
* Correspondence: hbawadi@qu.edu.qa; Tel.: +974-4403-4810

Received: 25 March 2019; Accepted: 27 April 2019; Published: 7 May 2019

Abstract: Anthropometric indicators can predict the development of diabetes among adults. Among them, a new indicator (Body Shape Index) was developed. Several cohort observational studies have demonstrated that A Body Shape Index (ABSI) is a prominent indicator for mortality and morbidity. Nevertheless, the predictive level of ABSI for diabetes varied among different ethnicities. This study aimed to assess the predictive level of ABSI for diabetes compared to BMI in the Qatari population. Date from 2536 Qatari adults aged 20–79 years attending the Qatar Biobank Study were used. Body height, weight, and waist circumference were measured. Blood samples were measured for glucose. The association between ABSI, BMI, and diabetes was assessed using a logistic regression. Both ABSI and BMI were positively associated with diabetes after adjusting for potential confounding factors. ABSI had a stronger association with diabetes than BMI. Per 1 SD increment of ABSI and BMI, the z-score had an odds ratios of 1.85 (1.54–2.23) and 1.34 (1.18–1.51) for diabetes, respectively. ABSI and BMI are significantly associated with diabetes in the Qatari population. ABSI is a better predictor for the risk of diabetes than BMI after the adjustment for age, gender, education, and physical activity.

Keywords: ABSI; BMI; Qatar Biobank; Diabetes

---

1. Introduction

The prevalence of diabetes mellitus is high among Qatari adults reaching 16.7% [1]. The progression of type 2 diabetes is accompanied with several complications such as neuropathy, retinopathy, cardiovascular disease, infections (e.g., monilial skin infections), and cognitive impairment [2]. The increase in the Type 2 diabetes prevalence is associated with a change in sedentary life style and obesity [3]. Different researches demonstrated that obesity, particularly abdominal obesity (AO), which represents both subcutaneous and visceral fat accumulation, is associated with an increased risk of cardiovascular and metabolic diseases in both adults and children [4]. It is well-known that obesity is linked with insulin resistance, which plays an important role in the pathophysiology of type 2 diabetes and other metabolic disorders [5,6]. Body mass index (BMI) is a widely accepted and easily applicable measure for obesity; it, however, cannot distinguish between fat and fat-free mass. Therefore, an elevated BMI might not necessarily reflect an increased adiposity [7]. To overcome this weakness, waist circumference (WC) has been used as indicators of abdominal obesity and is closely related to noncommunicable diseases [8,9]. It has been shown that an excess of WC is associated with an increase in the prevalence of cardiovascular diseases (CVD) and the risk of premature death even when BMI is within a normal range [10]. It was also reported that the association between insulin resistance and WC is better than that with BMI [11,12]. In 2012, Krakauer and Krakauer developed a new tool called a body shape index (ABSI) that accompanies waist circumference, height, and weight [13]. According to the authors, ABSI emphasizes the elevated risk of diseases related to central and general adiposity. Therefore, ABSI is capable of depicting a crucial risk factor for premature mortality [13]. ABSI showed a predictive power to the risk of CVD and cancer [14]. ABSI can estimate both visceral abdominal and general overall adiposities and can predict premature mortality better than WC and BMI [15]. ABSI has been validated to predict the risk of diabetes in several countries. However, the findings are mixed. Some studies suggest that ABSI is a better predictor for diabetes [16,17]. However, other studies showed ABSI is not a better predictor of diabetes than BMI [18].

The aim of this study is to assess the predictive level of ABSI for diabetes compared to BMI in the Qatari population. We also aimed to assess the interaction between ABSI and BMI in relation to diabetes.

2. Methodology

2.1. Study Design

The study is a population-based cross-sectional survey carried out between 2012–2014 for 60,000 men and women Qatari nationals and long-term residents (individuals living in the country for ≥15 years) (Qatar Biobank study); the detailed methods of data collection and sampling has been published elsewhere [19]. Exclusion criteria were a history of terminating diseases such as muscle wasting, athletes, age <20 or >79, and pregnant women. A random sample of 2802 adults aged 20–79 years was obtained from the Qatar Biobank survey data. Participants with incomplete measurements were excluded ($n = 266$). The final number of participants included in this analysis was 2536 (1275 males and 1261 females). Qatar Biobank recruitment and data collection protocols were approved by the Hamad Medical Corporation Ethics Committee. The Institutional Review Board approval for this study was obtained from Qatar Biobank.

2.2. Outcome Variable Diabetes

Diabetes was defined as having fasting glucose ≥7 mmol/dL, random glucose ≥11.1 mmol/dL, HbA1c >6.5%, or self-reported doctor diagnosed diabetes [20]. Anthropometric measurements including weight, height, and waist circumference were measured by competent registered nurses in Qatar Biobank clinics. The participants were asked to wear light clothing and to be barefoot. The weight was measured by kg and recorded to the closest 0.1 kg. The standing and sitting height were measured and recorded to the closest 0.1 cm with the subject's head in the Frankfurt plane. The waist circumference (WC) was measured at the midpoint between the last rib and the top of the iliac crest with stretch-resistant tape; the participants stood with their feet close together, arms positioned on the side. The weight and height measures were used to calculate body mass index (BMI, kg/m^2). The BMI status (normal, overweight, and obese) of the participants were assigned based on WHO BMI cutoff points [21]. DEXA-Full Body iDXA (GE) scan-scanners were used in measuring the body distribution of visceral and trunk fat. It works by passing a low dose of x-ray radiation that goes on the whole body of participants who were directed not to wear anything that might interfere with the x-ray of the device like metal belts or jewelry. They were asked to wear a gown and to lie flat on the screening for about 5 to 10 min, and for clear not blurry Full Body iDXA (GE) scan images, participants were asked to hold still without moving and to hold their breath for a few seconds.

A body shape index (ABSI) was calculated using the Krakauer and Krakauer equation: WC/(BMI$^{2/3}$height$^{1/2}$) [13]. The ABSI score was converted to a z-score using the following equation: ABSI minus ABSI$_{mean}$ divided by ABSI$_{SD}$. BMI was also converted to z-score. The z score was used to measure the association of ABSI compared with BMI and the risk of diabetes. The z-score was used as it makes the comparison meaningful because the unit change in the regression analysis is different for ABSI and BMI.

2.3. Covariates

The education level, age, and physical activity of the participants were obtained through a main questionnaire. Education was divided into three levels: Low education (up to secondary school), medium education (technical or professional school), and high education (university and above).

Leisure time physical activity levels (expressed as metabolic equivalents (MET) (hours/week)) were calculated based on the frequency and duration of different types of physical activity.

2.4. Statistical Analysis

The association between ABSI z-scores and diabetes was assessed using a logistic regression. Four models were used: model 1 adjusted for age and gender; model 2 further adjusted for education; model 3 further adjusted for physical activity; model 4 further adjusted for BMI. The association between BMI (z-score) and diabetes was also assessed using the same approach. Subgroup analyses were conducted and visually presented using a user-written syntax ipdover in Stata. All the analyses were conducted in Stata 15.1. A p value < 0.05 was considered as statistically significant.

3. Results

Table 1 shows the sample characteristics by gender. The mean age was 38.3 in males and 40.1 in females. More than 60% of the participants had a high education level. The prevalence of obesity was 39% (32.6% in men and 45.4% in women). Females had higher mean BMI and total fat mean than males. Males had higher waist circumference and visceral fat ($p < 0.001$). Sample characteristics by incidence of diabetes is presented Table S1.

Table 1. Sample characteristics by gender.

	Total	Male	Female	p-Value
	n = 2536	n = 1275	n = 1261	
Age (years)	39.4 (11.1)	38.8 (10.6)	40.1 (11.6)	0.004
Education				<0.001
Low	251 (9.9%)	94 (7.4%)	157 (12.5%)	
Medium	707 (27.9%)	388 (30.5%)	319 (25.3%)	
High	1576 (62.2%)	791 (62.1%)	785 (62.3%)	
BMI (kg/m^2)	29.0 (5.6)	28.4 (5.0)	29.6 (6.1)	<0.001
BMI categories				<0.001
Normal	603 (23.8%)	316 (24.8%)	287 (22.8%)	
Overweight	944 (37.2%)	543 (42.6%)	401 (31.8%)	
Obese	989 (39.0%)	416 (32.6%)	573 (45.4%)	
Waist circumference (cm)	89.2 (13.5)	93.5 (12.4)	84.8 (13.2)	<0.001
ABSI z score	0.0 (1.0)	0.7 (0.7)	−0.7 (0.7)	<0.001
Total mass (kg)	79.3 (16.3)	84.3 (15.2)	73.5 (15.7)	<0.001
Total fat (kg)	30.9 (10.7)	28.6 (10.3)	33.4 (10.6)	<0.001
Trunk fat (kg)	16.2 (6.4)	16.2 (6.6)	16.2 (6.2)	0.90
Visceral fat (kg)	1.0 (0.7)	1.3 (0.8)	0.8 (0.5)	<0.001
Leisure time physical activity (MET hours/week)	18.2 (38.6)	22.4 (45.3)	13.9 (29.8)	<0.001
Diabetes (%)	413 (16.3%)	191 (15.0%)	222 (17.6%)	0.073

The data are presented as mean (SD) for continuous measures and n (%) for categorical measures.

Table 2 shows the association between ABSI and BMI with diabetes using different logistic regression models with progressive adjustments. After adjusting for age and gender, both ABSI and BMI were positively associated with diabetes with an OR (95% CI) of 1.84 (1.54–2.21) and 1.38 (1.22–1.56) respectively. With a further adjustment for education, the OR for the risk of diabetes with ABSI z-scores was 1.87 (95% CI: 1.55–2.24), whereas the OR for the association between the risk of diabetes and BMI z-scores was 1.34 (95% CI: 1.55–1.19–1.52). After being mutually adjusted for ABSI and BMI, the ORs for diabetes increased for both ABSI 1.94 (95% CI: 1.61–2.34) and BMI 1.40 (95% CI: 1.24–1.60). The association between ABSI, BMI and HbA1c was assessed using a multivariable regression model where both indices were independently associated with HbA1c (refer to Figure S1 in the Supplementary Materials).

Table 2. The association between A Body Shape Index (ABSI) and BMI with diabetes among Qatari adults.

	ABSI z-Score		BMI z-Score	
	OR (95% CI)	p	OR (95% CI)	p
Model 1	1.84 (1.54–2.21)	<0.001	1.38 (1.22–1.56)	<0.001
Model 2	1.87 (1.55–2.24)	<0.001	1.34 (1.19–1.52)	<0.001
Model 3	1.85 (1.54–2.23)	<0.001	1.34 (1.18–1.51)	<0.001
Model 4	1.94 (1.61–2.34)	<0.001	1.40 (1.24–1.60)	<0.001

Model 1 adjusted for age and gender; Model 2 further adjusted for education; Model 3 further adjusted for physical activity; Model 4 further adjusted for the BMI z-score or ABSI z-score.

Figure 1 represents subgroup analyses of the association between ABSI and diabetes. There was a significant interaction between gender and ABSI in relation to diabetes. The association between ABSI and diabetes was stronger in women than in men. ABSI and diabetes were associated in all subgroups of age ≥30. The highest association were observed in the second age (30–39 years) subgroup ($p < 0.001$). Participants with a normal weight did not show a significant association between ABSI and diabetes while overweight and obese did ($p < 0.001$); however, obese participants showed the highest association between ABSI and diabetes ($p < 0.001$). As BMI became higher, the OR gradient for diabetes associated with ABSI also became higher. The OR for diabetes associated with ABSI were 1.24, 1.79, and 2.20 among normal, overweight, and obese participants.

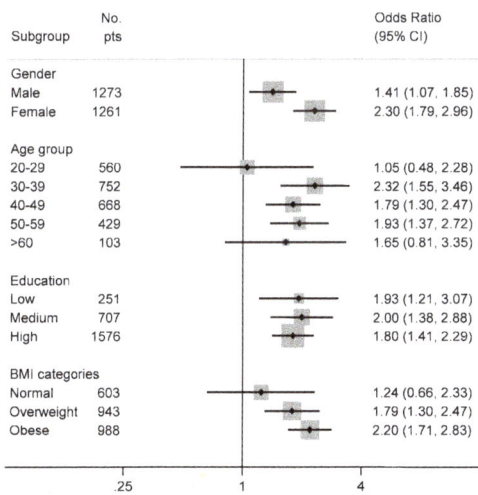

Figure 1. Subgroup analyses of the association between ABSI and diabetes.

4. Discussion

This cross-sectional study assessed the predictive power of ABSI and BMI on predicting the risk of diabetes in the Qatari population. It was found in the current study that ABSI is associated with a risk of diabetes to a greater extent as compared to BMI. Han et al. (2017) compared the predictive level of a body shape index (ABSI) to other anthropometric parameters including body mass index (BMI), waist to height ratio (WHtR), and waist circumference (WC) for the risk of developing type 2 diabetes mellitus (T2DM) in chinses adults [22]. After adjusting for different cofounding variables, ABSI differentiated between the cases and non-cases of diabetes; however, there was no difference in the predictive ability for T2DM when using ABSI or other anthropometric parameters [22]. Fujita and colleagues (2015) conducted a prospective cohort study aimed at addressing whether ABSI could be used as a predictor for the risk of developing type 2 diabetes mellitus and other chronic disease [23]. Researchers used annual health examination data (2008 to 2012) from Chiba City Hall in Japan. Their study included 37581 nondiabetic subjects followed up for 4 years. An increased BMI, WC, and ABSI elevated the risk of T2DM. Furthermore, the areas under the curve associated with ABSI regression models were smaller than that for BMI or WC models, which indicates that ABSI may not a stronger predictor for diabetes among Japanese population [23]. Similar findings were reported from an analysis of data from an 11-year follow-up study [24]. The authors reported that ABSI was an inferior discriminator of incident T2DM as compared to BMI and other anthropometric measures.

Interestingly, we found that the joint effect of BMI and ABSI is a better predicator for the risk of diabetes than the ABSI and BMI alone. This finding is in line with a recent retrospective study about the association between Body Shape Index (ABSI) with cardio-metabolic risk factors [16]. The study was conducted on 6081 Caucasian adults. Generalized linear models (GLM) were used to assess both sex and age and the adjusted association of the ABSI with binary and continuous cardio-metabolic risk factors. The results showed that the joint contribution of BMI and ABSI produced significantly improved associations for having a high fasting glucose, high triglycerides, and a low HDL but not high blood pressure [16].

5. Conclusions

ABSI and BMI are significantly associated with diabetes in the Qatari population. ABSI is a better predictor for the risk of diabetes than BMI after the adjustment for age, gender, education, and physical activity.

Supplementary Materials: The following are available online at http://www.mdpi.com/2072-6643/11/5/1018/s1, Figure S1: Association between ABSI, BMI and HbA1c; Model adjusted for age and gender. ABSI and BMI were mutually adjusted. Table S1: Sample characteristics by diabetes.

Author Contributions: Conceptualization, H.B.; formal analysis, Z.S.; writing—original draft preparation, S.A., M.A.; writing—review and editing A.K.; supervision, H.B.; project administration, H.B.

Funding: This research was funded by Qatar University, grant number QUEST-1-CHS-2018-7" and "The APC was funded by Qatar National Library".

Acknowledgments: Acknowledgement is due to Qatar Biobank for providing the data with all required support. The publication of this article was funded by the Qatar National Library.

Conflicts of Interest: The authors declare no conflict of interest.

References

1. Shaw, J.E.; Sicree, R.A.; Zimmet, P.Z. Global estimates of the prevalence of diabetes for 2010 and 2030. *Diabetes Res. Clin. Pract.* **2010**, *87*, 4–14. [CrossRef]
2. Massi-Benedetti, M. The cost of diabetes in Europe-Type II: The CODE-2 study. *Diabetologia* **2002**, *45*, 1–4. [CrossRef]
3. Tuomilehto, J.; Lindström, J.; Eriksson, J.G.; Valle, T.T.; Hämäläinen, H.; Ilanne-Parikka, P.; Keinänen-Kiukaanniemi, S.; Laakso, M.; Louheranta, A.; Rastas, M. Prevention of type 2 diabetes mellitus by changes in lifestyle among subjects with impaired glucose tolerance. *N. Engl. J. Med.* **2001**, *344*, 1343–1350. [CrossRef]
4. Britton, K.A.; Massaro, J.M.; Murabito, J.M.; Kreger, B.E.; Hoffmann, U.; Fox, C.S. Body fat distribution, incident cardiovascular disease, cancer, and all-cause mortality. *J. Am. Coll. Cardiol.* **2013**, *62*, 921–925. [CrossRef] [PubMed]
5. Orgel, E.; Mittelman, S.D. The links between insulin resistance, diabetes, and cancer. *Curr. Diab. Rep.* **2013**, *13*, 213–222. [CrossRef] [PubMed]
6. Ye, J. Mechanisms of insulin resistance in obesity. *Front. Med.* **2013**, *7*, 14–24. [CrossRef] [PubMed]

7. Kok, P.; Seidell, J.; Meinders, A. The value and limitations of the body mass index (BMI) in the assessment of the health risks of overweight and obesity. *Ned. Tijdschr. Geneeskd.* **2004**, *148*, 2379–2382. [PubMed]
8. Feller, S.; Boeing, H.; Pischon, T. Body mass index, waist circumference, and the risk of type 2 diabetes mellitus: Implications for routine clinical practice. *Dtsch. Arztebl. Int.* **2010**, *107*, 470.
9. Flint, A.J.; Rexrode, K.M.; Hu, F.B.; Glynn, R.J.; Caspard, H.; Manson, J.E.; Willett, W.C.; Rimm, E.B. Body mass index, waist circumference, and risk of coronary heart disease: A prospective study among men and women. *Obes. Res. Clin. Pract.* **2010**, *4*, e171–e181. [CrossRef]
10. Cerhan, J.R.; Moore, S.C.; Jacobs, E.J.; Kitahara, C.M.; Rosenberg, P.S.; Adami, H.-O.; Ebbert, J.O.; English, D.R.; Gapstur, S.M.; Giles, G.G.; et al. A pooled analysis of waist circumference and mortality in 650,000 adults. *Elsevier* **2014**, *89*, 335–345. [CrossRef]
11. Balkau, B.; Deanfield, J.E.; Després, J.-P.; Bassand, J.-P.; Fox, K.A.; Smith, S.C., Jr.; Barter, P.; Tan, C.-E.; Van Gaal, L.; Wittchen, H.-U. CLINICAL PERSPECTIVE. *Circulation* **2007**, *116*, 1942–1951. [CrossRef]
12. Sumner, A.E.; Sen, S.; Ricks, M.; Frempong, B.A.; Sebring, N.G.; Kushner, H. Determining the waist circumference in African Americans which best predicts insulin resistance. *Obesity* **2008**, *16*, 841–846. [CrossRef]
13. Krakauer, N.Y.; Krakauer, J.C. A new body shape index predicts mortality hazard independently of body mass index. *PLoS ONE* **2012**, *7*, e39504. [CrossRef]
14. Song, X.; Jousilahti, P.; Stehouwer, C.; Söderberg, S.; Onat, A.; Laatikainen, T.; Yudkin, J.; Dankner, R.; Morris, R.; Tuomilehto, J. Cardiovascular and all-cause mortality in relation to various anthropometric measures of obesity in Europeans. *Nutr. Metab. Cardiovasc. Dis.* **2015**, *25*, 295–304. [CrossRef]
15. Lee, D.Y.; Lee, M.Y.; Sung, K.C. Prediction of mortality with a body shape index in young Asians: Comparison with body mass index and waist circumference. *Obesity* **2018**, *26*, 1096–1103. [CrossRef]
16. Bertoli, S.; Leone, A.; Krakauer, N.Y.; Bedogni, G.; Vanzulli, A.; Redaelli, V.I.; De Amicis, R.; Vignati, L.; Krakauer, J.C.; Battezzati, A. Association of Body Shape Index (ABSI) with cardio-metabolic risk factors: A cross-sectional study of 6081 Caucasian adults. *PLoS ONE* **2017**, *12*, e0185013. [CrossRef] [PubMed]
17. He, S.; Chen, X. Could the new body shape index predict the new onset of diabetes mellitus in the Chinese population? *PLoS ONE* **2013**, *8*. [CrossRef] [PubMed]
18. Wu, Y.; Ding, Y.; Tanaka, Y.; Zhang, W. Risk factors contributing to type 2 diabetes and recent advances in the treatment and prevention. *Int. J. Med. Sci.* **2014**, *11*, 1185. [CrossRef] [PubMed]
19. Al Kuwari, H.; Al Thani, A.; Al Marri, A.; Al Kaabi, A.; Abderrahim, H.; Afifi, N.; Qafoud, F.; Chan, Q.; Tzoulaki, I.; Downey, P. The Qatar Biobank: Background and methods. *BMC Public Health* **2015**, *15*, 1208. [CrossRef]
20. Association, A.D. 2. Classification and diagnosis of diabetes: Standards of medical care in diabetes—2018. *Diabetes Care* **2018**, *41*, S13–S27. [CrossRef] [PubMed]
21. World Health Organization. *Waist Circumference and Waist–Hip Ratio: Report of a WHO Expert Consultation*; World Health Organization: Geneva, Switzerland, 2008.
22. Han, C.; Liu, Y.; Sun, X.; Luo, X.; Zhang, L.; Wang, B.; Ren, Y.; Zhou, J.; Zhao, Y.; Zhang, D.; et al. Prediction of a new body shape index and body adiposity estimator for development of type 2 diabetes mellitus: The Rural Chinese Cohort Study. *Br. J. Nutr.* **2017**, *118*, 771–776. [CrossRef] [PubMed]
23. Fujita, M.; Sato, Y.; Nagashima, K.; Takahashi, S.; Hata, A. Predictive power of a body shape index for development of diabetes, hypertension, and dyslipidemia in Japanese adults: A retrospective cohort study. *PLoS ONE* **2015**, *10*, e0128972. [CrossRef]
24. Hardy, D.S.; Stallings, D.T.; Garvin, J.T.; Xu, H.; Racette, S.B. Best anthropometric discriminators of incident type 2 diabetes among white and black adults: A longitudinal ARIC study. *PLoS ONE* **2017**, *12*. [CrossRef] [PubMed]

© 2019 by the authors. Licensee MDPI, Basel, Switzerland. This article is an open access article distributed under the terms and conditions of the Creative Commons Attribution (CC BY) license (http://creativecommons.org/licenses/by/4.0/).

MDPI
St. Alban-Anlage 66
4052 Basel
Switzerland
Tel. +41 61 683 77 34
Fax +41 61 302 89 18
www.mdpi.com

Nutrients Editorial Office
E-mail: nutrients@mdpi.com
www.mdpi.com/journal/nutrients

www.ingramcontent.com/pod-product-compliance
Lightning Source LLC
LaVergne TN
LVHW071954080526
838202LV00064B/6742